WHEN THE STUDENT IS READY…

WHEN THE STUDENT IS READY...

PUBLISH **MY** BOOK
.ONLINE

Angelo Campione

1st Edition 2018, paperback.

ISBN: 978-1-925764-55-0

Publishing services by: PublishMyBook.Online

Introduction

Thanks for purchasing *When The Student is Ready...*

In recognition of the sensational work the Khan Academy do, and in support of the free online educational community, all proceeds from the sale of this book will be donated to the Khan Academy.

I heard about Salman Khan in 2010 and was instantly impressed by what he was doing. I've had a dream of being able to provide free education worldwide since the early 2000's but had no idea of how to go about it.

Salman and I must have been on similar wavelengths because he seems to have created an online school that's even better than I'd imagined, and I'm thrilled about that. At some point, I hope to provide a FREE down-loadable version of When the Student Is Ready... through his site.

Finally, I trust you'll receive great value from this book, feel free to share both this book and the Khan Academy site with as many people as possible, if it's helped you.

I wish you well,

Angelo Campione

Foreword

OK, so there's something you need to know before you come along on this ride, and that is... this book is not a literary masterpiece and I am not a professional writer, I'm simply a finance guy that felt inspired to share a message based on my own experience. If you like the sound of being financially free, then you're at the right place.

Having said that, the basis of this book is about YOU helping yourself be free from the patterns that hold YOU back. This book is not going to magically transform you, that's your job, but you can definitely use the book as a framework to create change for yourself, if you choose.

If you're willing to take this ride, then you need to know that while money becomes a main focus in the book, money is not an end point. Sure, it allows you to live your dreams and not worry about how you're going to pay for things, but the belief that money will solve your problems is misguided.

I'm not saying there's anything wrong with wanting money, it's natural to desire bigger and better experiences, however money is ultimately a simple by-product of what you bring to the world. What you bring to the world is your unique gift and is a choice only you can make.

What you bring requires a YOU that shows up and says, "I'm here to shine as brightly as I can". Choosing to shine is living authentically and when you do this, you can't help but to ADD VALUE, everywhere. While adding value helps you get into the flow of living the life you were born to live, it's also important to know that managing money responsibly is a skill and like any skill, it requires knowing some of the basics.

When I worked in the accounting field, I saw people of all ages and all occupations (even those with high paying jobs) struggle with money and I really wanted to find a way to help bridge the gap for anyone that wanted to break free from the old conditioned patterns.

Having written this book now, I know there are still those that will struggle in their day-to-day life. This book is not intended to be a "fix all", but if you can slow things down enough and calmly ask, "What can I do to take care of myself right now?" Rather than asking (or expecting) others to do something to take care of you, you might be surprised at the openings that come up.

One other point, the story in this book is entirely a figment of my imagination, therefore fictional, but the principles aren't. If you take those principles to heart and consciously apply it in your own life, you'll open yourself up to a much greater learning and get a step closer to living the life you were born to live.

And a final point, the income and expenses used within these pages are estimates based on Australian living standards as of 2017. If you live in another country, your figures are likely to be different.

May you enjoy the journey,

Angelo Campione

Table of Contents

Part 1
SELF

A Chance Meeting

Beams of light shone through the cracks of Jane's bedroom curtains. Lying in bed, she slowly moved her arms up and out as she yawned and stretched at the same time.

She lifted the covers off with her left arm and bounced out of bed, opening the curtains with her right, in one smooth motion. Adjusting to the bright morning light, she stood there for a moment, enjoying the sun's warmth on her face.

Casually entering the kitchen, she sees her father, David, sitting at the kitchen table with a bowl of cereal in front of him, a spoon in his right hand and reading a newspaper to his left. Without looking up he says in a flat voice, "Morning honey, what do you have planned for the day?"

She yawns and says, "Well, it's Saturday, so I'll be going to gym first off, then catching up with a friend over a coffee and after that going to work in the afternoon. And of course, there's Mandy's 21st tonight, which should be fun."

"What a life, what it is to be 20 and care free ..." he says with a note of envy, as he looks up, reminiscing his youth. She gives a dismissive remark and sets about her day, completely unaware that today would mark a turning point in her life.

Later that evening, during her shift at work, a major spill in the kitchen caused her to stay back and help clean up. She watched the clock and knew she'd be late for Mandy's party.

By the time she arrived, the party was in full swing. The music was loud and the alcohol was flowing. Walking through the house, she saw various small groups chatting. As she continued, she saw some guys comparing their latest smart phones while another group were having a drinking competition, with the ones not drinking screaming, "Scull, Scull, Scull".

She headed for the backyard, looking for Mandy along the way. As she stepped outside, she saw a neatly dressed, well-groomed 30 something looking guy, extremely animated and speaking loudly with a small group of people.

She moved a little closer to hear what he was saying. "Money!!! Money's like sex, everyone loves it but no one wants to talk openly about it ..."

She thought, 'Oh-Kay, this sounds interesting!', and moved slowly to the outdoor fridge to grab a drink while listening to what the loud mouth had to say. " ... Money, just like sex, is one of those things we use for surviving and for thriving, but for thousands of years it's been used, abused and given all sorts of power over people, and now, we have the masses living with bucket loads of issues that stem from a general misunderstanding of money. The thing to understand is that money is not the *root of all evil*, as some might say, money is simply a tool, and like all tools, it can be used or abused. The question you have to ask yourself, though is, *Am I the user or abuser of it?*"

Jane had never heard anyone speak about money in this way. She'd never even given it that much thought in any event, other than what she wanted to buy with money. But now she was intrigued and wanted to know more.

As she pondered this for a moment, Mandy quietly crept up behind her, like a cat stalking its prey, then at the last second, pounced on her. "Heya Janey, glad you could make it." Mandy had clearly been drinking for a while and gave Jane a big kiss on the lips while making a 'mwa' sound.

Jane was stunned for a moment but was eager to find out about the loud mystery guy and said, "Uh, hey Mandy, oh, happy 21st... Sorry I'm late, you know work and that sort of thing."

Mandy was too drunk to care and said, "Don't sweat it Janey." In the meantime Jane was still transfixed on the loud guy and said, "... Um, I was just wondering, who's that guy over there?"

Mandy looked around, "Who, Arturo? ... he's an old friend of the family, he's always passionate about something and he loves an audience." Mandy then turns back around, looks at Jane, while taking a step back and smiles with a wry grin, then quickly grabs Jane's hand and says, "Come on Janey, I'll introduce you ..."

Without a moment to think, Jane is jerked over, "Hey Arturo ... " she says loudly, "this a good friend of mine, Jane, why don't you let her hear what you have to say?" Mandy then dances off, waving her arms in the air, while singing along with the music.

"Hey Jane, nice to meet you, my name's Arturo." They shake hands and he holds her hand for a moment longer than normal while looking at her intensely. "... We're having a discussion about money ..." he says.

"Uh, yeah, I overheard you speaking. I'm not sure I followed what you were saying but the way I see it, as long as I have enough money to get by, then I'm OK, I'm not really all that interested in having money so I can live in a mansion or anything like that."

Arturo looks at her inquisitively and says, "Hmm, knowing about money isn't about living a showy life, although if that's what you want, there's nothing wrong with that. The thing is Jane, money is a life skill, so how do you know what you're capable of if you don't master this skill? How do you know if you're the user of money or abuser of it?"

Her mind begins to race and she thinks 'What the hell was I thinking, why did I have to say anything, I should have just kept my mouth shut.' She finally responds with, "Uh well, I never really questioned it that much, I figure that you work, pay your bills and hopefully have some left over for entertainment."

Arturo smiles and says, "Jane, your innocence is very sweet."

'You condescending bastard!' she thinks to herself, while feeling diminished.

Arturo continues, "Let's put that aside at this point because what really needs to happen now is that we need to find a way to live in balance again ..." He turns to the group and says, "I say *balance* because in the past we've blamed people that have money for all the problems of the world, but I think that right now is the time to accept responsibility for what we've all created, and stop blaming others for where we are.

Each one of us has the power to create whatever we desire, but it takes awareness combined with focused action, for something new to show up. By stopping the blame game or what others should be doing, we can make some positive change for ourselves, and maybe then, we can start teaching kids about self-responsibility and of course, money.

The thing is, we should all be learning about money in schools from a young age but the whole system is designed to produce employees that don't really understand money, even those that end up studying business!

Big business and governments have come to rely on people not understanding money because it enables them to retain their edge in controlling the masses. It does this by encouraging you to buy now and pay later, enjoy now and bear the consequences later.

They want you to be in debt for as long as possible so that you'll always have to work to support this particular habit of spending today so you can owe tomorrow. It's insidious, but don't get me wrong, I'm not blaming them, they're simply a symptom of our society.

When you understand money, you take back your power and when you reclaim your power, being manipulated by anyone else disappears, you become 'responsible', the captain of your ship!"

He notices Jane looking at him suspiciously and says, "Is there a problem?"

"Well, it sounds like you're saying that it's a bad thing to be an employee, am I missing something here?" she says.

"No, I'm not saying that being an employee is wrong or a bad thing. What I *am* saying is that people buy things, get into debt and then have to be a slave to their job in order to finance their instant gratification lifestyles.

What's required is a level of awareness on how you spend. By having this awareness, you give yourself the ability to see different choices, rather than behaving like a programmed robot."

Jane could feel her anger increasing, 'Great, now this jerk is calling me a robot', she thinks.

He continues, "Look, schools do what they think is right but what we have in schools today, isn't really an education system, it's more of a training system. Kids are trained to be good little spokes in the wheel, as in obedient subjects, and as opposed to independent thinkers, that can make conscious and responsible decisions."

Jane was feeling a mixture of emotions now, on the one hand she felt offended by some of the things he'd said but on the other, there was an attraction to continue listening to what he had to say. He had a certain charisma but at the same time she felt a compulsion to antagonise him!

"Arturo, are you actually saying that education is a waste of time?"

"No Jane, I'm not saying that, however, while we're on the subject, what do you think really makes an education?"

"Uh ... well, I think that education is about preparing you for life, I guess, helping you to get a job in a field that you enjoy and, um ... OK, I'm not really sure, you've put me on the spot here."

"OK, well, the way I see it is that education is the process of learning, where students are engaged and interested. The teacher doesn't actually teach, the teacher simply provides the opening that allows learning to happen by providing an environment that facilitates and supports the enthusiasm of the student.

For a real education to happen, students need to learn how reality actually exists through reasonable perception and analysis. The subjects we should be offering are things like logic, science, ethics, history, important literature and of course, money.

These subjects are really designed to give you the ability to think clearly and make assessments of life for yourself. But, I'd add that to be a truly conscious participant in life, it's also necessary to have a calm and peaceful mind.

The mind is a great tool for helping with logistical things but it can't tell you who you are. As a result, an aspect of education today needs to include some form of meditation, where you practice the art of spending time in silence, with your eyes closed, and notice what goes through your head, without judgement.

Anyone can do it, but it takes practice to simply let the thoughts pass through you without attaching yourself to them or creating another story with them.

So coming back to education; what kids get today under the guise of *education*, whether in the early years or later ones, is not true education, but actually *training*.

Training is different to education because training is about rote learning with the intention of productive behaviour in the future. It's what you'd learn on the job, as an apprentice labourer. This would cover most high school and Uni courses, which are not designed to produce educated young people but useful employees, ready to enter the labour force. But in truth, these days they really struggle to even do that well.

The thing is, school is too rigid, it doesn't allow for failure. It encourages the 'right answer', instead of encouraging you to take a risk and try something new. It also doesn't do a great job in allowing you to get in touch with your creativity, to have creative thoughts, or how to sell creative ideas to others so that you can be part of the creative flow of life.

The bottom line is that the school system works on the basis of a 'perfect world' and 'all things being equal', when in truth, things are rarely, if ever, equal and in reality, we learn through trial and error. In other words, we learn by getting things 'wrong' or 'stuffing up'.

Henry Ford once said that, 'Failure is the best education you can have', but at school, the person that fails is considered a fool! Again, there's a certain disconnect between how things work in reality and what you learn in school."

Jane interjects, "Hang on a moment, Arturo ..." feeling that she's caught him out, "your argument certainly makes it sound like school is a waste of time, even though you said earlier that it wasn't!"

"OK, earlier you asked whether I was saying that education was a waste of time and I said no. I stand by that because I see education as something different than what we actually get through the 'education system'.

If you were asking me whether participating in the higher education system is a waste of time, then I'd say ... absolutely it is. I think there are vastly better ways to get a true education than via the higher education system.

For example, if I were 18 now, I'd spend a year travelling the world, most likely spending one month in 12 new places, learning the culture, working with the locals and learning to rely on my own ingenuity to survive and enjoy life. You really get to see what you're capable of when there's no safety net!

Think of it this way, when you jump in deep water, you sink to start with and then you rise to the surface, because the air in your lungs always bring you back to the surface. If you don't panic, you'll float for a while and then swim and enjoy your new environment. That's what travel can give you and it can be one of the best educations of your life."

He then waves his arms in the air and screams out, "Right, I've ranted for long enough, I've got another party to go to." He then turns to Jane, looks into her eyes, reaches into his pocket and says in a low voice, "Jane, here's my card, call me if you want to break out of the rabbit trap." He hands her the card and walks off.

She looks at the card, *ARTURO—Life by Design*. She thinks, 'What a wanker! Who the hell does this guy think he is? He's just a bit too weird for my liking.' She looks around and sees a bin by the outdoor setting. She walks over, looks at the card again and just as she's about to throw it away, she stops and decides to throw it out at home.

A New Day

The next morning Jane sees Arturo's card on her desk, she remembers some of the things he'd said, has a chuckle and again goes to throw the card out, but as she held the card, his last comment kept reverberating in her mind. '... What the hell did he mean by, 'break out of the rabbit trap'? This guy's a whack job, maybe he thinks he's Morpheus out of *The Matrix*.' She chuckles again and goes to the kitchen for breakfast. "Morpheus ..." she says out loud as she walks and breaks out into loud laughter.

"Morning Jane, you seem to be in a good mood this morning." David says as she sits down.

"Yeah, it's nothing really, it was just something I remembered from the party last night."

"Well, give me the juice Jane, don't leave me hanging here."

"Um ... OK, as I say, it's nothing really, it was just that this guy gave me his card as he was leaving and said that if I wanted to break out of the rabbit trap, to give him a call. It was really weird and as I was coming to the kitchen I thought to myself, maybe he thinks he's Morpheus out of *The Matrix*, and I cracked up laughing."

"That does sound pretty funny, good one Jane. I have to say, that's an unusual pick-up line. I hadn't heard of that one in my day."

"Oh, uh, no, I don't think he was trying to pick me up, he was just a bit of a loud mouth and he said some weird stuff that's all, it just seemed funny to me." she says while feeling a little embarrassed and quickly changes the subject.

Later that day she decides to call Mandy to find out a little more about Arturo. "Hey Mandy, great party last night, you must have quite a hangover ... Um, you know, I wanted to ask you something. You know how you introduced me to that Arturo character last night ... well it was a bit weird. When he left he handed me his business card and said if I wanted to break out of the rabbit trap, I should call him, what's your take on that? Does he think we're in *The Matrix* or something?"

Mandy laughs, "... Actually Jane, Arturo's a lovely guy, I don't know what he meant with that comment but I do know that if he said to call him, there'd be a reason for it. I know he seems a little weird and he can come across as opinionated and all that, but my dad speaks really highly of him and he just seems to have this way of knowing what people need. If he asked you to call him, I'm pretty sure it'll be worth your while."

Jane went silent, she hadn't expected Mandy to be so positive about him, she thanked her and hung up. She sat on her bed, staring at the card. On the one hand she felt unsure of what this guy was about but on the other hand, she knew that Mandy wouldn't have said those things if she didn't mean it, and that gave her some comfort.

'Maybe I'll see how I feel about it in the morning', she says to herself and places the card on her desk again.

She woke up early Monday morning still thinking about Arturo's words and the way he spoke, there was just something about him she couldn't shake. "Right, I'll call him and see what he has to say." she says to herself.

During her mid-morning break, she walked out to the university grounds and calls him. As the phone starts to ring she notices her heart pounding. Arturo answers with a confident greeting, his voice was deep and reassuring.

She slowly says, "Uh hi, Arturo? ... It's Jane here, we met on ..."

He quickly cuts in, "Yes, yes, of course Jane, how are you? Are you ready to break out now?"

Still feeling nervous she says, "Uh, well, what exactly do you mean when you say, *break out*?"

"Jane, what I'm talking about goes beyond words and is only something you can experience directly. If you want to give yourself the opportunity to experience it, then be here at 5pm today."

"What! Today?? But, um, that's so soon."

"Jane, I'm not forcing you to do anything here, this is a choice that you can make now, and if not now, when?" She gulps and says, "Um ... OK, I'll be there."

"Oh, and Jane, I take appointments very seriously, it's important that you are here on time, if you get here after 5.00pm, even by just 1 minute you may as well turn around and go home, is that OK with you?" he says gently.

There was silence over the phone as her nervousness was now replaced by anger, her mind began to race, 'Who the hell does this guy think he is, how dare he be so demanding'. Arturo waited quietly for a response and then, gently but firmly says, "Jane, is that OK with you?"

She bit her tongue and quietly says, "Yes, OK, got it."

She hangs up and feels anger raging through her, she has no idea what this guy is on about and now he's even demanding that she be on time!

She's normally punctual anyway but having someone be so precise with the time feels like excessive pressure and just a little over the top. She starts to question whether she should go and begins pacing, saying to herself, '... I hardly know this guy ... I feel like he's pushing me around ... what's he up to anyway? Why is he being so anal? For all I know he could be a hustler, trying to take advantage of me in some way, the arsehole.'

She then remembered Mandy's words, *he's a lovely guy*. 'Really? I just don't see it. But Mandy's usually a really good judge of character. But argh, he's so frustrating.'

She decides to go this one time, just to see if she can get a better gauge on him. 'If he tries this pushing around thing again, I'm gonna let him have it.' she thinks to herself as her anger turns to resentment.

The Meeting

Jane arrived at Arturo's office and looked at the time, 4.49pm. She was relieved on the one hand, but on the other felt it was too early, so she went for a stroll.

She noticed that his office was in a trendy part of town, where the socialites hung out. 'He's probably pretentious too. Great, just what I need!' she thought, which only added to her resentment.

She made her way back and cut it super fine, arriving at 4.59pm. Arturo happened to be at the door as she arrived and welcomed her in with a warm smile, "Welcome Jane. Come on in ..."

Her underlying resentment was suddenly neutralised as she looked into his eyes. They were large, deep blue and somehow felt very calming to look at. At the party, the light was too dim to see the colour but now his eyes were truly striking.

"Come on in Jane, take a seat, and thanks for coming on such short notice." She walked in and noticed that his office was very neat and tidy, everything seemed to be perfectly in place. It had a minimalist feel while being stylish at the same time.

She sat in front of his desk and now wasn't sure of what to say. She'd run through a whole series of different scenarios in her head in the lead up and could still feel her heart beating at an elevated rate. But now, in his presence, all her preoccupations seemed to dissolve.

Arturo paused as he looked across the desk into her eyes, it was as if he were looking into her soul. After a few moments she began to feel awkward in the silence and said, "Um, so what is it exactly that you do here?"

He continued to look for a few moments longer and calmly said in a soothing voice, "Jane, it's best that you not get bogged down with another story, there's a reason why you're here and it's important that we start that journey now.

At this point, simply understand that I am here to help you. The help I'll be giving you is not going to be the type of help that does *something for you* though, but rather it'll be the type of help that may inspire *you* to help yourself."

She listened intently, trying to work out what he was saying and said,

"You know, you seem to speak in riddles, you say all these things but I really have no idea what you're on about."

He smiles and says, "I'm glad to hear you say that Jane because it means we have a relatively clean slate to work with. I know this may seem confusing to you but focus more on the feeling of what I say rather than the words themselves, that's what will help you get in touch with the next step."

She starts to feel agitated now and says firmly, "You know Arturo, I'm still trying to get my head around this, am I supposed to be paying you for something? Like, I'm guessing you do this for a living and if so, what's this going to cost me?"

He smiles again and says with the same gentleness as earlier, "Jane, you will not need to pay me anything, let's just say that I have a gift, and from time to time I share that gift with another. While this is a gift I give freely, it will however still cost you something. But it won't be measured in terms of dollars, it'll be measured in terms of thought."

'Thought!! What the ...!' she thinks. "Arturo! You're doing it again, you're speaking in riddles, what-does-that-mean?" she emphasises.

"It's OK, I know this is probably somewhat overwhelming at the moment, but I assure you that it will make sense in time. Just bear with me for now.

OK, so here's the way I see this working, you'll come here every Monday at 5pm, for one hour, we'll have a chat and I'll probably give you a project that will need to be completed before our next meeting.

Now I want you to know that this process will be quite simple but it won't be easy ..."

Interjecting, she says, "There you go doing it again Arturo, what do you mean it'll be simple but not easy?"

"OK, OK ..." he chuckles, "let's say that you want to get through a dense forest, it's not easy because there's all this thick scrub to get through. You need to cut your way to get through and then there's the risk of getting bitten by snakes, spiders, etc. All of this takes a lot of effort, it's definitely not simple and it's not easy.

Then, let's say you had someone with you that knew of a path that had already been cut out, would that make the journey easy? No, but it would certainly make it a lot simpler. You'd still have to walk through it and face some risks but it'd be relatively simple compared to blazing a trail out yourself.

The journey would only be truly easy if you had someone with you that had an air-conditioned four-wheel-drive that was able to drive you through. But let's face it, you wouldn't really get a true experience of the forest like that, which means you wouldn't really get as much enjoyment out of it either.

Life tends to be more joyful when there's desire and at the same time, a bit of a challenge. We usually like to feel the wind in our hair, the heart pumping with excitement, and maybe a little risk. The challenge of the situation often adds a sense joy when we look back and realise how far we've come. It also provides us with a sense of adventure.

When things come too easily, we tend to give them little worth or even discount them altogether. It's a basic human trait.

Now, speaking of living joyfully, we have two choices:

1. We can see everything as precious, by treating the most trivial thing as the most amazing thing, in which case, there's no need to feel challenged in order to get that sense of joy, things being easy is our joy, or;
2. Look for the path that's most in alignment with us, which feels simple in terms of a next logical step but may not be so easy to start with.

Either path is joyful because joy is the basis of life. Struggle and hardship is a perspective that only serves to have us move. Joy, is where it's ultimately at."

Her mind focused on Arturo's last sentence – 'Joy, is where it's ultimately at.' She'd never heard anyone speak of life like this before, and had always believed that life *was* about struggle and striving to achieve things. Joy was reserved for the achievement of things, for brief moments after you've worked hard at something. But to hear Arturo speak of life as joyful had something within her say – 'YES, that's true.'

"OK Arturo, so life is meant to be joyful, I get that, but that's not a reality for most people, like, it wasn't joyful for me in feeling pressured to be here at 5 for that matter. Why even be so finicky about the time?"

"OK, good, let's take care of one thing at a time. What was happening for you that had you not feel joy? In other words, what were you telling yourself that caused you to not feel good about me asking you to be here on time?"

She thought for a moment, "Well, I felt like I was going to get into trouble, that you were putting this pressure on me."

"So you made me responsible for how you felt?"

"Huh? Uh, yeah, who else was pressuring me?" she says with a note of haughtiness.

"Well, YOU. When you called, I gave you a choice, you could have said no, if you wanted to, but you didn't, that was *your* choice. I was simply stating my truth in being clear about the appointment. After that, it's up to you to accept that for *you*, and honour yourself in that. That then releases any angst you may have towards me for being the imposer as opposed to someone that was providing you with a choice."

"So what you're saying is that you weren't pressuring me, I just interpreted it that way, is that right?"

"Yes, exactly. You see there's always two sides—there's what happens, in this case, me asking you to go back home if you didn't get here on time, and then there's what you DO with what happens, in this case, you feeling pressured.

While it looks like it was me doing the pressuring, that was simply a perspective that *you* had. From my perspective, I was simply being clear, it wasn't my intention to 'DO' anything to you.

It's important for you to know this Jane, when we meet, you'll always have a choice, you may not like the choices at times but you are always free to stop these meetings and to stop seeing me. I'm not here to be a father figure or someone that has authority over you. You're a free spirit and if you come, you come because it feels right for you to do so. Is that clear?" He says with a gentle tone.

"Uh, yeah, quite clear." she says while feeling the wind had been taken out of her sails.

"Great, now having said that, there's also freedom in discipline. Just because you're a free spirit doesn't mean that you're directionless. Each one of us has a journey that is ultimately a joyful journey, but we only realise that, when we've accepted full responsibility for being here.

Being disciplined is a part of this responsibility, but I'm not talking about the rigid thing that sucks your life energy in order to get to a desired result, like forcing yourself to do something just because you hope you'll get something good out of it down the track.

I'm using the word, 'discipline' but it's really about consciously choosing something that you embrace because it feels good to you. When you do this, this thing called discipline, becomes a natural flow of your joy. Not something that's imposed by someone else!"

He continued as he looked at her with intensity. "You could choose to see discipline as the desire to focus on one thing and be fully aligned with that one thing.

For example, keeping your room neat and clean might require you to have the *discipline* to clean it once a week. If a parent has asked you to clean it, it may seem like they're imposing their will on to you, and in that, you may feel as if they're *disciplining* you. But, if you decide that it feels good to have a neat and clean room, being *disciplined*, becomes a natural choice that you accept and do with joy.

Remember, you always choose what you choose because that's what you believe is the best path for you in that moment, whether that's a conscious choice or not.

By consciously choosing to be disciplined, you stand in your power. You don't blame any-one or any-thing, you accept full responsibility and love the journey—because the journey is ultimately joyful!

Are you still with me Jane?" he says gently.

"Um, sort of, I was just thinking that I've never heard it put that way before. I mean, I can feel the difference in what you're saying between something being imposed versus accepting it and doing it by choice, but I just hadn't heard it that way before."

"OK, good. Now let's move onto the next thing. Why I'm so 'finicky' about you being here on time for our appointment. This is a standard I hold for myself, and it boils down to awareness and respect for myself. In other words, if I respect myself, I'm more likely to honour my agreements and therefore respect others.

The practicalities are that for me to get somewhere on time requires an awareness of where I'm at and what I'm doing in the moment. It requires some planning, some conscious choosing and shows that I care enough to do all that.

If the person I've made an appointment with, in this case you, doesn't see it that way, then it's probably best we don't connect at that point."

"... But wait a minute, what if something happens along the way that's out of my control? That stops me from getting here on time?" she says defensively.

"Well Jane," he says wryly, "if that were to happen, you could always call and we would meet the following week." The look on his face implying there was more to what he was saying.

"Why are you saying it like that, Arturo?"

Smiling, he says, "Well, the way I see things is that nothing happens by 'accident', if I'm to be responsible, then even the things that happen that seem to be out of my control, are my creation also.

I may not be consciously creating it but nonetheless, I am creating it. It's neither right nor wrong. So if I'm late because of something that happened that seemed to be 'out of my control', I still chose on some level for that to happen, and there would be some unconscious reason for that."

Jane's head was spinning and he sensed that. "OK Jane, look, let's leave it there for today, we're getting to the end of our hour anyway. Now, is your room as neat and clean as you'd like it to be?"

Jane, looking down, still trying to get her head around the last thing he'd said, says, "Huh? What!! What was that about my room? What's that got to do with anything?" she says defensively.

He reminds her about the example he gave her around self-discipline as opposed to feeling imposed on by someone else.

She looks up and thinks for a moment and instantly hears her mum saying, 'Jane, for goodness sake, would you please tidy up your room!' She regains his gaze and says sheepishly, "Well, as a matter of fact, no, cleaning my room tends to be one of those things I tend to put off. I figure I can clean another time, there's usually more interesting things to spend my time on."

"OK, good. Then that time has come!" he says cheerfully, "Your project for this week is to clean your room to a point that feels good to YOU.

Remember, you're doing this because there is joy in your NOW moment and a clean environment is a natural extension of that joy, not because someone else has asked you to do it.

This may be coming from me but you accept it because it feels good to you. Now Jane, is this true for you?" He looks intently at her. "Is this something you can embrace for you, as your own?"

"Well, I guess so." she says reluctantly. "OK, so do you accept this project?" Jane could feel the same pressure she was feeling when he asked her to be on time.

With a caring look, Arturo says calmly, "Remember Jane, I'm not forcing you to do anything here, you have a choice, what do you choose?"

She notices a slight release of pressure and with a cheeky smile says, "And what if I say no?"

"Well, our time together would come to an end. What we're doing here is a dance, I take a step by showing you a new way of being, if you don't take your step, the dance ends, I'm not going to dance on my own. Do you see that, Jane?"

"Um, wow, you certainly have an unusual way of explaining things." She still felt some residual resentment but before she realised it, she heard herself say confidently, "OK, YES I'LL DO IT."

"Great, see you same time next week."

As she walks out she thinks, 'Clean my room! What the hell am I agreeing to here??'

SHE ARRIVES HOME just as the family are about to sit for dinner. "Will you be joining us for dinner tonight, Jane?" Elizabeth calls out.

"Uh, yeah, sure mum, thanks." she calls back.

As Jane enters the kitchen, David notices her looking disoriented, "Hey Jane, how was your day today?"

"What? Um, yeah, good."

"Come on Jane, I know you better than that, what's up?"

She stops for a moment, crosses her arms and fidgets with her hair, "Oh, ah, OK. Well, you know how I told you yesterday about this guy that gave me his card at the party and we cracked a few jokes about it?" David nods, "Well, I met up with him this afternoon."

Andy, her 15-year-old brother, quickly comes out with, "Ooh, Jane's got a new boyfriend ..." while making a kissy-kissy sound at her.

"Andy! Just grow up would you!" she snaps back.

"And, is there a problem now, Jane?" David says, ignoring Andy's antics, while sensing her concern.

"Uh, no, not really. It's just strange that's all."

"Yeah? In what way?"

"Boy, uh, yeah, it's difficult to explain dad." She takes a breath and then says quickly, "OK, it goes like this, his name is Arturo and from what I can tell he's some sort of Life Coach. Anyway, I spoke with Mandy about it and she vouched that he was a nice guy and that it'd probably be worthwhile seeing what he had to say. I was curious so I called and went to see him today, and now he's given me a project to clean my room, can you believe that!"

He stared at her for a moment, not knowing whether to be concerned or burst out in laughter. He decides to keep a straight face and says, "Right, OK, that does sound quite strange. So what are you going to do about that, honey?"

"Well, I said I'd do it, so I'm going to do it."

"And, how old is this boy, Jane?" David implying that there could be a romantic interest.

"Oh, uh, no, he's not a boy, dad, I think he's in his 30's. But no, it's not like that, as I said yesterday, I didn't think he was trying to pick me up. I get the sense he genuinely wants to help me."

"And why would he want to help you? What help do you need? Like, what's in it for him anyway?" he says with concern.

"Whoa dad, one question at a time. I don't really know why he wants to help me, he just said that he has this 'gift' and he shares it with people from time to time. And there's no charge."

"What! I'm not sure about this sweetheart, this all sounds very suspicious to me. I'd be asking him why he wants to do this because something just doesn't smell right here."

Putting his protective fatherly voice on, he says, "Jane, you be very careful, just let me know if you want me to have a chat with this Arturo character. In fact, it's probably a good idea for me to meet him anyway, just to be on the safe side ..."

"No dad, it's fine, he's a friend of Mandy's family and she spoke very highly of him, so it should be fine. In fact, Mandy tells me he's helped *her* dad out also, so it's cool, don't stress it, but thanks all the same, dad."

After dinner she started on her homework but couldn't stop thinking about the things Arturo had said. She'd never heard anyone speak about full responsibility before and not blaming anyone for anything and that life is supposed to be joyful. In that moment, it suddenly came together for her, 'Cleaning my room is about respecting myself, I clean it because I have respect for myself!'

"Whoa ..." she couldn't believe it, it suddenly made sense. Something as trivial as cleaning her room now seemed so profound. She felt a new zest and desire to clean her room and the words kept reverberating in her head, 'I clean my room because I care about myself!!'

The next day she got up early and began tidying up her room, she noticed that it didn't feel like a chore this time. It actually felt good! She felt clear that she was tidying and cleaning because she liked to look after herself. She couldn't believe what a difference this was compared to every other time she'd set about cleaning her room.

On the surface nothing had changed, she was just cleaning, but within her, she felt a huge shift. This time she was doing it with complete acceptance, she actually wanted to do it now. She then remembered Arturo's words, 'There's what happens and then there's what you do with what happens.'

She then says excitedly, "The cleaning is what's happening, and that is the same as before, but what I'm doing with what's happening, is different!"

'I'm not blaming mum for having to clean my room! How about that, I'm taking responsibility!' She patted herself on the back as she continued cleaning with a smile on her face.

Week Two – The Present Moment

Jane arrived at 4.50pm and waited in reception this time, without feeling the same level of anxiety as the previous week. As she sat, she noticed that the whole place had a consistent neat and tidy feel to it and it felt good. There were some tasteful magazines on the coffee table that were neatly fanned out and some low volume, gentle music playing in the background. It was all very calming.

Just then Arturo pops out of his office and says enthusiastically, "Jane, great to see you, come on in." They sit and again he pauses for a few moments while looking into her eyes.

Uncomfortable with the silence again, she says, "Why do you do that?"

"Do what exactly, Jane?"

"Stare into my eyes when we sit down."

"Well, it's my way of connecting with you before the words come along and take the stage. Plus, I find eyes very interesting—is that OK with you?" he says gently.

"Uh, yeah, sure." She blushes, feeling embarrassed for asking.

After a few more moments he asks, "So how's your week been Jane? What did you observe in completing the assigned project?"

She quickly perks up and says, "Wow, yeah, it was amazing. Initially I thought you were pulling my leg or something but I then started remembering some of the things you'd said and then I had one of those light bulb moments where I suddenly realised that cleaning my room is about respecting myself, I clean it because I have respect for myself!"

"Fantastic Jane! You got it. You got a taste of what it's like to do something from a place of joy. The thing is, no matter what you do, you can always choose to bring the same level of enthusiasm to it that you just experienced with your room. Whether it's tying your shoelaces, brushing your teeth or digging a hole in the garden. It's not *what* you do that's important, it's *how* you do it.

Think of it this way, when you get into your car, you have a destination in mind and most people simply want to get there as quickly as possible, they turn on the radio to help them forget about the 'boring' drive and they just get lost in thoughts or in whatever is being said on the radio.

They're not really there in that moment, they're there in a physical form, but they aren't present to life, they're on an autopilot mode, waiting to get to a more interesting moment. The destination often seems more interesting than what's happening NOW, so this NOW moment gets discounted.

But in truth, nothing happens in any other moment. When you get to a destination, it's now, when you brushed your teeth earlier this morning, it happened in a now moment.

Nothing happens in the future or the past, whenever something is happening, it's happening in a NOW moment. Past and future are abstracts of the mind that help us create some semblance of order, but reality happens right here, right NOW.

Once you truly get that reality is happening now, you don't need to spend much time thinking about what has happened and what will happen. You can appreciate and enjoy this moment, right here!

Now there's a secret that not a lot of people know and that is, if you can be interested in whatever is happening right NOW, you'll never, ever be bored again. And in fact, you'll find much greater joy in even the simplest of moments. You won't need to look *forward* to things because NOW is exquisite." he says with excitement.

"Wait a sec, are you saying we shouldn't look forward to anything?"

"No, I'm not, what I'm saying here is that when you find the joy in this very moment, you won't *need* to hang your hat on the thought that the future will be better than where you are right now, because NOW is where it's all at, NOW is your point of power, the point where YOU ARE.

It's like this, let's say you plan a holiday, feel excited about it but until the NOW moment arrives for the holiday, it's just a nice thought that you're having. Why not accept that the holiday will be fine, AND, that this moment here and now is fine too?

Or think of it this way, you're in a canoe, riding the rapids, getting a huge thrill, are you looking forward to another moment? Chances are, you're simply enjoying the exhilaration of the ride and not thinking about the next moment. Nothing else matters in that moment because your mind isn't engaged in thought, the moment is too thrilling and it's joyful!

That feeling of wanting to look forward to something happens when there isn't much to grab your attention in this moment and so your mind kicks in and looks for that future moment in the hope it'll be better than right now.

What I'm saying in a long winded way, is that when you learn to accept fully THIS MOMENT, and whatever you happen to be doing in THIS MOMENT, then the future no longer holds power over you. You then know that now is an exquisite point and you also know that because the next moment is born out of this moment, it will be exquisite too!"

"Whoa, wait a minute Arturo, are you saying that no matter what you're facing, you can not only accept it, but find that it's exquisite too? Like, even in a war zone or a third world country with no food and water??"

"OK, you want to go there, huh? ... Well, I know this may be difficult for you to hear right now, but yes, the acceptance and the exquisiteness isn't in the circumstances, it's in YOU. You find the allowance within yourself first, because your true nature is one of flow with *what is*. From there, whatever situation you find yourself in is an extension of you, and you can choose to see it any way you want.

Another way of looking at it is that the world, your circumstances, have both positive and negative aspects, the two coexist and in fact, depend upon each other. It's not about being joyful by needing the positive in your circumstances and rejecting the negative. It's about accepting the totality of your experience and *choosing* to be at ease, by knowing that there's more to you than your circumstances.

There's an Italian movie called *Life is Beautiful*, where the main actor plays a Jewish man during the Second World War. Without giving the plot away, he manages to find humour everywhere, despite finding himself in the worst of circumstances. Now I know this is just a movie and not real, but it does show that we have this ability to see things as we want to see things.

Remember that there's what happens and then there's what you *do* with what happens. If you were to find yourself in a war zone or a third world country, that would be what happens and then it's up to you on what you do with what happens in that moment."

"You've got my head spinning again Arturo ..." She pauses while taking a deep breath, trying to absorb what he'd said. "OK, I get that I have a choice on what I do with what happens, but what if I just can't find any joy in the moment and I choose to get angry or upset instead?"

"Would you really be *choosing* that, Jane? Being angry or upset are generally reactions, not responses out of choice. Anger, for most people, is an emotion that stems from fear. The fear of being hurt in some way, that someone or something external is going to hurt you and so you feel threatened and react angrily as a defence mechanism to protect yourself. That's not a choice that is made, it's a reaction to a situation or circumstance.

Remember this Jane—true choice only comes when there's a gap between you, and what you perceive. If you can see yourself as whole and safe, beyond the physicality of things, then whatever is happening around you is just a play of forms and nothing can truly hurt you.

Again, this may be difficult for you to process, but know this, the fact that you can be aware of your thoughts means there's an aspect of you that's separate from the thought. Without this aspect, you wouldn't even know that the thought existed. There is the thought and there is the one that is aware of the thought, and the two are not the same."

With a pained look on her face, she brings her right hand to her forehead and slides it down the side of her face slowly, "OK, let me see if I get what you're saying. Are you saying that the ME that's sitting here now, that I take myself to be, is somehow different to the thoughts in my head, is that what you're saying?" she says dejectedly.

"No, not quite. The 'ME' that you take yourself to be is your body ... And your body actually encompasses both your physical and mental attributes. Your perception of reality then, is merely an interpretation by your brain.

Let's use your eyes as an example, light enters your eyes, makes its way to the optic nerve, which then sends an electrical signal to the various parts of the brain for processing. Your brain then creates the image that you see, based on the data bank of matches that have been accumulated over time. Once this is established, it's not easy to change because it becomes part of your belief system. What you believe, the data bank match, is what you see!

If you doubt what I'm saying, it's because your brain doesn't have a match for it, but to see this in action, look up one of those *magic tricks revealed* video's on YouTube and you'll see that the mind can be tricked into believing something simply because there's a certain match in our brain for it. Have you seen this sort of thing on TV or the internet, Jane?" She nods.

"Good, so just like the information that the eyes take in can trick the mind, so too it is with thoughts.

Thoughts are little bits of information, just like light, which the brain processes to work out what needs to be done with that information. If there's no match for that information, it gets put to one side for possible use later, but for now it's disregarded.

If there is a match, then the information gets reinforced as a more valid piece of information and something to be on the look out for from the other sensory perceptions.

For example some people see rain as a wet inconvenience and sunshine as hot inconvenience and therefore both are negative. Over time, they have developed a negative thought process around the weather.

On the other hand, there are people that see rain as nourishment for the plants as well as life giving, and the sunshine, as glorious warmth. It's the same rain and sun but perceived differently based on whichever dominant thought pattern has been developed.

Now, with this understanding, what I'm really saying is that there's a YOU that is beyond words, beyond forms, beyond anything you can think about, that is more akin to essence than anything else.

This YOU, can be called an observer, a presence that's always there but is happy to stay on the sidelines for you, as Jane, to diminish your preconceived ideas (thoughts) about who you THINK you are."

She could feel herself become defensive now, "Arturo, you're making no sense and speaking in riddles again, how could any of what you're saying be true?"

"OK, I'll see if I can put it another way ... see this pen?" He picks up a stylish looking pen from the side of his desk and puts it in front of her. "Well, you are aware of the pen, right? ... But are you the pen?"

"Of course not." she snaps. "Exactly, so you can be aware of the pen but you are NOT the pen?"

"Where are you going with this Arturo?" Feeling herself becoming more impatient as she perceives him being patronising.

"Jane, please bear with me, this is a key point. OK, so it makes sense to you that you can be AWARE of the pen but not be the pen, but it doesn't make sense for you to be AWARE of your thoughts and not be your thoughts!

The fact that you can have an awareness of something means that there's a gap between you and that thing, which means that you, as the awareness, CAN'T be the thing that you are aware of, even your thoughts!

I said this earlier and I'll say it again, the fact that you can be aware of your thoughts, means there's an aspect of you that is separate from the thought. If that weren't the case you wouldn't even know that the thought existed. There is the thought and there is the one that is aware of the thought, and the two are not the same."

She sits back, stunned at the comparison. Her mind racing and she says quickly, "But that can't be right, that's like one of those magic illusions you were talking about earlier to trick the mind, I don't believe it—"

"Jane, Jane, I know this isn't easy to accept, but the logic in the comparison is valid. If you can be aware of something, it means that you're seeing that something as separate and distinct from you and so you can't be that thing because it *is* separate to you, and thoughts, are 'things' as well!

I tell you what Jane, let's leave it at that for this week because it's a lot to take in. Your project for this week is to simply notice your thoughts, don't judge them, just watch them and see what that's like. You may want to write some of your observations in a journal and then share them with me next week. Will you do that?"

Her head was throbbing and she still felt some anger around what he was saying but she agreed to the project. As she sat there for a moment, her doubts around Arturo arose again and she thought he must have been playing some sort of joke on her.

As she was getting up to leave, Arturo says, "Oh, and Jane, have you embraced the idea of keeping your room clean as an ongoing thing?"

"Uh, I hadn't really thought about it, but … yeah, I plan to keep on top of it now."

She walks out and starts to feel even more anger and resentment come up, thoughts start flying around her head, 'Who the hell does he think he is? Why is he telling me what to do? What the hell is he up to, anyway?'

Then all of a sudden she stops and thinks, 'Shit, my thoughts are running wild here!' She then remembers that her project was to watch her thoughts without judgement and realises that there's some really nasty stuff happening in her head.

She walks to her car, shocked at the thoughts she's having and feels as though there's some little demon within her, causing her to have these thoughts, as if she has no control over them.

She then remembers what he'd said, "The fact that you can be aware of your thoughts, means that there's an aspect of you that is separate from the thought. If that weren't the case you wouldn't even know that the thought existed. There is the thought and there is the one that is aware of the thought, and the two are not the same."

As she arrives at her car, she gets in and sits for a moment. She still feels a level of confusion but at the same time also feels a shift, as though something vaguely made sense.

SHE GOT HOME and David says, "So Jane, how did you go with that guy today, was it still weird?"

"Uh, yeah, it sure was. We mainly spoke about thoughts, how we can be aware of thoughts and that because we can be aware of thoughts, it means that we are not our thoughts!"

He looks at her with a scrunched up face and says, "What!! Just be careful Jane, make sure you don't get brainwashed here. This guy is starting to sound as though he could have ulterior motives. And for that matter, did you find out why he wants to help you?"

With those words, she suddenly felt a rush of doubt flood in again. The thought that Arturo was somehow using her for some sinister bigger plan sent a shiver down her spine. "Um, no dad, I didn't ask him." she says and walks away.

Later that evening, in her room, her dad's words kept going around in her head. She noticed that ever since David said those words about Arturo, she wasn't feeling good.

She decided to write down her observations in her journal:

After my meeting with Arturo, I noticed a lot of negative thoughts, as though something had taken me over and was running wild in my head. There was quite a lot of anger but when I noticed the thoughts, it was like they didn't want to be seen and the intensity of the feelings reduced.

My dad cast some doubt around Arturo and I noticed that I wasn't feeling good. When I looked at the thoughts I was having, it was all about doubt, that I was being a fool, that Arturo was going to hurt me in some way, that he'll abuse my trust and somehow get one over me.

Again, when I looked at these thoughts, I saw that they were like little imps all working together to have me feel bad, but looking at them directly seemed to reduce the intensity again and I then started to feel better.

She suddenly got an insight that her thoughts were not only NOT helpful, but that they actually seemed to be designed to have her feel bad!

"What the hell? My thoughts are against me!" she said aloud. She then thought, 'Who am I if I'm not my thoughts?' She sat with this thought, but no answer came, she was completely blank.

She spent the rest of the week noticing her thoughts and writing down her observations, but the *Who am I* question kept bugging her.

Week Three –
The Opposites

Monday had arrived and Jane was eager to share her observations about the week, with Arturo. "Come on in Jane." Again he spent a few moments looking into her eyes. "... So, how was your week, Jane?"

"Well, I've had quite an interesting week, but first, my dad's been hassling me to ask you why you're wanting to help me, so why *do* you want to help me?"

"OK, let's just say at this point, that I see a certain potential in you. All will be revealed when the time is right, but for your dad, you can say that this is a sort of 'paying it forward' type of thing. So please continue, how was your week?" he says with a note of dismissiveness.

"Oh-Kay, well I noticed that a lot of my thoughts are automatic, and negative, and that when I get into this spiral of negative thoughts, I end up feeling like crap!

The other thing I noticed was that when I simply noticed the thoughts, they would reduce in intensity, like they didn't want me to see them or something like that."

"Jane, that's excellent!" he says with surprise.

"Huh? Excellent!! What do you mean? I mean seriously, how can it be excellent when I feel as though my thoughts are against me? And then there's the issue that if I'm not my thoughts, like, who the hell am I?"

He leans forward and with a smile, quietly says, "... Again, excellent. You've experienced something about yourself that most people will never experience in a whole lifetime!

While it doesn't feel so good to think that your thoughts are against you, it's a key part of evolution. But before I tell you why, I'd like to ask you something and then I'll come back to this.

Jane, why are you here?"

"Huh!! Why am I here?" She fidgets around, "Um, uh ... you've put me on the spot here, I don't know, I guess I thought you were helping me for something or other." she says as she scratches her head in confusion.

"No Jane. Why are YOU HERE, as in why were you born, why are you alive, here and now?"

"What the, you really know how to throw some curve balls." He remains still and stares at her with intensity, as he waits for an answer.

"Uh, OK, well ..." Her mind races as she tries to come up with an answer. "I don't know Arturo! OK? Why the hell are you asking me these questions anyway?" she snaps back angrily.

He replies in a soothing voice, "OK Jane, I see the pattern, you try to shrug off the uncomfortable questions but when pressed, you get angry as a way of defending yourself or gaining some control back. It's OK, it's a very normal reaction.

The thing is, while the question I asked is a simple one, it's not easy to answer and the reason why it's not easy is because it's linked to the purpose of life. Now, do you have any inkling as to why you might be here?"

She feels her tension release and feels some ease now. She looks up and thinks about what her purpose to being here might be. After a few moments she says, "Well, the only thing that comes to me is that I'm here to continue living."

Still looking at her with intensity, he says, "OK, good. That's a good answer at this point, it's not complicated and it'll be good for you to have this as a reference point for when you're making plans about your future."

"What about you Arturo, do you have an answer for what the purpose to life is?" she says, thinking he might have another weird way of seeing life.

"I do have an answer but I'm not going to share that with you right now." he says and moves on. "OK, let's go back to why having thoughts that work against us is a key part of evolution. Now I'll take this slowly:

1. At a base level, our main focus is on survival, because as you said, we want to continue living;
2. Due to this focus on survival, our brain is sensitive to potential dangers and anything that could possibly stop us from surviving;
3. This hypersensitivity to danger helped us when we faced the danger of being eaten by some ferocious animal, but now, that threat doesn't exist for most of us, and yet this hypersensitivity remains, which generates an underlying sense of unease;
4. This happens unconsciously, that is to say, without us consciously knowing that we're doing it, for example, being concerned about

what someone might have said behind our back might be taken as a danger, unconsciously;

5. This unconscious unease feeds into our thoughts, which creates a loop of feeling bad, which then leads to having negative thoughts and then to feeling bad again. In other words, the emotion leads to a thought and the thought leads to an emotion and around it goes in a loop of negativity;

6. Overall, we don't enjoy feeling bad, so we start to look for ways to break this cycle and start to feel better;

7. We start off by looking outside of ourselves, by wanting more money, a bigger house, nicer clothes, the latest gadgets, a better partner, etc. In the hope that better external circumstances take care of the unpleasant feelings internally; Eventually, at some later stage in life, we exhaust ourselves of all the external 'stuff', and realise that even though we have all this stuff or achieved worldly success and status, nothing has really changed on the inside and the same old feelings remain;

8. At this point, one of two things happens, either depression sets in and the cycle of feeling bad continues, or we start to look within. We might take up meditation, go for alternative healing methods, etc.

When we start the looking within process, we give ourselves the opportunity to experience a state of being that is simple yet profound at the same time. What we inevitably find is the unfolding of our unique journey. Of course, this doesn't mean that we never get lost again and create another story out of that inner world also, but eventually we realise that we are IT, that we are everything that we've been looking for and that we are whole as we are. In other words, there's nothing that can be added or subtracted from us to make us better. This process is one of REALISATION.

The interesting thing though, is that if it weren't for unease, negativity and bad feelings, we wouldn't feel the compulsion to look for anything else. Another way of saying this is that **to know who we are, we must first know who we are *not*.** In order to know the light, we must first experience the darkness.

Can you see how the negative is necessary for the journey now, Jane?"

"Whoa, that's quite a theory! Uh, yeah, I can see the logical sequence but I'm having a tough time accepting it. Like, when you say that we need the negative before we have the positive, what's that about?"

"Actually, I didn't quite say that, I said that if it weren't for unease, negativity and bad feelings, we wouldn't feel the compulsion to look for anything else. But OK, it's probably a good time to talk about positive and negative aspects at this point.

The aspects of positive and negative are the same as the up and the down, the left and the right, the front and the back, and the in and the out. It's all the same thing. They're *the opposites*.

We all grow up with the desire for good (positive) things to show up in our life, but invariably something happens that feels bad (a negative) and we then live in a state of looking for the positive side of the coin to be there in a consistent way.

People look for that elusive positive side, while at the same time fearing, unconsciously, the negative and then hoping that they don't get that side. People say things like 'touch wood' or 'good luck'. They don't know how things are going to turn out and they fear that it won't go the way they'd like it to go. That reminds me, I'll discuss the idea behind 'luck' with you at some point also, I think you'll get a kick out of that one, but that's a topic for another day.

So back to the issue that remains, would you know that something was positive if you didn't first have some idea of what negative was? If the only colour you could see was blue, for example, how would you know it was blue, if you'd never experienced any other colour? You need something different to contrast in order to compare it and notice a difference. Is this making sense?"

"Um, no, not really, blue is blue, as long as I know blue, I can identify that colour anywhere."

"OK, let's try this from another angle. Please close your eyes ... now tell me what you see."

"Well, nothing, of course!"

"OK, you sure about that?" She nods. "Alright, you can open your eyes now. Why do think you couldn't see anything?"

"Arturo! Is this line of questioning really necessary? Isn't it obvious that I wouldn't see anything, because my eyes were shut!" she says sarcastically.

"Jane, please bear with me here. The reason why you couldn't see anything was because there were no distinctions or inputs hitting your optic nerve to register that you had seen something. You need to have some contrasts 'to see' something, but because your eyes were closed, all you had was uniformity and therefore nothing to contrast.

For all you know, there are things to see with your eyes shut but they just aren't registering for you because you don't have the refinements in place to see the subtle distinctions. Are you getting this now?"

"Whoa, OK, let me see. You're saying that I can only see something when I have something else that is not the thing that I'm seeing. A contrast! And so out of this, you're saying that I only really experience the positive because I have the negative to contrast it to? ... I don't think I like the sound of that."

"Sure, that's understandable, you've experienced pain and you know that you don't want any more of it. Here's the thing though, when you know that the pain and negativity are there as simply a contrast, the grip it has on you starts to diminish."

"But wait a sec, are you saying that we *need* to have people like murderers, rapist, etc., because we *need* this contrast to get in touch with the positive??"

"Hmm, you're wanting to go to the extremes again ... OK, now please listen very carefully Jane. In no way whatsoever am I condoning what murderers, rapist, etc. do.

People that behave in this way are all part of the way the world has operated for a very long time, I don't feel aligned, nor agree with that behaviour but I can accept that this is what still happens in the world at this point.

OK, so with that in mind, you want to know if we *need* this in order to know the positive? The answer is NO, because we already know about this, it's already imprinted in our consciousness as something undesirable, so no, it's not needed anymore.

Just like you said earlier, you know the colour blue now, so you don't need to see it to know what blue looks like.

What's important to understand here though, is that the ability to experience great pain means that you also have the ability to experience great joy. Knowing the pain allows you to appreciate the joy when you find yourself there. Does that make sense?"

"Uh, I think it's getting clearer. So what you're saying is that these people that do terrible things aren't really needed but they're still here at this point. But I don't have to agree with their behaviour, and simply knowing that, means I can appreciate goodness and joy when I see it..." she looks down, "... But the thing I don't get is that it still doesn't feel good when I see all the bad stuff out there, like in the news for example."

"Sure, it's not easy to feel good when there are lots of people around you, or on TV, that are in pain. Remember how you said that noticing your thoughts actually reduced the intensity of the feelings? ... Well it's the same with negative events that show up. If you can start to not resist them or wish that things would be different, you'll start to notice that things change.

It's like I said in our first meeting, there's what happens and there's what we do with what happens. Start to look at things that happen with curiosity, say to yourself, 'Hmm, isn't that interesting?' Just notice without judging one way or the other. The aim is to be neutral, you can notice that the feeling isn't good but you don't have to be enveloped by it. You can allow a gap to simply be there within you."

"But Arturo, everyone has opinions and judgements of things, and when it's in your face everyday, it's not realistic to be completely neutral!"

"Jane, you're wanting to hang on to your current mind patterns, your beliefs. See if you can be open to the possibility of something else being true. I know it's not easy, but you CAN do it. And you don't *need* to watch the news either, there's nothing of real value there for you. Just start to notice what happens around you."

"OK, OK, I'll give it a go."

"Don't give it a go Jane, bring your focus to it and allow yourself to experience it, or don't. Giving it a go is like *trying*, it's wishy washy." he says sternly.

"OK, OK, sheesh, you really can push it sometimes. Yes, I-WILL-DO-IT."

"OK, good, we're in agreement then. Now as for a project this week, I'd like you to still notice your thoughts as well as notice what happens within you when you see something that you would normally judge as bad or wrong.

When you notice the judgement, see if you can just come back to a place of curiosity, 'Hmm, isn't that interesting?' and make notes in your journal if you want. Remember Jane, this isn't about getting a right answer, simply be curious and notice what comes up.

Right, that's our time, I'll see you next week."

"OK, thanks Arturo."

AFTER THREE WEEKS, David is aware of Jane's routine with Arturo and waits for her by the door as he hears her pull into the driveway. She enters and he says keenly, "Hey Jane, so what was it this week? Have you found out why he wants to help you yet?"

"Uh, hi dad, boy, give me a chance to take my coat off and settle in ... OK, yes, he said that it was a type of 'pay it forward' project, he sees potential in me and wants to help. Are you satisfied now?" she says with an edge.

"Hmm, it still sounds a bit strange, but if you feel he's genuine, then OK. So what else happened, was it still weird?"

"Yeah, still a little weird but it's making more sense to me now. He spoke about the opposites, how you can't have one side without the other, as in you can't have left without right, up without down and so on."

"Uh, yeah, that seems obvious, that's what relativity is all about. Was there something more to it?"

"Yeah, he was using that as an example as to why negative things happen. Like, we all want positive stuff but we can't have positive stuff without first knowing that there's negative stuff. That it's only in the experiencing of the negative in some form, that we can experience the positive.

So instead of getting upset and resisting all the bad stuff that happens, just accept it as a part of life and be curious about it and see how that feels. Oh, he also said to not automatically judge it as bad."

"I'm not sure I'm liking that line of reasoning, Jane. So someone can come along and attack me and I should just sit back and take it? And be curious about it? That sounds pretty stupid to me!"

"No, I don't think that's what he means, dad. I think it's more about when we see bad things on TV or people in pain around us, it triggers something within us, which is then an opportunity to understand that this is all part of the opposites."

"Hmm, OK, so what he's saying is that for one thing to exist, its opposite must also exist, which is relativity, but he's relating it to the emotional level of positive and negative!" David turns his hands so that his palms are up and looks at them, while moving them like he's weighing things up. "That actually makes a lot of sense, I can see how that's logical when you relate it to all the other opposites that exist. Was there anything else?"

"No, not really, I have a project for the week that involves watching out for when something happens that I would normally judge as bad and see if I can not automatically judge it but just notice the feeling without doing anything with it."

"Hmm, that sounds like it'll be quite challenging, I don't know how I'd go in doing that."

"Yeah, I'm not sure how I'm going to go with this one either, but it was good to hear Arturo say, 'just be curious', and that it's not about getting a right answer."

The next morning, as she gets out of the shower, she hits her big toe against the bottom lip of the shower base, "... SHIT!" she screams out. Her toe was throbbing with pain and she started limping around the bathroom. She then noticed her thoughts, '... damn thing, why did that have to happen, it bloody hurts, ouch, damn, shit, shit, shit, why did this have to happen to me?'

She gently presses on her toe to relieve the pain and the pain slowly dissipates. She then remembers Arturo's words, 'there's what happens and there's what you do with what happens.' As she thinks about this she says sarcastically, "*hmm, isn't that interesting!*" and laughs out loud.

Later that day at the college cafeteria, Trent, a good friend, comes up to her in a panic and starts talking quickly, "Jane, Jane, I was sitting in traffic this morning when a guy rear ended my car, neither of us have insurance and he can't pay for the damage, what I am going to do?"

He looks at her expectantly and she could feel the injustice and pain that Trent was feeling and felt the urge to join in with his anxiety, but she remembered her toe and just thought, 'hmm, isn't that interesting!' Trent was still waiting for an answer and screams out, "Jane!! What's going on with you? What am I going to do?"

She became still and said calmly, "Trent, I really don't know, but I can see you're in a lot of pain right now. What do *you* think you can do about it?"

He hadn't seen Jane this calm before and with confusion said, "Huh? I don't know, it's a shit of a situation. I just don't know... You always have an answer, can't you think of something for me?"

"Well, try it this way, what if you did have an answer for yourself, what might it be?"

He thinks for moment, "Uh ... I guess, I could see if I can arrange some sort of repayment plan with the guy?"

"Well, that sounds like a pretty good plan to me." She then walks off with Trent scratching his head, wondering what had just happened.

As she walked off she thinks, 'Wow, that was amazing, I didn't react! By just noticing it, I was able to ask him what he thought about it and he came up with a solution, himself!'

She thought she was getting the hang of this noticing thing when a few days later her aunt Louise came over sobbing. Louise told the family that her brother in law had been suffering with depression for years and had now killed himself. She was inconsolable.

Jane knew John very well, he was 9 years older than her and had been like a big brother to her while she was growing up. She felt a deep sorrow come over her and tears welled in her eyes, followed by an uncontrollable sob.

As she sat there with tears streaming down her face, she noticed her thoughts, '... how is this possible? He seemed fine whenever I saw him, how could he do that? I'll never see him again! He was always so nice to me.'

Then, like a person pushing their way through a crowd, the words, 'hmm, isn't that interesting!' came along. '... Oh shit, not now, I just can't do this now. No, he just can't be dead.' She began to sob uncontrollably again.

Week Four – Selfishness

Jane was eager to meet with Arturo, as Monday afternoon rolled around. She'd been to John's funeral in the morning and was still in denial about the whole thing.

"... So Jane, how was your week?"

"Well, I've had better. I had some terrible news during the week and I'm struggling with it. A good friend of the family, someone I looked up to like a brother, killed himself!

I wasn't able to allow the statement of, 'Hmm, isn't that interesting!' It was just too painful. I'd handled a few other things that came up and thought I was getting the hang of it, but this was simply too much to deal with." she said as tears started streaming down her cheek.

He passed the tissue box over and when she settled he said, "Jane, look at me ..." With his deep blue eyes penetrating her soul, and his calming voice, "this is a process, it's a gradual opening where you come back to an understanding that there are things that happen that you can't explain, and that that's OK.

This friend of yours must have been in a huge amount of pain for him to do what he did. It's not easy to accept that someone you care deeply about is gone or that they directly chose to end their time here, but it *is* their choice.

You may not want to hear this right now, but you too have a choice. You can choose to see that at this moment he chose to resolve his pain by leaving this world and that for whatever reason, this was the best way for him to find peace for himself. Or, you can choose to resist and make it wrong that he killed himself.

I know this is difficult to accept, but we are all here to live joyfully and sometimes when people feel like they have no way of finding joy, then taking steps to end it can seem like the only option. It's difficult for the people around them but ultimately each one of us is responsible for taking care of ourselves, even if that means dying!"

Doing her best to hold back the tears she says flatly, "Well that just sounds really harsh and it feels selfish to me. I think that if you care about the people around you, you should take their feelings into consideration.

And killing yourself is just not on!" Tears again welled in her eyes and she reached for another tissue.

"Hmm, you're hurting right now, but are you saying people should disregard themselves, that they should follow what others think is important, even if that means living a lie and a life without joy? ... Wouldn't that actually make *you* the selfish one?"

She leans forward, while bringing her hands to her face at the same time, and starts to sob. After a few moments, she blows her nose and says quietly, "Well, I don't know, maybe you're right ... But it just doesn't seem right, somehow."

"I get it, we don't want people killing themselves under any circumstance. There's always help for anyone considering doing away with themselves, but ultimately, each of us are on a path and have the freedom to choose whatever we want, even if it *looks* selfish to others.

Think of it this way, when you take a plane trip, the air stewards go through the emergency procedures and they always say you should fasten your own breathing mask first, before helping anyone else. Why would they encourage people to focus on themselves first? Are they really encouraging selfishness?

It would seem they are, and the reason they encourage this is because without taking care of yourself FIRST, you're of little use to anyone else. When you give to yourself first, you create the space within you to be there in a more complete way for another.

The issue is that we tend to have a natural tendency to want to help others, because it feels good to help. It releases the feel-good hormones into our system and this can become addictive. The problem is, it's a short-term gain for a longer-term pain, just like any other vice.

What we don't see is that when we do this, we send a message to our psyche, the message is that I'm not worth it. I'm not worth taking care of myself, but I justify it to myself because the payoff is that others like me for helping them. In other words, gaining love from others becomes more important than giving myself love!

All of this has a substantial cost at an energetic level, and we can only do this for so long, at some point we either feel the desire to be whole and well and we take steps towards that or our life starts to fall apart and we aim to fix that as best we can. Either way, we'll do what's in our own best interest to do.

"You're messing with my head again! I don't get it, how does John killing himself have anything to do with what you're saying?" she says angrily.

"Jane, please take some deep breaths ... I don't know what caused John to take the steps he did, but for whatever reason he reclaimed his power in the only way he thought was best in that moment. I know it doesn't look like it but he made himself a priority and did what was in his own best to do. Regrettably for all those around him, he chose to do it in a destructive way.

Whether you like it or not, his death makes a very powerful statement and you can be sure that you and others that knew John, will think of life in a very different way from now on.

Some of you will learn and grow from the experience, and see it positively, while others will continue to resist and see only the negative. In the bigger tapestry of life however, I have no doubt that this will help everyone involved.

But, please don't misunderstand my point, I'm not saying that it's good that he died. I'm saying it was OK for him to choose to make himself important enough to stop pretending for others."

Looking down, she says in resignation, "Maybe you're right ... I just don't know. I guess, it's just really painful and I wish he could have reached out for help."

"Jane, it's important to understand that the way you see your world, is the world of how it affects YOU personally, it's your world. The best you can do is know that your world is safe, loving and joyous and it only gets that way when YOU REALISE that IT IS!"

She takes a deep breath and says, "OK, so how do I REALISE that 'my world' *is* safe and loving when so much crap happens?"

"OK, the thing to understand is that each of us constructs the world around us based on our perception. Perception is the building block that leads to a belief which then leads to what we consider reality. That's why how you see the world is just that, how YOU see the world. Someone may be standing right next to you and may literally be seeing something completely different.

So when you say 'so much crap happens', this is a perception in that moment, it's not set in stone and it doesn't have to be your world. Remember, there's what happens and there's what you do with what happens. When you practice this, you start to introduce a choice within you on how you want to see the world. One of those choices is that the world is a safe, loving and joyous place.

So coming back to selfishness, I want you to know it's not only OK to put yourself first, it's also OK to accept that the universe revolves around you. When you truly know this in your heart, you know that nothing can be added or taken away from you to make you more or less. When you realise this, you find that the love you feel for yourself, is the same love you feel for another – is this clearer now?"

"I think so... But why is it that people make it wrong for putting yourself first?"

"Here's the paradox, when you know that you're safe and whole, you naturally *want* to help others, and it *looks* as though you're putting them first. But you're not, you've already taken care of yourself, so helping another becomes a natural extension of you, and leaves everyone feeling good in that moment.

There was a time where the powers that be saw an opportunity in controlling the masses and exploited this by making it sinful or wrong to focus on yourself, and virtuous to help others. In so doing, the message was that you have no worth if you don't put others first. The result is that people have discounted the importance of taking care of themselves first because it *looks* better to show that you're helping others first.

Most people know unconsciously that it's important to take care of themselves first, but it's covered up by layers of dogma and in most cases, they simply don't want to do the work to uncover the truth."

He stares at her with intensity now and says, "You need to know, Jane, you are extremely important and you should always treat yourself as such. If something doesn't work for you, you don't have to bend yourself to suit anyone else, only do it if it's right for you. Remember, it's all about joy."

She leans back, looks up for a moment and then says, "But, what about compromises? Like when you're in a relationship? If each person is just looking out for themselves, without regard for the other, I don't think the relationship is going to go very far."

"Well, you're right. And it'd be easy to say, just don't get into a relationship if you haven't taken care of yourself enough, but the truth of the matter is that you often don't know how much you still need to take care of within yourself, until you *do* get into a relationship.

But before I get into the relationship side, I want to be clear about something—What I'm talking about, when I say *you don't have to bend yourself to suit anyone else,* is that ideally your aim is to be as clear minded as you can be, with a feeling of peace in your heart, and from there make a decision on whether something is right for you or not.

I'm not saying that you arrogantly walk around, looking down on others, with no regard for them. That's just more of the same consciousness that we've had for millennia. So again, what I'm saying is a relatively simple concept but it takes awareness and then courage to honour yourself, with love. Is that clear?"

"Yep, that's good, got it."

"Now, relationships, these are often a great environment for knowing what you need to take care of for yourself because the more you get upset when the other doesn't meet your expectations, the more you need to take care of something for yourself.

Your partner is going to behave in ways that are different to the way you operate and you're generally going to react against that. This then, becomes an opportunity to see what's true for you.

For example, you might like to spend time outside, walking in nature while your partner may prefer to sit in front of the TV, watching sports and drinking beer.

Through awareness, you can choose to come back to a place where you can feel whether the relationship is right for you or not, or whether what is being asked of you is right or not. From there, you make a choice and what your partner does with your choice is up to them.

Often, the best relationships happen when the individuals involved are comfortable with who they are and they come together with mutual respect, love and a desire to share common interests with each other. They don't need the other to bend for them to feel good and they give each other space whenever it's needed. They don't blame and they don't complain.

From the outside, it could look as though they compromise but they don't because the desire of one is not resisted by the other, and whatever needs to be taken care of, happens without a fuss."

"Wait, that sounds like no relationship I've ever heard of, do they really exist? And for that matter, what would be the point of being in relationship if people don't need each other?"

"They sure do Jane and I hope you get to experience that for yourself. The point of the relationship is simply to be in joyous union with another.

But first, remember that these relationships don't just happen automatically, they take work and a willingness to reflect on what the other has triggered for *you.*

It's this willingness to come back, where you bring awareness and accept responsibility for your part of the argument or disagreement, that's what makes the difference. From there, the ability to discuss your part and look for a resolution is what connects you."

"But what happens if I do that but my partner can't, what happens then?"

"Well, when you accept responsibility for yourself, you open the door for your partner to do the same. If they don't and just use the situation to blame you even more, then it means that their pain is still active and you can't connect at that point. In this case, if you can stay clear and not get triggered again, then one of two things happens, either they see their behaviour for what it is, or they'll leave because the two of you are no longer a match for each other.

Now, the challenging part is if others aren't used to you making yourself number one, they're not going to like it. When we make ourselves number one we make a statement and that statement is, *I am important.*

For someone that needs the other to give them the love they don't feel for themselves, this statement is going to trigger a negative reaction. The reason being is that they feel that the other doesn't care about them, and of course, they don't like the way that feels.

So when two people come together that don't need each other, they joyfully come together to share their path with each other. They walk the path together, without being *joined at the hip,* so to speak."

"Whoa Arturo, I'm going to need to sit with that, but I hear you and it makes sense. I just need to come to terms with the feelings I have around it."

"OK, but I do want to emphasise what I mentioned earlier though ..." He leans forward and with an intense gaze says, "... that being focused on yourself doesn't mean that you put others down, or are disrespectful towards them.

While others may still feel that you're being selfish by not bending to what they want, you can stay clear within yourself and know that they are a glorious manifestation of life, just like you. The only difference is that they're looking to you to give them something so *they* can be OK. They haven't realised their own gloriousness yet and so they look to you to give them something.

Have you ever noticed how a child reacts when they don't get their way? They throw tantrums, kick or scream and because most people haven't yet grown emotionally, the child within them still throws a form of tantrum by getting angry or pouting when they don't get what they're looking for.

Jane, this is key ... to truly grow up and be an adult means that you have all that it takes to take care of YOURSELF and that you're free of needing anyone to take care of you in any way.

You don't condemn anyone for not meeting your needs or standards and you understand that YOU are the one to look after you. You also release the need to blame anyone if something doesn't work out as you planned. You can still ask people for help, if that feels right but you don't turn it into drama if they don't."

"Oh Arturo, my head is really spinning now." She brings both hands up and shakes her head a little. "OK, so are you saying that no one can ever do anything wrong by me, that I somehow stand as this peaceful guru superhero or something??"

"Firstly, doing something *wrong* is a judgement that you make, you may not agree with what someone does and it may have consequences for you, but ultimately it's up to you on how you choose to deal with it. It comes back again to what happens and what you DO with what happens.

Secondly, I'm not saying that you're never going to feel hurt by the actions of others. Most likely, it'll feel quite painful but you're able to feel the pain while knowing that the pain is not who you are. You can cry, get angry or let out whatever is within you to let out, but you'll know that ultimately, you're OK and that you have what it takes to be all you can be in this environment.

She lets out a snort, "You are full on. You know that? OK, I think I get it."

"Good. OK, let's leave it at that and for this week's project, notice what you do and notice when you're doing things just to make someone happy or to simply keep the peace. I'm not saying to do anything differently, just notice, and if you want to do something differently then that's fine too."

"OK, thanks Arturo, see you next week."

"So Jane, what did you talk about this week?" asks David, the moment she steps in the door.

Her head was still in a spin over the conversation with Arturo, "Uh, just give me a minute, dad ... Well, the main thing that's got my head spinning is that Arturo was essentially telling me about how being selfish is necessary before we can really help anyone else."

"What!!!" he retorts, "What the hell is that about?" he says shaking his head in disbelief.

Remaining calm, she says, "Well dad, he actually makes a really good case for it."

"Oh yeah? This'll be good, let's hear it ..." he says while tilting his head up and crossing his arms.

"Well, he gave the example of when we take a trip in a plane, how the air stewards go through the emergency procedures and they always say that you need to fasten your own breathing mask first, before helping someone else. The reason being that unless you can breathe, you won't be able to help anyone else."

"Yeah I understand that, but that's different, that's an emergency situation of life and death, you can't go around living your life like that!"

"It was more about how our tendency is put others first because we like how it feels to help others, as in our brain releases certain hormones that feel good, when we help others. But if we do this without taking care of ourselves first, or neglect ourselves altogether, it has a cost on an emotional level, which eventually causes us to take drastic action because we ultimately want to live more joyfully."

He scratches his chin and looks up, "Hmm, I think I'm getting what you're talking about. In many ways I've put the family ahead of me because of the responsibilities involved with that and also because it feels good to take care of the family. But I can see that if I'm not taking care of what's important to me, then my own mental health or wellness suffers and then I can't help the family anyway."

He then becomes serious, "You know Jane, I think I haven't wanted to believe this, but you're right, we do need to take care of ourselves first." He sits down slowly and digests what he said, "... And of course it makes sense that you need to take care of yourself first before you can be of any use to anyone else, I've just been so absorbed in my role as husband and father that I haven't really stopped to think about it before." he says, now stunned with his own realisation.

"Yep, and as long as we feel there's something lacking in ourselves, we can't give to another." she says while sitting down slowly next to him.

Speaking softly, he says, "So what are we going to do about this, how do we live life by taking care of ourselves without it looking selfish to others? Did he say anything about that?"

A little stunned by her dad's candour, she says, "Uh, not really, he just said that others won't like it because it'll highlight their own insecurities, or something like that, but what I understand is that the more I take care of myself, the more I'm likely to *want* to help others.

I'm guessing that if I feel good about myself and what I do, then if or when someone accuses me of being selfish, I can calmly say that I'm taking care of myself first before I can help others ... Oh, he also said that being focused on yourself doesn't mean that you become arrogant or put others down in any way. People might still think you're selfish if you're not bending to what they want, but you can stay clear within yourself and know that they're still valuable beings.

Um, I think there was a bit more to it also ... ah that's right, he said that the only difference between them and me is that they're dependent on me giving them something so that they can be OK."

With a pained look on his face he says, "Oh, that all sounds quite tough."

With a burst of energy, she says, "Dad! Don't you get that we've bought a pack of lies, why do we have to tiptoe around people? It's because we're scared that they won't like us! I don't want to play that game anymore."

She continues, "You know what? I know I'm a good person and if others don't like me, it's their issue. I have to live as honestly as I can, even if it means others don't like me for not doing what they want."

With a shocked look on his face he says, "Wow Jane, I don't think I've ever heard you speak quite like that before, I kinda feel proud and scared at the same time, but I actually feel an inspiration to be more assertive myself.

I think you're right in that too often we tiptoe around people for fear of offending them or being disapproved of in some way, it's time to take a stand isn't it?" They looked at each other with a knowing that they'd uncovered something they could no longer hide from.

THE NEXT DAY, while having lunch at the Uni cafeteria, Trent runs frantically towards her. "Jane, Jane, boy am I glad to see you. Listen, I was wondering if you could do me a favour, remember how my car was rear-ended a few weeks back? ... Well my car's getting fixed today and I really need a lift to go and pick it up after class, can you drop me off?" he says while he puts on his best puppy dog look.

"Um, I'm going to work straight after class today but if it's on the way, that should be OK. Where is it?"

"It's not far, Jane ..." "Trent, I need to know exactly where it is?" she says gently but firmly. He points in the direction and says, "It's about 5k's that way." She looks at him realising that it's not on her way. "Trent, that's not going to work for me, that's the opposite direction that I'm heading in and I'll probably be late for work if I drop you off, so I think you're going to have to find another way."

"Oh Jane, please don't do this to me, I'm really stuck here, I don't have anyone else to ask, you gotta help me out, please Jane, pleeease."

Arturo's image popped into Jane's mind and she remembered the conversation about putting herself first and that others won't like it, so she looks at Trent in the eyes and says calmly, "Look, I don't expect you to understand this but I need to do what's right for me. I'm sorry, I can't help you right now."

Trent stands there for a moment looking at her in both disbelief and disgust. He then walks off, shaking his head and saying loudly, "What the hell happened to you, Jane?"

She looks at him walk away, she can't help feeling bad that she's let him down and it feels painful. As she sits with the feeling, she becomes aware of a feeling of clarity, that it was definitely the right thing to do. She knew in her heart that had she done this for him, it would likely have caused issues for her at work, and while the pain of Trent's disapproval really hurt, it was the right decision.

Week Five – The Journey

The moment she sat at Arturo's desk, she couldn't contain herself and quickly began to share the experience she'd had with Trent. Arturo remained still and when she finished speaking there was silence as he continued looking intensely at her. She sat there eagerly waiting for a response but then became calm and still herself. She then said gently, "Arturo, why are you doing this? I mean, why are you even helping me like this?"

He remained still for a few moments more and then said, "OK Jane, it seems the time has come for you to know. You see, it's like this, I see things in people, quite literally. You could call it a sixth sense or something like that, but sometimes I come across someone that has a very strong calling in life, someone that's yearning at a deep level to evolve and be an agent for change as part of a bigger picture ... Jane, YOU are that person."

She sits there, blankly looking at him, she then thinks, 'Is he shitting me?' Eventually she says, "Um, I'm not sure I understand what you're saying, I mean, like, how is that possible? I'm just an average person, living a normal life, how do I know you're not just giving me some sort of motivational pep talk here?"

He moves forward, places his elbows on the desk and clasps his hands together, "Jane, I would like to show you something, can I do that?" She nods suspiciously, "OK, put your hands in mine and close your eyes ..."

He puts his arms out on the desk with palms up waiting for her to put her hands in his.

Her mind starts to race and she feels a level of anxiety in not knowing what he's going to do, but then feels herself relax as she looks into his eyes and senses calmness. She then moves her seat closer to the desk, puts her hands in his and closes her eyes.

In an instant she feels herself jolt and move at lightning speed down a corridor towards a bright light. In that same moment a scene opens up and she finds herself standing in the middle of a well-lit ballroom with Arturo by her side. She looks at Arturo and says, "What the hell!! What just happened? Where are we?" He turns to her and says, "I want to show you what I saw on the night I met you at Mandy's party. Look around ..."

She looks around and sees hundreds of well dressed people sitting at tables, in what seems to be a swanky reception, and in that moment everyone stood and began clapping, while an elegantly dressed middle-aged woman walks across the stage towards a man that had just introduced her. He then hands her some sort of trophy and they shake hands.

Jane's distance from the stage prevented her from getting a clear view of the woman but she could see that this was a confident woman. The woman then stands in front of the microphone and pauses for a few moments. She looks at the trophy and then begins to speak as the applause slows.

"Thank you ... thank you. I'm deeply appreciative to all of you for coming out tonight, it's a huge honour to be here right now and to be honest, I could never have imagined all those years ago when I went down this path that I'd be standing here tonight in front of you ..."

The applause erupts again. "Thank you. Even though my goal, right from the start, was to help children become healthy, responsible and independent adults, I really never saw a point where I would be standing here receiving this amazing award.

My aim on a day-to-day basis is always quite simple, and that is to enjoy the journey and trust that everything unfolds in a way that's beneficial for everyone involved. It's a way of thinking that has guided me very well over the years and I really have to give credit to my good friend and mentor, Arturo Vincetori ..."

Jane suddenly realised who this person was and with a look of absolute horror, screams out, "HOLY SHIT! ARTURO!! Is that ME in the future??"

Her head starts turning violently from the stage to Arturo and back again. Arturo looks at her with gentle eyes and a little smile and puts his arm around her shoulders, "Jane, it's OK, breathe. You're safe. Just breathe, this is why I knew I had to reach out to you."

In an instant Jane was back in Arturo's office, she opens her eyes, looks at her hands still in his and pulls them away quickly and puts them on her head as she tries to work out what just happened "What the hell!! Was that a dream?? What just happened? How did that happen? What's going on here?"

"Jane, look at me, I know it's a lot to take in, breathe, just take some deep breaths and focus on the air coming in and going out. The first time is always a head spin, but keep focusing on the breath and I'll get you some water ...

OK, as I mentioned earlier, I have this ability to see certain things and

I can also show others what I see. I have shared this with you in order for you to better understand why you and I are doing this work together."

Jane was still reeling from what she had just experienced and was focusing on her breath. "Jane, look at me, I want you to know that there's nothing to fear, you're absolutely safe here, I know it's a bit much to take in at the moment but you *are* safe, just keep focusing on the breath."

She calms down a little and he continues, "I want you to know something very important Jane, and that is, there's nothing that you have to do about this, it's a glimpse of what's possible for you, that's all. You've simply seen an aspect of you that exists within you, right now."

Breathing heavily again and bringing her right hand to her head, she says, "But, I don't understand what just happened, it just can't be real, I mean, it had to be an illusion, right? Or some sort of figment of my imagination, right?"

"Jane, whether it was an illusion or whether it wasn't, the question is, did it feel any less real than what you're feeling right here and now?"

"Uh ... no, it felt just as real as this." she gestures with her arms waving around. "But how, how is that possible? Are you some sort of magician, is that what this is about? Or is this some sort of hypnotherapy type of thing?"

"No Jane, I'm not a magician or anything like that ..." he chuckles, "look, just know that what you saw was a future that is a possibility for YOU, it's not guaranteed or set in stone in any way. It's simply an idea that's there for you, if that feels like the right path for you.

Remember, you never have to do anything that doesn't feel right for you. Right now, your old conditioning of what you consider as possible or not is causing you to feel anxious. But you *can* choose what feels good and go with that. Just focus on this moment, here and NOW."

Speaking a little calmer now, she says, "I'm still grappling with this. Was this something you've created?"

"No, not in the way you think, this *is* your creation and I am simply a link that allows you to tap into a greater aspect of you. As I said, I saw this in my mind's eye when I shook your hand that night at Mandy's party and that was my signal to reach out to you. From that moment on, it was all up to you."

"So, if I didn't call you, that would have been it? You wouldn't have called me?"

"That's right. It's important that I not push it. If I 'tried' to make this happen between us, you would most likely have pushed me away as some sort of madman. So it's quite delicate at the start, I open the door, but you take the steps to walk through, and the choice is all yours."

She looked down for a moment and thought, 'Wow, I came so close to throwing that card out!' She then looked up and said, "So are you able to you see the future of everyone you come into contact with?"

"No. Only those that have a strong calling and out of those, an even smaller number that I get a further impulse to reach out to."

"My head's spinning Arturo, I have so many questions..."

"Jane, listen to me, for now, just sit with what you've seen and know that this potential future is not a certainty, it's a probability that exists in this time-space reality, based on your current energy imprint. The only true point of power is right here and now, the past was a now moment that's already happened and the future is a now moment that *you* create out of *this* now moment.

I know it's not easy to let go of what you saw, but you need to know that it's definitely NOT guaranteed. You are a creator by nature, exploring and experiencing this exciting journey called life, it's up to you to create whatever feels right to you out of this NOW moment.

At this point, simply understand that you create out of this now moment and you have the power to create something completely different if that's what you choose.

It's also important to know that your life won't be any easier for knowing that this exists for you. Right now this exists as a possibility in your mind, you can think about the outcome and the accolades but I recommend that you don't focus on that too much.

What's important is to stay focused on what feels good to you here and now and trust that everything else will unfold in ways that you can't even imagine at the moment.

Your project for the week ahead is to focus on your breath every time your thoughts take you to what you saw about your future."

"But Arturo, this is going to consume every waking hour, my head is in spin and I automatically keep thinking about the woman on the stage, I just still can't believe this whole thing!"

"OK Jane, if you find that focusing on the breath doesn't help, take out your journal and write out what you're thinking. Write down questions as well, and see what answers come to you, and then write those down also.

You will find a place of peace around this Jane, you're more powerful than you realise but also know this, you and I wouldn't be doing this if you didn't have what it takes to hold this information!

Oh, and one more thing, I recommend that you don't tell anyone about this, most people can't handle this sort of thing at this point in time and so they're likely to put you down as someone that has lost the plot or gone crazy."

"But, my dad, I have a chat with him every Monday after our sessions, what will I say to him?"

"You'll work it out Jane. When you're with him, something will come to you that will allow you to still honour yourself."

SHE ARRIVES HOME to David's usual curiosity, "So Jane, what was it this week?"

"Um, well, how can I put it?" she says, scratching her head and looking up, "... We, um ... spoke about my future and how the future exists as a probability but not as a certainty."

He remains still, in anticipation for some earth shattering statement, "Dad, stop looking at me like that, I'm doing my best to convey this."

Smiling, he says, "OK honey, it's just that every week there seems to be something big that happens and I'm just waiting for that."

"Well, it *was* big, I'm just finding it hard to put it into words. OK, let me try this again. Most people make plans for the future, whether it's a plan for a holiday or a plan to get a certain job. Now, depending on what we bring to this moment, which is our point of power, we begin to shape whether those plans will turn out as we planned. But ultimately, we don't know whether they'll turn out as we think they will. But, if it's something we feel confident about, they probably will, but it's by no means certain that they will.

I'm not sure I'm making this clear still, I guess what I'm trying to say is that, this moment, here and now, is the most important moment. It's fine to have plans for the future but the key is to enjoy the journey NOW, before you get to the destination. The destination or outcome is just a potential point down the road, what matters most is the journey along the way.

It's fine to think about the future and feel good about it but if the destination is your only focus, when you get to that final destination or outcome, it only feels good temporarily, it doesn't truly fulfil you and you then need a new outcome to go for so that you get more of those temporary hits of accomplishment.

What happens is that you end up spending all your NOW moments chasing these future points that you hope will give that permanent feeling of being whole and you miss the only point where you can be whole, and that's NOW." She stops for a moment, looks to the side and thinks, 'Where the hell did that come from? ... I don't know, but it sure sounds good.'

"Jane, Jane—earth to Jane, are you there Jane?" he says, seeing that she's lost in thought.

"Um, yep, yep, I'm here, I was just thinking how true this is."

"OK Jane, it does sound quite deep and I think I get a sense of what you're saying here, but sometimes we just need that carrot at the end of the stick to keep going."

"What!! NO Dad, that's not it, maybe that's the way it used to be but it doesn't have to be that way now. Now we can choose. Even when something doesn't feel great, we can still choose to focus on something that does.

Look, what's the point of busting your gut and being miserable just because you hope that it'll be worth it for a pot of gold down the road? For all you know, when you get there, you'll die and still won't be able to enjoy it. No, find the joy now and trust that whatever comes along down the road will be fine too."

"Wow, this Arturo character has really brought out the feisty one in you. I understand what you're saying but I'm just not sure it's as easy as you make it sound." he says, feeling uncomfortable and a little defensive with her outspokenness.

"Of course it's not easy dad, we've all grown up with false ideas, work hard, get a good job, fight as hard as you can to get what you want, struggle, struggle, struggle, and then one day, maybe when you're 65, you can relax and enjoy the fruits of your labour ... HEL-LO, I don't think so. If you're miserable now, you'll be miserable down the track as well, when the shine of whatever you've achieved has gone.

We treat life like some sort of game, where you've got to fight hard to score and defeat the opposition, in the hope that you get the shiny cup in the end and then you can rest and enjoy. Dad, that just feels like crap to me and I don't want to be a part of that game anymore."

Feeling even more defensive now, he says, "OK Jane, I'll play along. How are you going to live? Are you going to go all hippy on me and think that things are going to magically appear for you out of thin air, that you won't have to work or go to Uni, and just live in this la-la sort of state?" he says sarcastically.

"Jane, you live in a cocoon right now, you have limited living expenses and you really don't have many obligations, how do you think your life would look in this state of utopia you speak about?" he says with agitation now.

Having noticed his defensiveness, she started focusing on her breath and now says calmly but firmly, "No dad, I won't be living in a 'la-la sort of state', and you're right, I do live in a bit of a cocoon here. You cover all the family bills and all I have to do is maintain my car, my phone and a few other bits and pieces. Maybe I should experience what it's like to be self-reliant and see if I can find the joy while having to cover bills."

Suddenly realising that he may be pushing her out and that Elizabeth would hit the roof if Jane moved out on his account, he quickly says, "Well, just hang on a moment honey, I know I'm putting you on the spot here but we're just talking, I'm not suggesting in any way that you should move out or anything like that, I'm just wanting to make a point on the facts ..."

"And your point is valid, dad. I think I *am* old enough to be looking after myself, there are people that move out at a younger age than me, so it's not a totally foreign concept." Sensing that he's about to go into panic mode she says, "Look dad, I'll just think about it, I won't do anything without thinking it through, so don't stress, it'll be fine."

He quietly breathes a sigh of relief and says, "Um, OK Jane, you do that, OK." and walks off.

Later that evening, in her room, she was still thinking about the experience she'd had with Arturo, '... how the hell was that possible? Am I really destined to help kids be responsible, independent and healthy adults? This is just crazy. But it felt so real, how is that even possible??' She then remembered to focus on the breath, but after a short while, thoughts of her future started pouring in again.

'Argh, this is driving me crazy. OK, let's get the journal out.' She starts jotting down some points and eventually falls asleep.

That night she dreams of herself walking through a meadow on a sunny day, there are kids everywhere, of all ages, running, playing games and having fun. The kids then see her and run to line up behind her. They then start to follow the way she moves, and she playfully dances while the kids start to dance and laugh with her ...

A New Beginning

Jane wakes up remembering the dream from the night before and it fills her with joy. She thought, '... if people are going to follow me, maybe I should be the best example they can follow!'

She then felt a burst of enthusiasm to explore what it would take for her to be a healthy, responsible and independent woman, now. She decides to spend some time in the library at lunchtime to make some notes.

AT LUNCH, SHE took out her journal and made three columns on a page with the headings, HEALTHY, RESPONSIBLE and INDEPENDENT. She then began to think what the characteristics for each were, and came up with the following:

HEALTHY	RESPONSIBLE	INDEPENDENT
Body—Eat well, exercise, grooming **Mind**—Positive attitude, believe in myself **Spirit**—Meditation, awareness of thoughts and feelings, be at ease and joyful, feel compassion for others	• I accept the circumstances I'm in now • I blame no one for the way my life is • I accept that I have the power to change and create • I am no one's victim • I trust that people are basically good • I contribute to the well-being of the world	• I think for myself • I question whether something is right for me and follow my own intuition • I don't follow the crowd without knowing it's right for me • I cover my living costs • I move around freely

She put her pen down, picked up her notebook and stared at what she'd written. She then felt more excitement than she'd felt in a long time. At that point she suddenly realised that Graphic Design was no longer the path for her.

With that thought, fear crept in, '... shit, how am I going to break this to mum and dad, I haven't got a clue on what I'm going to do next!' Her anxiety started going through the roof.

She decided to skip her afternoon classes and spent some time in the sun. She sat on the grass, closed her eyes and focused on her breath. As she became aware of thoughts, she'd let them pass through and come back to noticing the air entering her nose and exiting her mouth.

She then remembered something that future Jane had said, 'Arturo was her friend and mentor', she hadn't thought about him as her mentor but it felt right. She then thought, 'maybe Arturo could help me with what I wrote at lunchtime.'

That afternoon she wrote an email to him explaining that Graphic Design was no longer the path she wanted to go down and that being a healthy, responsible and independent person is what she now wanted to focus on. She also said that if it was OK with him, whether he would be her mentor.

Arturo replied later that evening simply with, 'Let's talk on Monday. Arturo.'

The next day she felt a little nervous but still excited about her decision, she skipped classes again and spent the day in the library.

She pondered on some of the conversations she's had with Arturo and thought, '... if now is always where my point of power is, then it's probably best that I look at where I am right *now!*'

She wrote the following in her notebook:

Health

Body:
Eat well—*I mainly eat good food, maybe a pizza or burger and chips once in a while, but mostly salads, rice, pasta, fruit, vegetables and cereal*
Exercise—*I go to gym 3 times a week, doing cardio workouts*
Grooming—*I shower daily, look after my skin with moisturiser and use sunscreen when in the sun, I also look after my clothes and dress neatly*
Mind:
Positive attitude—*I'm generally optimistic and have a can-do attitude*
I believe in myself—*I generally achieve anything I set my mind to, I have the confidence to take a little risk*
Spirit:
Meditation—*I don't really do this, maybe I'll start*
Awareness of thoughts and feelings—*Arturo has helped me focus on this, I need more practice with this*
Be at ease and joyful—*I can get a little anxious at times, so I need more practice with this too*

Feel compassion for others— *I need more practice with this too*

Responsible:
I accept the circumstances I have now—*I'm a little uncomfortable with this because I feel a bit nervous about making a major change*
I blame no one for the way my life is—*This is a little scary too, that I can't blame anyone if things don't turn out for me*
I accept that I have the power to change and create—*I do feel my strength when I come back to this moment, but I don't know if I can do this consistently*
I am no one's victim—*Similar to not blaming anyone, feels a little scary to be fully responsible*
I trust that people are basically good—*I do, but I still feel like I might be taken advantage of because of my lack of experience in life situations, I could be a 'victim' if I'm not careful!*
I contribute to the well-being of the world—*Not yet*

Independent:
I think for myself—*I'm getting there, Arturo has helped me to see things differently*
I question whether something is right for me and follow my own inner guidance—*same as above*
I don't follow the crowd without knowing it's right for me—*I need to practice this more*
I cover my living costs—*Sort of but not really, I live with my parents and also money isn't something I've thought about, maybe I need a plan*
I move around freely—*Not yet, I still live under my parents' roof, I'm not really independent!!*

She stared at what she'd written and thought, 'hmm, now what? What's the next step to take? ... there's so much stuff I need to work on!' She decides to keep it all to herself and not tell her family until she's at least had a discussion with Arturo.

Week Six – The Drop Out

As Jane drove to meet with Arturo she kept thinking about what he might say to her about her decision to drop out and whether he would mentor her. Every now and then she'd remember to focus on her breath but the anticipation was running wild in her head.

She arrived at Arturo's and studied his face for clues, but as usual, he simply sat and looked into her eyes.

After a few moments, he leans forward, and with a smile says, "So Jane, you're biting the bullet, going down the road less travelled, getting out of the rat race and all that sort of stuff ... How do you feel?"

"Um, I'm feeling a little anxious at the moment, and, to be honest, I'm concerned about what you're going to say."

"Really!! What I say? ... Jane, if you've made a decision that feels good to you, what does it matter what I say about it?" he says empathically.

"I guess it was how you simply said in your email, that we'd talk today, I took that in a way that maybe something was wrong."

"I see, so you were looking for a certain response from me in the email?"

"Uh ..." feeling embarrassed now, "well, I guess I was looking for some sort of recognition or maybe approval. I think I was feeling a little vulnerable, sharing my decision and asking for your help, that maybe you'd ridicule me or something."

"OK ..." he says firmly but with a gentle face, "what would a person that was healthy, responsible and independent do in this situation?"

She thinks for a moment and feels a little pressure building, "Uh, I guess that that person wouldn't shy away from the decision nor the request they made?"

"OK then, and so, what's your request?"

She sits up and says confidently, "Ahem, Arturo, would you be my mentor in helping me to be a healthy, responsible and independent person?"

With a smile on his face but jokingly trying to be serious, he says, "Jane, it would be my pleasure ..." They both burst out laughing.

When they stop laughing, she takes her journal out, turns to the page where she'd written her thoughts about being healthy, responsible and independent and places it in front of him, "I've made a start on what I think it is to be a healthy, responsible and independent person."

He looks over the pages briefly and says, "OK, good, I'm glad to see you've made a start. Now we need to look at why you would do this ..." he says while moving the journal to one side.

She stares at him incredulously, "What! What do you mean? You just said that if I've made a decision that feels good to me, that it doesn't matter what you say about it, and now you need to know *why*?" she snaps angrily.

"Whoa Jane, what's going on here, what's been triggered in you? Your reaction seems way out of proportion."

She stops for a moment, looks down and focuses on her breath, "You know, I'm feeling quite sensitive about this because I'm scared. I haven't told my parents that I want to change direction yet, and for that matter, I don't even know what that direction really is, I just have this knowing that it feels right to change now.

You know, my dad and I had a discussion last week around me living in a bit of a cocoon because he and my mum cover all the family bills, and I hinted at the possibility of moving out to get the experience of being self-reliant, and he almost went into full panic mode at the thought of it.

I suspect that they're both going to be super disappointed in me when they find out that I'm dropping out, let alone that I'd still like to move out and be self-reliant!"

"OK, I see. Making a big change when there are established expectations in place is never easy. So first off, I suggest that you don't drop out just yet, wait until you're clear on the steps that lie in front of you. It's great that you feel the inspiration to change but a part of being responsible is to consider the consequences of what you're wanting to do and then, if it still feels right, go for it."

"Phew, that feels like a weight has just been lifted off me. I think I'd worked myself up into thinking that I had to do it all as quickly as possible, and my anxiety was going through the roof." she says while letting out a big breath.

"Right, remember this Jane, you don't have to do anything that doesn't feel right in this moment, and most importantly, YOU NEVER NEED TO RUSH. When the step feels right, you take it. If you're feeling overwhelmed, stop and regroup. Take that time to find the way that gives some clarity on the next step.

There's a saying I like, I don't know who said it first but it goes like this,

Change happens slowly but when it happens, it happens quickly. If you look at a flower bud, it sits there, growing at an imperceptible rate until one day, boom, it blossoms. That's the way change happens.

For you, you may be in a cocoon, but you're growing and when you're ready, you'll burst out of that cocoon and be the lovely butterfly you were born to be.

OK, so let's go back and explore, why do you want to change course now?"

She takes a deep breath and then says, "When I saw that vision of myself in the future and what I'd said on stage, it struck a chord within me. I didn't fully realise it at the time but when I wrote the notes of what a healthy, responsible and independent person would be, I got this tingling feeling within me that said, 'YES, this is it, this is for me'. And I really don't know why I need to let go of Graphic Design, it just feels like Graphic Design isn't the area for me to focus on anymore."

"OK Jane, the reason I ask you this is because it's really important that you're clear on the feeling. The feeling is your indicator of whether you're on track or not. Without the clarity of knowing, chances are you won't be able to handle the consequences of your choices, and there are always consequences to these sorts of things.

Just know that you don't have to let go of Graphic Design in order to live as a healthy, responsible and independent person, you can still do both, if that feels right to you."

"OK, thanks for making that clear, but I *am* clear that I no longer want to study Graphic Design, but I take your point and won't drop out until I've worked out a plan of action, and the consequences I can see."

"Good, now before we go any further, I think it's important that we look at the definitions of what it means to be healthy, responsible and independent. So shoot, let me hear your definitions."

"Um, OK. I see a healthy person as someone that is free of any illnesses, able to exercise easily and move their body easily.

I see a responsible person as, someone that does what they say they are going to do and doesn't blame others when things don't go well.

I see an independent person as, someone that can stand on their own and doesn't need help to look after themselves."

"Thanks Jane. OK, let's break it down a little.

Health—starts with the mind. A healthy mind is a calm mind, not concerned about what has happened or anxious about what will happen. A mind is at ease with the present moment when YOU, the conscious observer are present and at ease with what is. You, as presence, then use your mind to work out things where logic is needed.

There's no need for stress, no need for concern and no need for worry of any sort. The healthy mind trusts that all is well because YOU are here, watching and knowing that the one that you are is beyond the physical body and the world of opposites, and that one is Love.

The level of health I'm talking about here is not concerned about the state of the physical body. You, as conscious presence is all that matters, your physical body is simply an extension of your consciousness and is taken care of through your own inspiration for life.

Now, this level of health all starts by breathing to your heart, becoming still and knowing that all is indeed well. The more you practice this the more that the joy of life flows through you."

"Wow, that sounds amazing, it seems to take care of the whole body, mind and spirit thing that I thought I needed to work on as separate things."

"Yep. Now let me ask you this—Why do you think it's important to sit, stand and walk with a good posture?"

"Um, because it's good for the body?"

"Yes it is, and more importantly, when you do this, you make a statement to yourself, you say, I'M HERE, I'M READY and I RESPECT THIS BODY and the LIFE FORCE THAT FLOWS THROUGH IT.

This doesn't only apply to posture though, it applies to what you eat, the way you eat, the way you talk, the things you say, the things you think, the clothes you wear, the way you wear them, and on and on, it's all the same. It's all a statement that you make and the more conscious you are, the more harmonious that statement becomes.

The thing to understand in this though, is that there's a difference in doing something because you *think* it's good for you, as opposed to choosing something because you *understand* your nature behind it and it feels right to do."

"Hmm, that's deep. I never thought of it that way. I really like that!"

"Now Jane, remember, this isn't easy to do at the start, and I'm not expecting for you to suddenly change the way you do things just because you've heard me say this. What you're gaining now is an understanding of a new way of being that's vastly different to what you're used to.

This is about knowing yourself at your core, the essence of YOU, and being OK with whatever shows up in your world. Here's the thing though, you can only do this when you know, at your core, that you are pure love and as love, you are ONE WITH ALL.

So, being one with all leads us to being responsible!

Being responsible is all about YOU, where there's nothing that happens, that isn't to do with you. In other words, whatever you become aware of, is your creation, either consciously or unconsciously.

This is a tough one to accept because you might think, 'how could I have created the stars, the planets, the creatures and everything else?' But it's not you, as the skin and bones sitting there on the chair, that creates, it's the deeper part of you that is one with every aspect of the universe.

While you may not be conscious of this deeper part of you yet, you can still choose to be responsible for all of it."

"Hang on a moment, I don't get that. Are you seriously saying that because I happen to be aware of something, let's say, John killing himself, that I'm responsible for that??"

"OK, I understand that the thought of you being responsible for what someone else does seems ludicrous. As if you're to blame for everything, right?

But that's not the way this works. Being responsible goes beyond blame, fault or wrongness. From your deeper perspective, there are no problems, all is in fact well, there's nothing that's ultimately 'wrong'.

The one that says or feels that something is wrong (or right), is a mind judging it that way, based on preconceived ideas about the matter.

You, as Jane, are a limited being and you can't be responsible if you see yourself as small and separate from everything around you. But when you get in touch with the aspect of you that's ONE WITH ALL, that's where you flow and unite in a deeper way with the totality that is, LIFE.

OK, please close your eyes for a moment and focus on your breath, in ... and ... out ... relax and feel all resistances leave your body. Feel yourself become as light as a feather. There's nothing to do, just notice the breath and enjoy this beautifully relaxed place ... And when you're ready, open your eyes."

She opens her eyes after a few moments and feels noticeably more relaxed, "That was nice." she says.

"Tell me Jane, what did you experience just then?"

"Well, just hearing you say those words helped me to let go of the tension I was holding in my body and I really did feel as light as a feather! It felt really peaceful."

"Good, now this peacefulness you experienced, how does it differ from what you experience in your normal day-to-day life?"

She looks up and thinks for a moment, "My day-to-day life feels like it's quite heavy and a bit chaotic at times, like there's always something to do or somewhere to be, but closing my eyes like this and being at ease feels really light and freeing!"

"Great, so there's a clear distinction between these two states of being. One is inner space and the other is outer stuff, and while it seems as though nothing happens in the inner state, as in there's no 'stuff' there, it's nonetheless a state of being that opens you up to experiencing ease in the outer state as well."

"Really? I don't think I can experience that level of ease and peace with my eyes open." she says doubtfully.

"Well, I won't kid you Jane, it does take practice, but it's definitely available to everyone. It's about not hanging on to your opinions so much, and in that, allowing life to be OK as it is. From there, you begin to find an ease with things."

"And how is that supposed to help me be responsible, exactly?"

"By being at ease and peace, you connect with others at a deeper level. From here, you're able to have compassion for others because you know that they're no different to you, they're simply playing a different role than you are in this moment."

"Oh, wait, wait, I think I get it ..." she says while looking up to gather her thoughts, "by coming back to this place of ease, it's the same as the practice you asked me to do the other week, about releasing the automatic judgement by being curious with the 'hmm, isn't that interesting' statement.

By doing that I put a gap between me and the thing I would normally judge and that helps me drop my resistance for wanting things to be a certain way, which brings me back to ease. Is that right?"

"Yep, and how are you responsible out of this?"

"Um, well, because I haven't judged the situation and I'm at ease with it, I'm OK with it from the bigger picture perspective and that helps me to connect with everyone through this place of stillness."

"Good, you're getting closer, this is a big one and you're definitely on the right track with it.

Now please write this down ..." He hands the journal back to her, "*your responsibility lies in everything you think, say and do, you can't control the actions of others but you take responsibility by taking care of your own thoughts, words and actions in relation to what the other has said or done.*

Your job is to always find a place of ease by first noticing what's floating around in your head. If you notice something negative, you take responsibility by finding forgiveness for both yourself and the other, and let it go with love.

Now I want to come back to what you said about being responsible as someone that does what they say they are going to do. That's a good point because if you do what you say you're going to do, by when you say you're going to do it, you'll be standing head and shoulders above the crowd. It's basic, but you'd be amazed at how few do it and yes, that's an aspect of being responsible.

Having said that, if something changes for you and you can no longer honour your agreement, let the other person know that things have changed. Responsibility is also about respect for others that are involved.

OK, two down, one to go – so in summary, health begins from your inner Being and responsibility flows from accepting that everything is your creation.

Now with Independence, this flows on from health and responsibility because to be independent requires you to first and foremost, be an independent thinker, free from the chatter of what you see on TV, read on the Internet, or hear from the people around you.

A truly independent person isn't swayed by the beliefs of others, they may hear what another has to say but they trust their own inner knowing, regardless of how they'll be perceived by others.

This doesn't mean they go against what others say just for the sake of looking like they're being independent. No, they listen and carefully, assess what the other is saying to see if it resonates for them.

If it does, they may agree with the other, which may look as though they're not being independent, but they're not. Independence is for you to know, regardless of how others may judge.

Now it's also important to mention that to be independent doesn't mean that you stand alone or do things exclusively on your own. It's true that an independent person stands on their own, but it doesn't mean that they don't seek help when it makes sense to do so.

An independent person knows how to allocate their time so that they make the best use of it by doing what they enjoy and paying someone else to do the things they're not aligned with in that moment.

For example, if your car needs a clean and you prefer to spend your time in other ways, then you would pay someone to do that for you. You're not dependent upon them doing it, it's simply a choice you make based on what you find more uplifting.

Being independent is about being clear on where you stand and then making conscious choices to take care of things. You seek help and may even rely on people but you don't abuse your circumstances, you stand free and clear and know that if those people weren't around, that you would still find a way to handle things, without fuss.

And by the way, it also means that you stand clear of expecting hand-outs from the government, your parents or anyone else that you may think owes you. You let go of the sense of 'entitlement', as though society or family owes you something. You can never be truly independent if your survival depends on handouts."

She scratches her head, "But, what if you can't find a job and need some temporary help, what happened to asking for help?"

"Jane, it all comes back to being clear within yourself, you always know if you're abusing a situation or not. Asking for assistance to help you get through a tight spot is totally fine.

But all too often people ask out of expectation or entitlement, there's no responsibility in that, and they unconsciously abuse. The tendency is that the so called 'assistance' becomes a crutch and their creative nature to find solutions takes a back seat as they get addicted to the handout.

OK, so let's move on ..." he says while gesturing her to pass him the Journal again. "Right, I can see you've made a good start on what you think it is to be healthy, responsible and independent. What do you now see as the next step, now that you understand that all three are linked?"

She thinks for a moment, "Well, I'm still feeling a little anxious about it all but I can see that practising the awareness of what I think, say and do is a top priority as well as finding that place of ease and serenity within me.

But I can also see that I need to find a way to stop relying on my parents to take care of me financially. I'm thinking that if I earn enough money, I can then take care of myself, by moving out and getting my own place."

"OK, that's very good. And, a great way to move forward is to work on the inner while taking steps on the outer."

He now moves the journal towards her and says, "Please make some more notes, it sounds like we're going to need to focus on your finances."

He dictates the following instructions to her:

Aim # 1—Find out how much I earn and how much I spend, now.

Aim # 2—Work out how much money I need to survive as an independent person.

Aim # 3—Work out how much money I need to live comfortably.

Aim # 4—Work out how much money I need to live the life of my dreams.

Ongoing Aim—Present moment awareness practice

"Jane, what you've just written is the basis of a plan. A plan that will show you a reality of what it'll take to stand on your own.

For the week ahead your project is to complete the first aim. I'll send you a link where you can download some templates, tonight. Then, by this Sunday night, I'd like you to email me the completed spreadsheets. Would you do that?"

"Um, I'm not really sure what's involved here. I mean, what if I don't understand something and can't complete it by Sunday?"

"Jane, this isn't school, this isn't about getting the 'right' answer. The idea behind this exercise is that you do some research into understanding how you live now and seeing how independently you live. So, would you do that?" he says gently.

"OK, yes, I'll do it."

"Good, let's leave it at that. I'll see you next week."

JANE ARRIVES HOME with David on the couch, sipping on a glass of wine and watching TV as he waits for her. She walks over to him cautiously, knowing that she doesn't want him to know too much about her plans just yet.

"Hi sweetheart, how did it go this arvo?"

"Yeah, good, we've shifted the focus a little now. Arturo's a big fan of self-responsibility and of course taking care of yourself, but now we're focusing on finances. He's going to help me get my finances in order."

His jaw drops as he says, "Uh, right. Now there's something I never thought I'd hear you say... that you actually *want* your finances in order. That's great! ... Oh, hang on a moment, is this because of the conversation we had last week?" he says with a pained look on his face.

"Well, sort of. I suppose that conversation did spark something inside me that actually wants to live more responsibly. I feel like, I behave a bit childlike in allowing you guys to look after me."

Still suspicious, he says, "So what exactly is that going to look like, honey?"

"Well to start with, I need to fill out some spreadsheets and look at how I spend my money now, then later, look at what it's going to take to live the life of my dreams."

"It sounds like a bit of a dream building exercise, is that right?"

"Something like that, yeah." She then quickly says, "let's eat, I'm starving." Bringing the conversation to an end.

After dinner, she goes to her room, sees Arturo's email and downloads the files.

She starts to feel anxious at the thought of filling everything out, but over the course of the week she manages to complete her task. She completes the spreadsheet and sends it off to Arturo on Sunday afternoon.

Part 2
FINANCES

Week Seven – Anxiety

Jane arrives at Arturo's, visibly anxious. He spends a few moments attempting to look into her eyes, but her agitation causes her eyes to dart all over the place.

"Jane, has something happened?" he says in his usual calm tone.

"Um, not really, I just can't seem to shake this anxious feeling, I've tried the breathing and then writing in the journal, but there just seems to be this level of panic that I'm feeling at the moment and I don't know what's going on."

"When did you first notice this?"

"It seemed to start when I went through the spreadsheets and saw what I needed to be earning, just to survive! I'm now wondering what the hell I'm doing. Like, how the hell am I going to be this healthy, responsible, independent woman when I'm such a mess?

I can't handle it. I still have to tell my parents that I want to drop out, I don't know how I'm going to support myself and I'm supposed to help other people at some point. It's just too much, and I can't handle it!" she says as tears start streaming down her cheeks.

He moves the tissue box across and waits for her to blow her nose, "It's OK Jane, I understand." he says with empathy, "This isn't easy, and you're stretching yourself in a major way here.

What you're actually doing is taking a leap into the unknown, it's something that most people would never even dream of doing. So it's completely understandable that you'd feel this way."

"But, I just feel like a wreck, I'm fearful of what my parents are going to say, I'm fearful of being a failure and I'm even fearful of disappointing you!" she says as she starts crying again.

"... Jane, look at me ... right now you're hurting and I sense the fogginess in you that's causing you to feel confusion and an inability to see your way through this. It's OK, I'm going to take you through an exercise that may help you.

OK, please sit up, close your eyes and take a deep breath, keep focusing on the breath ... What do you know about yourself? Take your time and just allow the words to arise on their own."

"I know, that I'm a good person, that ... I can do anything I set my mind to, and that I'm quite strong inside."

"Good, that's very good Jane. OK, now that you have this clear knowing, I'd like you to imagine the worst possible scenario for yourself. You've told your parents that you've dropped out and you're going to live on your own, what happens next?"

"They disown me" she says quickly, "... I'm an embarrassment and shame to the family ... I struggle on my own and I live on the streets, I have no job, I'm alone, I'm cold and I'm hungry with nowhere to go, my life is over and I wait ... for death." she breaks down again.

"OK Jane, stay with that feeling, you're in the gutter, waiting for death to approach. With what you know about yourself, what do you do while you're waiting to die?"

She lets out a short laugh as she imagines the grim reaper coming to collect her in her despair. "Well ..." she says as she blows her nose, "I guess I would go and look for a soup kitchen for something warm to eat ... after that, I'd see if anyone knew where I could sleep for the night."

"Now let's assume that death still hasn't arrived, what do you do in the morning?"

"Um, I'd go and see if there's some work that I can do, I'd speak to as many people as possible for help to get back on my feet." her voice begins to get stronger the more she speaks.

"Yep, you would Jane, and things are generally never as bad as we think they might be. OK, open your eyes, so what did you get out of this little exercise?"

"Well, I guess that if the worst case scenario did happen, I now have sort of a plan for how I'd get back on my feet!"

"You sure do."

"Thanks Arturo, I'm actually feeling a lot better. I think a part of me doubts that I can do this, I'm really getting a sense of how much of a cocoon I've been living in and the thought of breaking out of the safety of that cocoon is freaking me out."

"It's great that you're realising that the cocoon is a safe place. That's a part of the role that parents play, providing a safe place for their children to step out and be healthy, responsible and independent adults.

So Jane, are you ready to take the next step?" She lets out a big breath, "OK, yes I am." she says confidently. "Now before we go on, keep this experience in the back of your mind and use it as a reference point for when it happens again, because it will happen again. Just go through the same process of seeing your worst case scenario, accepting it and then looking at how you can move forward."

He now opens the manila folder that was sitting on his desk and looks at the pages. He looks at the spreadsheets she sent him the day before and says, "OK Jane, let's see what we have here, where you are now, your Income Statement:

Jane's Income

(Annual)

Money In	Amount
Wages	$14,700
Total	$14,700

Jane's Spending

(Annual)

Money Out	Amount
Gifts (birthdays, Xmas, etc.)	$300
Mobile phone	$500
ATM withdrawals/incidental spending	$5,000
Grooming	$1,500
Clothes	$2,000
Car Fuel	$1,200
Car repairs	$600
Car insurance & Registration	$1,800
New fun experiences	$800
Restaurants/dining out/movies/concerts	$1,000
Total	$14,700 OK

And your Statement of Assets and Liabilities:

Jane's Assets
(Things I own)

Things that don't pay me to own them	Amount
Electronics—PC, Tablet, etc.	$1,000
Clothes, Shoes & Accessories	$1,500
Car	$5,000
Furniture & Fittings	$0
Things of value that don't pay me	
Cash at Bank – at call	$250
Artwork & Collectibles	$0
Gold & Silver (Including jewellery melt value)	$500
Things that pay me to own them	
High Yield Bank Accounts	$0
Businesses	$0
Stocks/Shares	$0
Property	$0
Total Assets	**$8,250**

Jane's Liabilities
(Things I Owe)

Things I might have to pay for in less than 12 months	Amount	
Credit Cards	$500	
Short Term Loans	$0	
Things I might have to pay for in greater than 12 mths		
Credit Cards – Long Term	$0	
Long Term Loans	$0	
School Loans	$25,000	
Mortgage	$0	
Car Loan	$0	
Total Liabilities	**$25,500**	****REDUCE DEBT****
Net Assets	**-$17,250**	

So how do you feel about your current financial position, Jane?"

"Well, not great but I can see that even though I don't earn a lot of money, I still get to live quite well, living in the cocoon." They both laugh.

"You're right Jane, you have a car, a phone and you seem to have a good amount of money for incidentals. You don't pay rent nor contribute to household bills at all, you're living the cocoon dream!" They erupt in laughter again. "OK Jane, so do you have any idea of what your next step might be?"

"Uh, not really. I spent so much time on research for the spreadsheets and then felt the anxiety come up, that I haven't really thought of anything else."

"OK, let's take the time now then. You know that you want to drop out of Uni, you know that you want to live as an independent, responsible person and, you know that your part time job doesn't provide you the income to live independently.

What feels like a clear step, no matter how small, for you to take now?"

She thinks, and after a few moments remembers aim number two and says with excitement, "Oh, I can look at how much money I need in order to survive as an independent person."

"Excellent Jane, that will be your project for the week ahead. You'll see those templates in the same place you got the last ones. Just email them to me by Sunday."

"OK, see you next week, Arturo."

SHE ARRIVES HOME to David sitting on the couch with his glass of wine again. "How goes it Jane? How's the dream building going?" he calls out.

"Very slowly, dad ... we're just taking it one step at a time at the moment. Actually, if you don't mind, I'm going to take a quick shower before dinner, I'm feeling really tired."

While she showered, she appreciated the warmth of the water on her skin, she was grateful for the clean, hot running water, and that she could take a shower whenever she wanted. Thoughts of being destitute popped in and she thought, '... I really appreciate what mum and dad have done for me.'

Over dinner she says, "Mum, would it be OK for me to cook dinner for the family tomorrow evening?" Elizabeth almost choked on the mouthful of food she had just taken, "... Uh, sure Jane, that'd be fine." Elizabeth couldn't believe what she was hearing and after a few moments says, "Jane, I have to ask, what's brought this on?"

"Well, I've been thinking, and I've decided that if I want to be a responsible, independent person, then I need to start behaving like one. I've realised that I really don't do much around here, nor do I pay you guys for the privilege of living in this great home, so my way of being more responsible is to contribute more to the household in non-cash ways."

Elizabeth was trying to stop her mouth from gaping open as she turns to David, "Do you know anything about this?"

"Uh, yeah, I know that Jane is starting to talk more about being independent and I already went through a bit of shock myself, last week, when she said she wanted to get her finances in order. So I'm not surprised that she wants to do this." He turns to Jane and says, "Good on you honey ..." while feeling a level of discomfort.

Andy sat quietly, eating his meal and hoping that no one would notice that he doesn't contribute to the household chores.

Jane bursts out, "Guys! Please relax, and stop making such a big deal out of this. OK, I get it, I've tried to get out of doing housework whenever I could and I've treated this place like a hotel at times but I'm now clear that it's time for me to grow up and behave like an adult."

Elizabeth's mouth was now agape as she looked at Jane and thought, 'Wow, my baby girl is finally growing up.' At the same time, she felt a sense of pride, as though she was responsible for bringing this out in Jane.

"OK Jane," Elizabeth says, "I'm impressed, I look forward to your meal tomorrow evening."

Over the course of the week Jane came up with a schedule of tasks that she'd do for the household on a regular basis as her way of contributing and being responsible. She also completed the project that Arturo had assigned her.

She noticed that she felt good about doing the schedule of tasks. She had a sense that it was somehow helping her for when she *was* ready to break out of her cocoon.

Week Eight – Survival

"Hi Jane, come on in ..." After the usual quiet time of looking into her eyes, he says, "Is there anything you want to share?"

"Yeah, I had a bit of an epiphany last week, I realised how blessed I am to be living the lifestyle that I live and how much my parents have done for me. Up until this point, I've really been taking it all for granted, but I realise now that I really have an amazing life!

Out of this realisation, I found the wanting to be more responsible and created a schedule of tasks that I'd do for the household on a regular basis."

"Go Jane! Good for you. Was there anything else?"

"Well, I completed the spreadsheet but it was a real eye opener on what it's going to take to survive on my own. To be honest, I have no idea how I can move out while I'm at Uni. And even if I get a full-time job, I really don't know if I'll earn enough to move out of home either."

He opens the manila folder that was sitting on his desk and takes out the latest spreadsheets.

"OK, let's see ... right, survival, and the minimum you need to live is ...

Jane's Minimum Spend to Survive

(Annual)

Money Out	Amount	
Electricity & Gas	$1,000	
Gifts (birthdays, Xmas, etc.)	$300	
Home & Contents insurance	$0	
TV, Internet	$500	
School Fees	$0	
Club dues	$0	
Life insurance	$0	
Body Corporate Fees	$0	
Health Insurance	$0	
Medical, Dental	$0	
Travel	$0	
Mortgage/Rent	$12,000	
Property rates, taxes & water	$0	
Subscriptions	$0	
Mobile phone	$500	
ATM withdrawals/incidental spending	$3,000	
Groceries	$4,000	
Storage units	$0	
Just in Case Funds	$1,200	
Grooming	$600	
Clothes	$600	
Home accessories	$0	
Public Transport Costs	$2,000	
Car Fuel	$0	
Car repairs	$0	
Car insurance & Registration	$0	
Donations	$0	
Build up Cash to cover debt	$6,000	
New fun experiences	$0	
Restaurants/dining out/movies/concerts	$300	
Total	$32,000	**Minimum Net Income Needed**
ADD Tax @ 20%	$6,400	
	$38,400	**Minimum Gross Income Needed**

…And what you need on your Statement of Assets and Liabilities…

Jane's Minimum Assets Needed
(Things I own)

Things that don't pay me to own them	Amount
Electronics—PC, Tablet, etc.	$500
Clothes, Shoes & Accessories	$500
Car	$0
Furniture & Fittings	$0
Things of value that don't pay me	
Cash at Bank – at call	$2,000
Artwork & Collectibles	$0
Gold & Silver (Including jewellery melt value)	$0
Things that pay me to own them	
High Yield Bank Accounts	$22,000
Businesses	$0
Stocks/Shares	$0
Property	$0
Total Assets	**$25,000**

Jane's Liabilities
(Things I Owe)

Things I might have to pay for in less than 12 mths	Amount
Credit Cards	$0
Short Term Loans	$0
Things I might have to pay for in greater than 12 mths	
Credit Cards – Long Term	$0
Long Term Loans	$0
School Loans	$25,000
Mortgage	$0
Car Loan	$0
Total Liabilities	**$25,000**
Net Assets	**$0**

Right, you're saying you need $38,400 just to survive. And you feel as though you might not be able to earn that if you worked full-time?"

"Yep, when I drop out of Uni I'm not going to have any qualifications, I'll be a drop out! So I'm guessing that the only jobs I can get will be a low paying service type of job."

He moves forward and says, "Jane, the time has come to share with you how money works. Right now you have a set idea of the choices you have in front of you, and those ideas are limited by what you believe.

What you see is a path where you work one hour and receive one hour of pay. But, if you can be open to learning other ways of having money flow in, you might find a new world of choices, are you open to that?"

"Um, sure, as long as it doesn't involve anything illegal." she says flippantly.

"O-K." He pauses and looks at her suspiciously. "You seem to have a resistance, do you think it's not really possible to have much larger amounts of money flow in legally?"

She suddenly feels heat rushing to her face and says quickly, "Uh, no, I was just joking, of course there are legal ways for more money to flow in."

"It's OK Jane, I'm not saying this to attack you, this is about uncovering what lies underneath the surface. OK, do this, close your eyes for a moment and focus on your breath.

Now, ask yourself this, *Can I have more money come in without working at a job for it?* And sit with it, wait for an answer then open your eyes when you're ready."

She closes her eyes and follows his guidance. After a few moments of silence she slowly opens her eyes, "Whoa, uh, I'm kind of feeling embarrassed now, you were right. The answer I got was NO! I can't believe that, it's a bit of a shock really."

"It's OK, it's good that this has come up now and you've seen it early on."

"But why? Why is that there? Why would I be blocked like that? It doesn't make sense." she says, scratching her head, while feeling a level of annoyance.

"Jane, what you don't realise at this point is that what you've just uncovered is extremely common, you're perfectly normal. Be gentle with yourself and know that virtually everyone has some sort of blockage when it comes to money.

These blockages form at a very early age from how we perceive the world around us. As a child, we have no concept of how the world works or how we fit in, so we take in every experience and make some judgement about it to figure out what's safe and what isn't.

We then naturally absorb a heap of stuff from our parents or the people that we spend the most time with. We watch how they behave in various conditions and then make an assessment of how the world works. This perception then gets tucked away in our psyche and forms part of the story that is our life.

This is a complex area because how you see the world is how YOU perceive it. It really all depends on how you process the information that comes in through your senses.

So at this stage, simply understand that how you see the world may not be the same as how someone else sees the world, your *truth* may not be theirs.

If you can understand this, you'll be open to the possibility that other things exist and that there are other ways for money to flow in, other than working on a time basis.

Now I'd like to leave you with one thing before we wrap this up. As a general rule, money flows to those that bring value to another. The perceived value is what has people feel good in paying for something. It's very simple really, the more value you provide, the more money flows to you.

OK, let's leave it at that, Jane. And your project for this week is to think about what we discussed today and make notes for yourself on it."

DAVID APPROACHES JANE as she enters the house, "Hey Jane, how did it go today?" he says tentatively, knowing she's undergoing some sort of transformation and that he's now feeling apprehensive about it.

"Uh, OK. Arturo and I discussed some mind stuff ..."

Interrupting, he says, "... Do you want to sit and talk about it?"

"Um, not really, I just need to spend some time on it to get clearer. I think we'll leave it for now, if that's OK."

"Sure, sure, that's fine honey."

After dinner she made a start on her project. By this stage she no longer did any of her Uni work, her focus was entirely on Arturo's assignments.

Week Nine – Belief and Judgement

"Hi Jane, come on in." His kind smile quickly has her feel at ease. "Jane, today we're going to do something different."

'Different! Every week is different with him', she thinks. "I'm going to ask you to sit back, relax and think about something. So sit back, close your eyes now and see what comes up when I ask you the question, then open your eyes when you're ready to share. The question is ... Do you believe that anything is possible?"

She sits there with the words floating around in her head, 'Do I believe that anything is possible?' After about 15 seconds she opens her eyes and sees Arturo looking intensely at her. "OK, at first I thought, sure, anything is possible, but then I thought, 'wait, I don't believe that I can fly or that I can walk on water', so to answer honestly, I have to say that I don't believe that anything is possible. I believe that there are certain limitations to what is possible because the basic laws of the universe apply to all of us equally."

"OK, good, thanks for sharing that, Jane. Are you open to the possibility that while your beliefs may be true for you, they may not be true for someone else?"

"Huh? No, these are physical laws that I'm talking about and they're quite black and white. If you run off a cliff, gravity's going to bring you down to earth at a fast pace, there's no two ways about it!"

"I see ..." he says while sitting back, "so how do you explain the experience you had in seeing an older version of yourself?"

"Aw, I knew you were going to bring that up. I can't. Okay?" she snaps back. "All I know is that it felt real but that somehow it wasn't part of the basic laws that cover the physical universe. I don't know how that happened or why you're even able to do that, for that matter."

"OK, so you accept the experience as feeling real, but not as being part of the physical universe. Then let's start again, do you believe that anything is possible?"

"Alright, I see where you're going with this, okay, yes, I believe that anything is possible, on some level, even if it's not this particular universe." she says in a begrudging tone.

"Jane ..." he chuckles, "I'm not sure if you realise this, but you don't want to let go of your beliefs around how the universe works. You have your physical universe that has to conform to certain laws and then your other universe, which you don't really understand but everything else that doesn't fit or make sense gets lumped into that universe."

His smile quickly turns into a serious look as he leans forward and says, "That's all very convenient Jane, but it's not going to help you move beyond your current beliefs. I know it's not comfortable to think that maybe things aren't the way you've always known them to be, but until you can be truly open to the possibilities of something unknown, your old beliefs will always keep you where you are.

Remember, the mind needs things to match its understanding, it doesn't like things not matching and will discount them, unless YOU CHOOSE something else."

"O-Kay, so where do I go from here?" "Where do you think you might go?" She thinks for a few moments, "Um, to let go of the idea that I know how it all works?"

"Yes, that's good, and how do you do that?"

"Er, I don't really know. I mean, I've never really questioned it before. I've gone by the principle that if it looks like a duck and walks like a duck, then it's a duck. So I'm not sure how I let go of that type of reasoning."

"OK, there's nothing wrong with that type of reasoning. That's about probabilities, and yes, in most cases if something has several characteristics that point to a certain conclusion, it's probably right. But, what I'm talking about is learning to let go of making those assessments automatically.

What I mean by that is, using your duck analogy, just because the probabilities point to it being a duck, what difference would it make if it wasn't a duck? What if you let go of the assessment altogether?"

"Whoa, wait a minute Arturo, making the assessment determines how I relate to it. Like, if instead of a duck, it's a bear, well the assessment is going to help me get out of there so I don't end up as bear dinner!"

He chuckles, "So how often have you faced a bear?"

"Well, never, but that's not the point. The point is that the assessment is needed!"

"Jane, as humans, we're highly attuned in our ability to identify and react to life threatening situations, but most of us go through our whole life not facing any. But that doesn't stop the brain from constantly being on the lookout for them, it's hard wired in us and it's done a great job in helping us survive.

What I'm saying though, is what if you could hold off on being so quick to make judgements when you see things or hear people talk? In most cases the situations aren't life threatening, so you don't need to go into the fight, flight, freeze response.

Do you remember the practice of being curious? ... Well that's your ticket to holding off on judging and assessing things, and from there, you can see if you can be open to life being magical, where anything is possible, and all to benefit YOU!"

"OK, let me get this straight, the last time you told me to be curious was around noticing what I judged as bad or wrong, whereas now you want me to notice life in general with a sense of curiosity. Is that right?"

"Yep, you got it Jane. It's about refining your awareness. Step 1 is about noticing how much you judge things as right or wrong and step 2 is about going beyond right and wrong and being open to the wonderment of life, without labelling it in any particular way and then noticing what that's like."

"OK, got it, Arturo."

"Good, I think we'll leave it at that Jane and I'll see you next week. So just to be clear, your project for the week ahead is to notice life with a sense of curiosity, is that clear?"

"Yes, got it."

As she drives home, she says to herself, 'OK, notice life ... open to wonderment ...' She pulls up at a set of lights and notices some people in the other cars and in an instant thinks they all look like they're half asleep. 'Shit, that was a judgement.' She looks over again casually, and this time aims to look by just being curious, the way a child may look when they don't know what something is.

She suddenly notices a shift within herself, a sense of well-being and a special sort of connection with these people. It felt good, really good.

SHE ARRIVES HOME with David sitting on the lounge, watching TV. He turns to her and calls out, "Hey Jane, how's it going?"

"Yep, fine dad ..." and goes straight to her room.

She takes a moment to focus on her breath and re-centre herself before dinner, with the aim of noticing things with a sense of curiosity.

At dinner, she takes time to look at the food before putting a small mouthful in her mouth. She then takes time to notice the taste of the food and the texture, chewing it for a little longer than normal, before swallowing it.

Elizabeth notices Jane's slow movements and says with concern, "Jane, is everything OK?"

She looks over at Elizabeth and while nodding, she swallows and says, "Yep, all fine mum."

"Are you sure, you seem to be moving in slow motion or something."

She smiles, "Yeah, I'm just taking time to notice the little things more, that's the project Arturo gave me for the week."

With suspicion in her voice, Elizabeth says "And what purpose does this serve?"

"Well, it's really just to see what happens when you don't judge things. Often, we go about our daily life not really noticing what we're doing and we make all these automatic judgements based on what we think is true.

By taking some time to notice things, I'm giving myself an opportunity to be open to learning something new. It might be that my judgements around something isn't quite right but if I don't slow down and notice, I'd never know."

"Jane, it all sounds like gibberish to me, I think you're reading too much into things. I mean, you're young for goodness sake, just enjoy your life while you're not weighed down by the burdens. All this other stuff just seems like hard work and quite frankly, a waste of time." she says with agitation.

"Actually Jane, this reminds me, your father and I have been talking and we think that maybe this Arturo character isn't the best influence on you. I mean, I know you're stepping up and doing more around the house, which is great, but it just seems a little strange. Like, when was the last time you went on a date, or even a party for that matter?"

Jane noticed the agitation building up inside her, feeling that she had to defend herself, but she focused on her breath and said to herself, 'just be curious', "Well mum, I can see you're concerned about me and it seems you think I'm not enjoying life, or something like that. But all I can say is that Arturo is helping me question *why* I do things and he always encourages me to follow what feels right for me. In fact, It's like he's always looking for the best in me and, that helps me to find the best in myself, which feels really good.

I know that doing things like taking time to notice small things seems weird but it's just because we often don't question things, and do things in an autopilot type of mode.

What Arturo is encouraging in me is to make decisions for myself with greater awareness. So while I might not go out as often as before, I feel really good about the direction I'm going in."

"And what direction exactly is that, Jane?" Elizabeth says sternly.

"Well, that's hard to put into words. I guess all I can say is that when I hear Arturo speak, it feels good to me and I like feeling more confident within myself. So, I'm not sure exactly where I'm going at this stage, but I'm enjoying the journey, as corny as that sounds."

Elizabeth looks down and continues eating, not wanting to acknowledge Jane's point.

Week Ten – Interest and Debt

"**H**ey Jane, come on in ... OK, this week I'd like to go back to our money discussion, but before I do, is there anything you want to share about the project you had from last week?"

"Yeah, it's not so easy just noticing things without making some type of assessment automatically, although, once I was able to relax and just do it, it actually felt really good to notice without placing a judgement. There seemed to be a stillness and connection with people and things that I hadn't experienced before."

"Great stuff Jane, just remember to be gentle with yourself if you fall back into old habits. OK, moving on, what's your understanding of Interest, like say, bank interest?"

"Er, well, the way I understand it is that you put money in a bank account and if you have a certain type of account that pays interest, then you get this extra amount as a bonus."

"OK, let's see if I can make it a bit clearer for you. Now, to truly understand interest, it's important to understand the relationship between *giving* and *receiving*.

Look at your job, you *give* your time and skill in order to *receive* a wage, you exchange one thing of value, your time and skill, for another thing of value, money. Your boss has *received* your time and skill and *gives* you money for it.

In any relationship, there's always a two-way exchange of energy, a constant moving from one to the other. One gives while the other receives and vice versa. This type of movement also exists in nature.

For example, imagine yourself standing by the water's edge on a beach, the water moves toward you and then moves back out, there's an ebb and flow, an in and an out. Just like your breath moving in and out of your lungs.

Another example is buying and selling, where, a buyer gives cash and receives a good or service, and a seller gives a good or service and receives cash. Interestingly, while there's a flow of giving and receiving on both sides, generally the people that attract a lot of money to themselves, tend to be the ones that give more in USE value than they receive in CASH value.

When you consider this perspective, to have more cash to flow to you, it's simply a matter of aiming to be the giver of way more *use* value in any exchange. You then find that more value naturally moves towards you. Some interpret this as, *be a seller more than buyer.*"

"I like that, Arturo. I never actually looked at it like this before, even though it makes perfect sense, that by buying things, I'm handing over *cash*, for *use*. And so if that's my main focus, I might receive all this *use* value from the things I buy, but I could end up poor because I'm not really providing any *use* value to others, by selling something!"

"Jane, I'm really glad this point is striking a chord with you, and, it's super important to understand that providing *use* value doesn't necessarily mean that you 'sell something'. It's possible that you might provide *use* value through a pod cast service or some other community service, for example, and not receive anything tangible.

However, people that genuinely provide value like this tend to find that others want to help them back in some way. It's not out of obligation, that others give back to you, it's out of appreciation. Although some might still do it out of obligation, depending on their own filters.

All I'm saying Jane, is that if you keep providing value, the natural laws of flow that I spoke about earlier will find a way to bring balance back again. As a result, value, in some form, returns back to you.

Just make sure you don't try to manipulate this *value giving*. What I mean by that is that you can't fool Life, if you give with the *expectation* for something in return, you taint the whole thing and you end up messing with the elegant natural flow that exists in our nature.

OK, so let's go back to interest, let's say that with the money you received from your job, you go to your local bank and *give* them the money. They are thankful for your deposit and agree to *give* you 5% per annum (pa) in interest and in return for the money you deposited. At the end of the year, you *receive* your 5%, and the flow is happening.

This is what it looks like in actual figures at the end of year…" He moves over to the white board and writes the following:

Job money RECEIVED -> $100 -> bank deposit GIVEN -> Interest cash RECEIVED -> $5

He continues, "Now you might be wondering why the bank would be willing to pay you interest, when the money seems to be just sitting there doing nothing ... The answer is that while it looks like the money is just sitting there, it's not. The bank uses your money to *give*, i.e. 'lend', to someone else, at a higher rate of interest than you are being paid.

For example, they might give you 5% in interest and then they might receive 8% in interest from the person they lent the money to, which means they make a profit of 3% for running their banking business.

In other words, the bank says thank-you for putting money with them by paying you interest and this allows them to be in the business of banking.

This is how it looks to the bank:" Again he moves over to the white board and writes the following:

Your deposit received	—	$100
Interest paid to you @ 5%	—	$ 5
Your money lent	—	($100)
Interest received from lender	—	$ 8
Profit to the bank	—	$ 3

"Therefore, interest is what you *give* if YOU use money from another or it's what you *receive* if another uses YOUR money.

And it's often been said that it's better to give than receive but when it comes to interest you need to be careful because when you give interest to another, it means you're in debt, and you need to understand debt before using it.

So Jane, I've done a lot of talking here, please share with me what you've understood so far ..."

"OK, um ... What I've understood is that everything has a certain flow and money is no different. When I put money into the bank, they receive that money gratefully and pay me interest, as their way of saying thanks. Then they use that money to give to someone else and they (the bank) receive a higher rate of interest and that's how they make a profit for running their business. All of this works as part of the flow of life, ebb and flow."

"Great, you got it, that understanding should help you make better decisions when you face getting into debt. Speaking of debt, do you have any particular view on it?"

"Uh, not really, I just know that people get into debt when they want to buy a house or in some cases when they buy a car."

"Right, what about credit cards, would you say that's debt also?" "Oh, yeah, definitely, I forgot about that one!" "Yep, that's the way it works, credit cards allow you to get into debt without fully realising that you're in debt. It can burn a big hole in your pocket without you knowing it's even happening. Not that I'm saying credit cards are bad or that you shouldn't have one, you just need to know how to use them so that they work *for* you rather than *against* you.

So let's look at the basics, if you want to buy something but you don't have the money for it, you have a choice to make. You can:

1. Wait, and save the money until you have enough to buy it, or;
2. Buy it with borrowed money that you pay back over time.

In our western way of life we've learned that waiting to buy something is painful, we want everything now and credit is easily available, so we generally choose to borrow now and pay later. That pleasure in being able to buy and enjoy now lures people away from the pain of actually paying a much higher amount for it over time.

The problem is, it's a lot like the drug addict looking for that quick hit. They're so driven by the need for the high, they ignore the fact that there's hell to pay later.

It may sound a little dramatic to compare debt in this way but I suspect that at some basic level, we understand that debt can be very dangerous and that it should be treated with great respect.

In the olden days, credit for consumer goods wasn't common, if you didn't have the money to buy something, you'd generally wait, and you didn't have much choice about it. I remember hearing a story where a young couple in the 1950's saved for over a year to buy a fridge and while they waited, they filled a small icebox with ice every few days until they had enough money to pay for the fridge. On top of that, the cost of the fridge was equivalent to around 6 months' pay for the average worker!

If you speak to someone over 70, they'll tell you that it definitely wasn't an easy life back then. But I'm not going to get into a discussion around who's responsible for making credit easy, we just need to focus on where we are now and play by the rules of credit and debt.

Jane, what you need to know is that having the ability to get into debt is a bit like having the option to own a gun, if you get the gun without learning how to use it properly and responsibly, you might hurt yourself or someone else. In the same way, if you take on debt, without learning how to use it safely, you could find yourself in a world of pain.

I know I'm labouring this point but it's important to be aware of what's really happening when you take on debt.

And the most important thing for you to know is that debt *isn't* a necessity in everyday life. The 'buy now, pay later' motto was a marketing ploy to get people to buy cars, boats, furniture, electrical toys, clothes and holidays on credit, but they're not necessities, they're just nice things to enjoy, but only IF YOU ALREADY HAVE THE MONEY FOR THEM!"

"Wow Arturo, you really *are* labouring this point. I guess I never really thought about it that much. I'm starting to feel a bit anxious about it, I mean, I thought debt was OK if it was in moderation."

"Moderation is what gets you sucked into the system, remember the drug addict looking for the quick hit? ... Well, the drug dealer doesn't want the user to take so much that they die, they want him to take it in 'moderation', so that he gets the high and keeps coming back for more.

A drug dealer is in the business of looking for 'lifetime customers', he doesn't ultimately care about the customer's well-being, and it's not his job to care!" he says dispassionately, "... It's *your* job to take care of your own well-being. The sooner you understand that society is made up of people that are actually motivated by self-interest, the sooner you understand that the buck really does stop with YOU!"

"Whoa Arturo, you're blowing my mind here, are you seriously saying that just by using my credit card to buy a pair of jeans, say, I'm getting sucked into the system as if I was taking a drug??"

He sits back, takes a deep breath and says calmly, "Jane, it's all about forming habits. If you form a habit of paying for things with credit and then not pay it off before you're charged interest, then you become a great customer ... for the finance company.

They get you to repay your debt on a drip-feed basis so that you don't notice how much those jeans are actually costing you. You don't necessarily mind as long as you have enough money coming in to pay the minimum balance because you're not aware of what's really happening.

At some point though, when the amount you owe builds up to a point that's too big to handle, you then realise there's a problem. But by that point it's too late, the credit card company owns a piece of you, and you've become a lifetime customer!"

"You're scaring me now Arturo, I don't want to believe that we have a finance system that actually wants us to be like drug addicts!"

"Jane, it's OK. Remember, you have the power to choose, when you have the AWARENESS. At the end of the day every business is supplying something that is demanded for by a customer. It's up to you, as the customer, to demand their product or not!

This isn't about blaming the finance companies for making credit easy. I have no issues with credit cards because they allow me to pay for things without carrying cash and I get a statement at the end of the month that allows me to pay in one lump sum.

I never pay interest because I use credit cards under my terms. I always have the money sitting in a bank account, and could easily pay for the item if the credit company wasn't there. But the thing is, if everyone did this, credit card companies would probably just find other ways to make money.

Remember that whether it's alcohol, food or absolutely anything else, the availability of the product is not the issue. The issue is the awareness of the user, the more aware the user is, the clearer the choice.

If you're aware, you can determine whether the consequence is acceptable or not. If not, the choice is unconscious and habitual, and the consequences will most likely make you a victim of the system.

And of course, I get it, our awareness is often distracted by glitzy advertising and the desire to feel special or important in some way, and if you haven't practised being aware, you're likely to succumb to this."

"Wait a sec, can you repeat that? I didn't get that part about the availability of the product." she says with a pained expression.

"Sure, let me see if I can put it another way ..." he tilts his head up, as he thinks, "OK, there are various laws that say certain products are allowed to be sold and others that aren't, for example, alcohol is allowed but marijuana isn't, in most places. In theory, these laws have been designed to protect people from getting into too much trouble, but the fact remains that people still get into trouble regardless of the legality of the product. If someone doesn't question what they're doing, they can still have 'legal' ways to harm themselves!

It's not the product or the laws, that are responsible, it's the individual.

What this means is that, if your choice isn't conscious, then it's unconscious. The unconscious choice is made due to some tucked away belief from past experience, i.e. pre-conditioned patterns, and no law can protect you from your conditioning!

I'll give you an example, let's say you're at a party and the person throwing the party happens to love chocolate, which is obviously legal. So there's chocolate everywhere, there's chocolate drinks, there's chocolate mousses, there's chocolate blocks and there's chocolate cake, everywhere ... you get the picture.

Now, let's say you like chocolate because you've had good memories of it as a child and you find it comforting. The question is, what do you do? If you're like most people, you'll probably try at least a bit of everything on offer and then end up feeling sick or maybe just have a sore stomach.

So did you make a conscious choice here? You might say you did but if you stop for a moment before eating the chocolate and go beyond your mind saying, 'mmm, yes, let me at it', and check in with what your body is feeling, you'd probably get a message like, 'OK, let's have one or two types of chocolate and then that's enough'.

You see the thing is that most of us run on autopilot and when something is presented, we just do what we're conditioned to do. Let me ask you this Jane, do you eat more than you normally do when you're at a buffet?"

With a sheepish look on her face she says, "Uh, yeah I do, there's just so much to choose from and it's so delicious ... are you saying that's bad?"

"Jane, it's best to think about this in terms of helpful or not helpful, rather than good or bad. Does it help you to eat more than you usually do or not?"

"Well, I suppose not, I usually end up feeling very full, but it's still satisfying to have eaten whatever I wanted."

"OK, good, so a part of you is satisfied but another part has this feeling of being too full. So which is more helpful, does the feeling of satisfaction override the part of you that doesn't feel good about being very full? Or maybe to make it clearer, where does the satisfaction come from and where does the feeling of fullness come from?"

She thinks for a moment, "... OK, I think I get where you're going with this, the satisfaction is a thought that says something like, 'isn't this good, I've seized the opportunity and now have plenty of food in me, I'm not going to starve now', whereas the feeling of being over full is my body saying, 'you've really overdone it here, I didn't need this much food'..."

"And which is more helpful for you?"

"My body, of course! The other seems to be a mind pattern that's focused on survival!" she says, stunned at the realisation.

"Jane, that's excellent, you're a true star. Your mind's primary focus is on survival and it doesn't know when enough is enough for you, but your body exists in the present moment and is finely tuned to what it needs. If you listen, it'll always tell you what it actually needs. This is why, your AWARENESS is more important than the availability of any particular product.

OK, so let's get back to debt, having implied that it's not helpful to most people, there are times that it *is* helpful."

"Huh?" she says curiously.

He continues, "The trigger for whether debt is helpful or not is whether you're receiving income from the thing that you bought with debt. In other words, if the thing you're buying puts more money in your pocket than what you pay in interest on the debt, it's considered helpful debt.

This is a key point so I'll give you some examples:

let's say a friend needs money desperately and says to you, "Jane, if you can give me $1,000 I'll give you my collection of 500 mint condition comic books", you do the numbers and work out that you could probably sell these comic books on Ebay for $5 each, that means 500 x $5 is $2.500 and a potential profit of $1,500 over the $1,000 it cost you!

The only problem is, you don't have $1,000 to give to your friend, so you decide to get a loan from the bank.

The bank agrees to lend you the money for one year, at a rate of 10%. This means that after one year, you have to pay the $1,000 loan plus an extra $100 in interest (10% of $1,000).

You figure it'll probably take close to a year to sell all 500 comic books and so you agree to the arrangement. After one year, everything has gone to plan and you've repaid the loan. You've now made a profit of $1,400 ($2,500 in sales less $1,100 to the bank).

In this case, you started with nothing, and by using the debt of $1,000 you made $1,400. Congratulations, you used debt well and you've been rewarded. That's **helpful debt.**

Now, using the same example, let's say that when you got the loan, instead of selling the comic books, you started reading them and fell in love with them. After a year, the comic books are no longer in mint condition and you now need to find $1,100 to repay the bank. Debt has just bitten you.

You might say, "yeah but I can still sell them and at least get a $1,000 for them", and maybe you can. But until you do, it's just a potential that exists and chances are if you haven't done it by now, you probably couldn't be bothered doing it now. Especially when you consider that now they're all dog-eared and scrappy looking.

This was not a wise use of the debt and you suffer the consequences of not being able to pay back the loan. That's **unhelpful debt**.

It's important to note that the debt itself is neither good or bad, it was simply a flow that came to you via the bank, *how* you use it is what makes it helpful or not. Debt can be very useful, but it's *not* really necessary unless you know how to use it well."

"Hang on a moment Arturo, so what happens if that money can't be repaid to the bank?"

"The bank will try to set up a repayment plan with you, maybe $20 or $30 a month and they'll continue to charge interest until the loan is repaid, which is similar to the drip-feed credit card system!

If you still can't pay them, they'll sue you and if you have nothing of value, you'll need to go bankrupt to wipe that debt and start again. Going bankrupt is serious and leaves a black mark against your name, so you definitely want to avoid bankruptcy, if you can.

Now, what most people don't realise is that whenever you get into debt that is unhelpful, you give up a bit of your freedom. What I mean by that is that you personally have to do something whether you like it or not, to repay this debt.

This often happens when we buy homes that are beyond what we can really afford. Note, just because the bank is willing to lend you a large amount of money, doesn't mean they're doing it out of the goodness of their hearts, remember, they're in the business of giving you what you demand, as long as you can keep paying.

When banks make it easy for you to borrow money, be very careful. They have a keen interest in you borrowing, because like the credit card company, they want you on the drip-feed system also. They effectively get to own a piece of you!

I know that sounds ominous, but whether you like it or not, you're going to have to keep working to pay them back, and this is a restriction on your freedom. It may sound harsh but the point is that no one can put you into bondage without your consent, regardless of whether that consent was unconscious!"

"You're scaring me again Arturo, what I'm hearing you say is that when we buy a home, we effectively become a slave to the bank, is that right??"

"Well, let's look at that for a moment, how would you define a slave?"

"Um, I'd say, a person that is held against their will and forced to do things they don't want to do."

"OK, I wouldn't say a bank holds you against your will when you borrow money, but if you don't make your repayments, they have the right to kick you onto the streets and sell your home. This, by itself isn't slavery, but if you get to a point where you don't enjoy your work anymore and want to stop working for a while, you won't be able to because the consequences will be the loss of your home.

If that happens, you force yourself to keep working to satisfy the bank, you don't have the freedom to choose and therefore you make *yourself* a slave to your mortgage.

So when you're thinking about getting into debt, ask yourself two key questions:

1. How long will it take to pay this off? And;
2. How much will it cost me in total?

If you don't know the answer to the questions, don't get into debt, full stop. If you do, and you feel good about the answers, and of course the debt is helpful to you, then go ahead. If something isn't quite right, look for another solution. I'll give you some examples ..." He opens a file on his computer: "Let's say that you've gotten into the habit of buying things with credit cards. After a while, you notice that your credit card debt bill has ballooned to $25,000. You're outraged and decide to cut up your cards and get rid of the debt. You look at your finances and know that you can commit $450 per month to paying back this debt.

Now, how long will it take to pay off, and how much will it cost you? He keys all the information into the spreadsheet and says, "The answer may shock you, but it'll take 10 years to pay off your credit cards. You'll pay a total of **$54,153** and of that, **$29,153 will be interest**, assuming a rate of 18% per annum.

That's not a typo, you'd be paying more in interest than the debt itself!

And that assumes you don't buy anything else on credit from that moment on. It's shocking but this is why it's so important that you don't allow yourself to get lulled into a false sense of security when buying on credit."

"Shit Arturo, I can't believe that, how is that possible? Do people really get into these situations? It just sounds crazy!"

"You're right, it is crazy. And yes, people do get into these situations, more often than you know.

Have you heard the story on how to boil a frog? ... I don't know if this is actually true but it makes a good point. It goes like this, if you put a frog into a pot of boiling water, it jumps out, however, if you put the frog in a pot of cool water that heats *gradually* until it starts boiling, the frog doesn't realise there's a problem until it is too late.

With that principle in mind, this happens with people and credit. They get lulled into thinking that they're fine, paying off a small amount every month, until BOOM, the water's boiling and they're cooked!"

"Wow, I had no idea. That just sounds really sinister."

"Remember Jane, we don't want to make the credit providers wrong, they're providing a service and it's up to us to realise whether the temperature is being turned up!

OK, I'll give you an example with buying a house." He punches some numbers in the spreadsheet again. "let's say a house costs $400,000 and you take out a $320,000 loan with a 6% interest rate over 30 years. Your mortgage payments would be $1,918 per month, which, let's say, you can afford.

But how much will that house really end up costing you?

You'd end up paying $690,683 for it. Over half of that –$370,683– will have been in interest payments! Also note that 6% is a relatively low rate, if interest rates rise, it'll significantly impact how much interest you pay."

"Holy crap! You're really freaking me out here, why the hell would anyone want to get into that situation?" She sits back and digests the burden of debt "... boy, that means my parents are in this position too!" she says while shaking her head in disbelief.

"Jane, I know this doesn't sound good but you need to look at the bigger picture, and that is, you still need to live somewhere. The choice is either to pay rent to someone, or buy and get into a mortgage.

Yes, it can be a burden but don't be too incredulous, people often don't mind making this commitment because property has tended to rise in value over the long term. The real issue however, is whether you have a source of income that allows you to live with the debt comfortably."

"But hang on Arturo, you said to always ask the two questions and to look at whether the debt was helpful, how can the debt be helpful on a home that you live in, when it doesn't put any money in your pocket?"

"Good question, and you're right, the home you live in doesn't give you an income, unless you rent some rooms out. The truth is that it actually costs you money to maintain a home but, this is where it helps to know the numbers.

What I mean is that if you can find out what the total cost per annum to rent the place you want, versus the total cost per annum to buy the place, then you can work out which is a better deal. In that way you can work out if the debt is helpful or not because you still need to live somewhere.

Ultimately though, no one knows how high property prices will rise, so the best you can do is base the calculation on the current state of affairs and work with the income you have.

OK, so here's what you need to know about debt: As a general rule, aim to live without debt. If you don't have the money to pay for something now, chances are you won't have the money to pay for it later either, that is if you don't get into the habit of saving first.

Also it's important to note that this applies to cars also. Borrowing money to buy a car doesn't make financial sense for most people. The best way to buy a car is to save for a few years and buy one that's two or three years old, with low kilometres. It'll still be like new but usually close to half the price of a new one.

I know that the temptation to buy now rather than waiting is high but remember that nothing you buy is going to give you lasting happiness when the joy of the purchase wears off and you're left with the monthly debt payments, that's when you'll regret the purchase and be left with a sour taste in your mouth, or maybe the smell of your skin cooking!

For that matter, don't buy anything with a credit card until you have proven to yourself that you have the discipline to only buy what you can pay for. The best way to do this is to use a debit card to buy clothes and groceries.

If you don't have enough money in your bank account to use your debit card for a purchase, then you don't buy it. In other words, if you don't have enough money in the bank to buy something, it means that something needs to change so that you do have money in your account at all times. Debt, in the form of credit card debt comes with a huge interest rate and is like a big hole in the bottom of your pocket. You have to plug that hole before you put another cent in there.

So if you find yourself in a position where you already have an accumulated debt on your credit card, shop around for a deal to get a lower rate of interest on the debt, then cut up the card and pay as much as you can as quickly as you can to seal up the hole.

OK, I've talked enough, the project for the week ahead is to talk with your parents about their mortgage, how much do they pay? When do they expect to pay it off? And, how do they feel about it?

Is that something you can do, Jane?"

"Ooh, uh, I think my dad will be a bit uncomfortable with that. But if I'm honest, I'm probably not all that comfortable with it either." She sits back, looks up and thinks about how she's going to approach it with her parents. After a few moments she looks at him and says, "OK, I accept. I think there's something in me that I need to face, so yes, I'll do it."

"Great, see you next week, Jane."

LATER THAT EVENING she approaches David and says, "Dad, can we have a chat about debt?" With surprise he says, "Uh, sure honey, why not? What's on your mind?"

"Well, today Arturo was explaining debt to me and I didn't realise how much debt can cost over a lifetime. Like, I know that you and mum have a mortgage on the house and um, how do you feel about that?"

David sits back, feeling some discomfort with the question, "How do I feel about it? Well, to be honest, I wish we didn't have the mortgage. Sometimes I feel like it's a bit of a weight around my neck and it's quite a chunk of money to payout every fortnight."

"Do you mind telling me how much that is?"

Feeling it was important to be open, he says, "Um, no, that's fine, it's $1,200."

"$1,200 every fortnight!!" she says as her eyes almost pop out of their sockets, "Wow dad, I had no idea. Why is it so much?"

"Hmm, OK, it's like this, we bought the house around 13 years ago for $400,000 and borrowed $300,000. Then after a few years we wanted to renovate the kitchen and bathroom and since the value of the home had gone up, the bank was happy to give us more money.

We thought that while we were at it, we'd upgrade your mum's car and so we ended up refinancing and borrowed another $100,000 over the original $300,000. The loan's over a 30 year period, so all going well, it should be paid off in another 20 years or so."

"Whoa dad, that seems like a lot of money, I can see why you feel like you've got a weight around your neck. Do you ever think about how much interest you'll be paying over that time?"

"Oh Jane, don't remind me ..." he says while putting his hands on the sides of his head, "I haven't calculated it, but I know it's a lot. But there's no choice, that's the way it is and if you want a home, these are the costs."

Just then Arturo's words came to her, *you always have a choice*, and she says, "Dad, if there was a choice, what do you think it would look like?"

"What? That's a strange question." She held her gaze. "OK, OK. Well, if I had a choice I suppose I would have bought a smaller home. I suppose a three-bedroom place would have been OK instead of the four we have. I probably wouldn't have renovated, it was OK before as well and I'd aim to pay off the mortgage as soon as possible."

With an upbeat tone in her voice she blurts out, "OK, so why not do that now?"

"What!! What are you saying, to move from here? ... No, no, this is our home, you guys have grown up here, it's a nice home, and it'd be such an inconvenience to move." he says, crossing his arms and legs in discomfort.

"So let me get this straight, you're paying $600 a week to the bank, which feels like a weight around your neck, when you could do something to ease the burden, but it's too inconvenient, is that right?"

He scratches his head, "Jane, it's not that easy, your mum would be very disappointed if we had to leave this place, she has a network of friends in the neighbourhood, it really wouldn't be that easy."

"Right, I think I'm getting the picture dad, you're uncomfortable with the debt burden, but not so uncomfortable that you would do anything about it, you prefer to stay a victim of the situation. And to top it off, it seems you don't want to upset mum, like your role as a man is threatened or something like that."

David leans forward and says angrily, "Now wait just one minute young lady! What's going on here? Why are you speaking to me like that?"

She wondered for a moment where those words came from and in a calm voice said, "Dad, I'm sorry if that came out harshly, I don't mean to hurt you.

I'm simply seeing something a certain way and calling it as I see it."

With that, he sat back in resignation and let out a big sigh, "... It's OK Jane, you're right, I feel like a wimp, I've been working my arse off for years and I really don't have anything to show for it. This house gives me the illusion that I've achieved something but the reality is that we still owe the bank a big chunk of change.

The truth of the matter is that if we downsized from this place, it'd be like admitting to myself that I *am* actually a failure, that I couldn't make a go of my life even though I've had every opportunity. I'm 48, with nothing to show for my efforts." he says, looking at the ceiling as tears well in his eyes.

Jane had never seen her dad in such a vulnerable state, her heart went out to him and she puts her hand on his knee. "Dad, hey, it's OK. Maybe you don't have all the stuff you'd like to have, but you have a good family. I think you've done a pretty good job with Andy and me, well I think *I've* got my head screwed on properly, as for Andy, who knows!" she says while chuckling. "Look, if there's one thing that Arturo is showing me, it's that we can always change for the better if we want to, the choice is always ours in this moment."

He wipes his eyes with the palms of his hands, looks at her and says, "How did you get so mature all of a sudden? ... You know, I may not say it often, but I'm really proud of you sweetheart. Maybe this Arturo character is having a positive influence on you after all ... Look, leave it with me, I think you've given me a lot to think about. Thanks honey."

Later that evening as David was getting ready for bed, he says to Elizabeth, "Hey Liz, you know, I had an interesting conversation with Jane this evening, we spoke about debt of all things!" Elizabeth's attention was piqued, "Debt! Why is she talking to you about that? It's that Arturo character again, isn't it?" she says with an edge.

"Yes, but it's OK, I'm starting to get the feeling that he really does have her best interest at heart. He's teaching her about debt at the moment and she's interested in finding out about our situation, like how much we owe."

"And, what did you say to her?" she says defensively.

"Well, I told her the truth. I told her that we borrowed 300k when we bought the place and then another 100k later in renovating and updating your car."

Elizabeth was now fidgeting uncomfortably, "And what did she say to that?"

"Well, she was quite shocked. She was surprised by how much we've borrowed and how much we're paying the bank every fortnight. I also told her that sometimes I feel like the mortgage is a real weight around my neck."

"What! I didn't know that, you've never mentioned it before. What did she say to that?"

"She asked what I could do if I had a choice, and I said that I would've gone for a smaller home, not renovated, and paid off the mortgage as soon as possible. But then she said, why not do that now!"

Elizabeth's fear was now triggered, "I hope you put her in her place David, I think that girl's just getting a bit too big for her boots."

David looked at her seriously, "You know Liz, I told her that you wouldn't want to move, but I have to say, she's given me a lot to think about and I think we should actually sit down soon and consider the possibility.

The truth of the matter is that we need to work for another 20 years just to pay this place off ... we'd be close to 70! We don't really need a place this size and the kids will probably be moving out at some point over the next 5 years or so anyway."

Elizabeth couldn't believe what she was hearing and says sternly, "David! Are you serious? Do you know what a major pain it'd be for us to move from here? I mean, we have some good friends and we've established roots here, it's just not something I want to entertain right now."

"Look, all I'm saying is that we should consider our options. Until Jane mentioned it, I was blindly going around day-by-day, not feeling great but not really realising that it was because of this debt burden I'm feeling.

If we could find a way to alleviate some of that burden, it'd really help ... Look, putting aside the friends and roots and all that stuff, how do *you* feel about the level of debt we have?"

Sitting up in bed now and looking down, she says, "Well, I guess like you, I kind of just accepted that this was the situation we were in. We wanted a nice house, we could afford the repayments and we did it. I never really considered what impact that might have on us, as we got older, or on you for that matter." she says forlornly.

"Liz, you know I love you and I've always wanted to give you the world, I'm sorry that I haven't been more of a success but I'm finding that I'm really feeling quite trapped with this debt situation and I think we can probably do better by downsizing."

She stops fidgeting, looks directly into his eyes and says gently, "Look, you're probably right, but I just can't bring myself to let go of this place. I love living here, it's a great home and a great neighbourhood. I just think that there has to be some other way that can allow us to still live here."

He thinks for a moment, "Well, the only way I think we can stay here is if our income rises substantially. Given that I'm already working full-time, I suppose that means you'd need to get full-time work also. We'd also need to look at our expenses and see where we could cut a few corners ... maybe not go on holidays every year, or something like that."

She brings her hands to her face and starts to sob.

He moves over and puts his arm around her, "Look, let's sleep on it and discuss it more when we've rested." He caresses her hair, holding back his own tears as he feels her pain, then kisses her gently on the lips.

The next evening, after dinner, David and Elizabeth sit to discuss their finances, "Liz, I've had a quick look at our finances and I think that if we can pay off our mortgage within five years, that would be sensational.

Currently, between your income from the two days a week and my full-time wage, we have around $1,650 each week after tax. We put $600 on the mortgage and that leaves us with $1,050 for living.

I've also worked out that to pay off the loan in five years, we'd need to pay an additional $700 per week. Now, we can't live on $350 a week, but if you started working full-time, that would add about another $450 a week, giving us around $800 a week to live on, and if we held off on holidays for the next five years, I think we could do it!" he says excitedly

Dashing his enthusiasm she says, "I just don't know, what you're proposing is tough, and I guess that I'm just really struggling with it at this point. A part of me just doesn't want to believe that it's come to this."

"Liz, I know it's tough, but if we want to stay here, we need to make sacrifices. If you want, I can look into the numbers for us to move into a smaller place, so that you don't have to go back to full-time work ..."

"No David! I want to stay here and if that means working full-time, I'll do that, damn it! But I need to know that it's not going to be for longer than 5 years. Can you promise me that David? Can you promise that I won't have to work full-time for longer than 5 years?" she says as she fights back the tears.

He looks down for a moment, thinking about what she'd just said and says in a low voice, "... Liz, I can't promise it because I don't know what the future holds. The best I can do is make a commitment that I'll do everything I can to help us be debt free within five years."

Blowing her nose, "OK, I'll let work know in the morning that I'm available for full-time work, if they have it. If they don't, I'll start looking elsewhere."

"OK, thanks Liz, I know this isn't easy and I really appreciate the effort. Also, I think we should sit with the kids and let them know what we've decided. I think all of us will need to pull our belts in."

"OK, let's do that tomorrow evening, and show a united front!"

At dinner, the next evening, David says, "Jane, Andy, your mother and I have been talking and we'd like to share something with you guys ..." They look at him intently, "After the discussion I had with you the other evening, Jane, I spoke with your mum and we decided that we would like to pay off our mortgage as soon as possible.

We considered moving to a smaller place but we really like living here and as a result, your mum has decided to increase her work hours to full-time." Jane and Andy turn to Elizabeth with surprise.

Elizabeth steps in with a brave face, "Yep, that's right kido's, I'm going to be working full-time and we're going to need to watch how we spend our money from now on. This is going to be a joint effort and all of us need to help out."

Andy says with concern, "What do you mean that we *all* need to help out? And what exactly is a mortgage?"

Elizabeth answers, "Firstly, a mortgage is just a fancy name for a loan we took from the bank to buy this house. This loan gets paid off over a long time usually, but we'd now like to pay if off as soon as possible.

Next, what I mean by helping out, is that all of us have been used to spending without thinking too much about how it affects us, and so in your case, young Andy, your allowance is going to be cut back and you may need to find a part-time job, like Jane has, if you want extra money."

He coughs, "... What!! But none of my friends have to work, their parents give them more than what you guys give me! I don't understand, why do I have to have my allowance cut?"

David sees Andy's anxiety increasing and says, "Andy, I know this isn't easy for you to get your head around, you've been used to being able to buy your lunch everyday and hanging out with your mates at the movies, but now you might need to look at what's more important, a bought lunch or entertainment with your friends, that is of course, if you don't want to get a part-time job."

"No, I don't want to. I like buying my lunch everyday and doing stuff with my mates, it's just not fair." he says pouting.

Speaking in a firmer tone, David now says, "Andy, do you think it's fair that I or your mother have to go to work? Sometimes in life you just need to do what you need to do to get through a situation. We're not saying that you can never have your bought lunch and amusements.

What we're saying is that rather than relying on us to pay for these things, if they're important to you, you need to find a way, an honest way, to bring money in so you can continue with the lifestyle you enjoy now. And most likely, that means some type of part-time work after school.

You can get all upset at the unfairness or the inconvenience of it, which won't get you anywhere other than not feeling good, or you can find a solution, it's really up to you which way you want to go, OK?"

Andy shrugs his shoulders in disapproval, looks down and resumes eating.

Jane had been listening to the conversation carefully and now says, "Look, I think this is great, I can help with some of the tools that Arturo has given me, maybe there are more solutions than what we see at the moment, also."

"Great idea Jane," says David, "let's get together on Saturday, after lunch and have a brainstorming session." Andy, still looking down and stuffing food into his mouth, acknowledges with a reluctant grunt.

Saturday Afternoon Family Brainstorming Session

Saturday rolls around and everyone gathers around the family dining table after lunch. David, whose had a spring in his step the last few days, begins by saying, "... Thanks for making the effort guys, I want you to remember that we're a team and I'm confident that with the changes we're going to make, we'll all be better off down the track. Now, does anyone have anything to say?"

"I do," says Jane, "I've printed out a couple templates that Arturo gave me a few weeks back. I think we can use this as a basis for working out a budget." She gives everyone a copy of the *Now Position* spreadsheet.

"This template is designed for us to put in what our position is right now, so that we can see how much money is coming in versus going out. I think if we fill this out first, we can then look at the minimum we need to survive."

They all begin to talk about the income and expenses and Jane keys the data on her laptop. After an hour of discussion, she turns her laptop around and shows them the spreadsheet for their current position:

Our Family Income

(Annual)

Money In	Amount
Wages – David – After tax	$67,600
Wages – Elizabeth – After tax	$18,000
Bank Interest	$0
Stock Dividends	$0
Rental Income	$0
Total	$85,600

Our Family Spending

(Annual)

Money Out	Amount
Electricity & Gas	$3,000
Gifts (birthdays, Xmas, etc.)	$1,500
Home & Contents insurance	$1,200
Home Phone, TV, Internet	$1,000
School Fees—Andy	$2,000
Health Club dues – David & Elizabeth	$1,200
Home owners association dues/Body Corporate fees	$0
Health Insurance	$2,500
Medical, Dental	$1,500
Travel/holidays	$5,000
Mortgage/Rent	$31,200
Property rates, taxes & water	$2,800
Mobile phones – D, E & A	$1,200
ATM withdrawals/incidental spending	$3,000
Groceries	$14,000
Just in Case Funds	$0
Grooming & Clothing – David	$500
Grooming & Clothing – Elizabeth	$1,000

Grooming & Clothing – Andy	$500
Home accessories	$0
Car Fuel	$3,000
Car repairs	$1,000
Car insurance & Registration	$2,800
Donations	$0
Andy's Allowance	$4,160
Money saved for a goal – e.g. New Car	$0
New fun experiences	$0
Restaurants/dining out/movies/concerts	$1,800
Total	**$85,860**

The family studies the spreadsheet and David says quietly, "Wow, no wonder we're not getting anywhere." Even Andy pipes up, "Boy, I can't believe I spend over $4,000 a year! All those lunches and movies really add up!"

David turns to Elizabeth, "What do you think, darling?"

"Well, yeah, it seems that we're just keeping our heads above water. Other than the money we spend for holidays, it doesn't look like we're really going overboard with our spending. But the thing that concerns me is that we aren't saving any money. We have no fallback position for an unforeseen situation. For that matter, if Jane was to get married soon, we'd probably have to borrow again!"

Jane quickly says, "What! Come on now, the purpose of doing this is just to get a snap-shot of where we're at now, it's about showing that we can do something to improve the situation from here on … Anyway, I don't think I'm getting married any time soon!"

"Fair enough Jane," says David, "we now have a clear view of where we stand and can do something about it."

"Before we do though," says Jane, "we need to also list what we own and what we owe, Arturo gave me a template for this also."

She goes through the template with them and after more discussion, they come up with the following:

Our Family Assets

(Things we own)

Things that don't pay us to own them	Amount
Electronics—PC, Tablet, etc.	$3,000
Clothes, Shoes & Accessories	$2,000
Cars (2)	$35,000
Furniture & Fittings	$8,000
Things of value that don't pay us	
Cash at Bank – at call	$2,300
Family Home	$700,000
Gold & Silver (Including jewellery melt value)	$3,000
Things that pay us to own them	
High Yield Bank Accounts	$0
Superannuation – D & E	$170,000
Stocks/Shares	$0
Investment Property	$0
Total Assets	$923,300

Our Family Liabilities

(Things we owe)

Things we might have to pay for in less than 12 months	Amount
Credit Cards	$1,000
Short Term Loans	$0
Things we might have to pay for in greater than 12 months	
Credit Cards – Long Term	$0
Long Term Loans	$0
School Loans	$0
Mortgage	$283,500
Car Loan	$0
Total Liabilities	$284,500
Net Assets	**$638,800**

Looking at the bottom line, Andy says, "Hey, looks pretty good to me, we've got almost 640 big ones!"

Before David could open his mouth, Jane says, "Andy, NO!" While shaking her head with a disparaging look. She then realised she was just triggered and says, "... Sorry Andy. Look, on the surface it looks like a lot of money but you need to understand that other than the Superannuation, that money isn't working for us, it's mainly tied in the house. We're always going to need somewhere to live, and living requires money, so until you have money working for you, you need to work to cover your living."

David and Elizabeth turn to each in shock in hearing Jane speak this way.

Andy starts scratching his head with confusion and says, "Um, can someone explain Superannuation?"

"Sure," says David, "just think of it this way, imagine if we said to you, we're going to give you $70 a week, instead of $80, but the $10 that we would've given you is going to be put in a special account that you can't touch until you're at least 55. That money then grows and ideally, when you retire, you can live on that money. Does that make sense?"

"What! You're going to force me to save my money, for someday when I'm an old fart?"

David smiles while saying, "Yep, that's about the size of it, it's forced saving. The government created these laws so that when we retire from work, they don't have to pay us a pension."

Andy again scratches his head, while looking up he says, "Hmm, very interesting, I never knew that."

Just then Jane announces, "Guys, we're going to have to wrap this up, I need to go to work."

"OK Jane," says David, "I think we've covered a lot, let's get together again tomorrow after lunch and look at the next step." Andy and Jane walk off while nodding their heads in agreement.

David turns to Elizabeth, "So, how do you think that went?"

"Yeah, I think it was quite an eye opener, seeing the figures like that really showed me that we do need to do things differently and I actually feel better about returning to full-time work."

"Oh, on that, did they get back to you about that?"

"No, they said they'd need more time to work out whether there's an opening or not for me."

"So where does that leave you now?"

"Well, I think I'll start looking in the papers to see if something else comes up. Obviously I'd prefer to stay where I am because I already know all the systems, but it might be worth seeing what else is out there, just in case.

The next day the family gathers around the table again and David says, "OK, I think yesterday was an eye opener for all of us, does anyone want to say anything at this point?"

"Yeah," says Andy, "I've been thinking about it and I think it would be good for me to get an after school job." He then turns to Jane and says, "Can you get me a job where you work?"

Before Jane could react, David says, "Andy, thanks for that, I think it's great that you want to get a job, but let's focus on how we can reduce our living costs first."

"Dad," says Jane, "I think we need to be careful to not go too overboard with cutting expenses, Arturo highlighted to me that life is supposed to be fun, so we need to find a balance when doing this."

"OK Jane, noted. So I think that if we look at the costs from the spreadsheet and take turns in saying where each of us think we can save, that would be good.

OK, I'll go first." says David, "I think we should keep the health club membership. I can review our mobile phone plans and probably save at least $40 a month there between us. Andy, I think it's a good idea if you just text with your phone rather than make calls, we can talk about that later.

Next, I can drop my incidental spending by $50 a month by bringing my lunch from home more often. Grooming and Clothing, I can probably find a cheaper barber and limit clothes purchases to socks and jocks, so that could reduce by half ... Liz, what do you say if we reduce our eating out by $50 a month?"

"Yes, I think that should be fine."

"OK, the other thing that needs a joint decision is the holiday expenses. Now Jane, I know you haven't come along on family holidays the last few years, so you're probably not fussed, but Andy, I know you enjoy that summer break at the caravan park on the beach. What I was thinking is that we could drive up and back each day for maybe four days, would that work for you?

Andy thinks for a moment, "Uh, would we stay all day, so that I could play with my friends in the evenings?"

"I think we can do that, we've got a big beach tent and some camping gear, so at least we have some shelter and a way to cook some food. Liz, what do you think?"

"Hmm, I think that it'll take some extra organising, but it can be done. But we'll all need to help, don't just expect me to do it all." she says while glaring at Andy.

"Yeah, alright mum, I hear ya. Yeah, I'll help out."

"Great," says David, "I think that we can reduce the costs down from $5,000 to say $1,000, to cover food, fuel and incidentals. OK, Liz, do you want to go next?"

"OK, well, I can cut my Grooming and Clothes bill by half to $500 and I'll cut my incidentals by $50 a month also by cutting down on my coffees. Andy, your turn."

"OK, I suppose I can cut my Grooming and Clothing down also ..."

Elizabeth interjects quickly, "Actually, no. You're still growing, so I think we need to leave it as is, for just in case you do need something new."

"OK, well then it's really just my allowance, what if I cut this in half as soon as I get a job?

"Actually Andy," says David, "I think it's a good idea we cut it in half regardless of whether you get a job, you may need that incentive to help you find a job quicker."

"Aw what! That's a bit rough, can't you at least give me a month to find a job?"

Elizabeth steps in to back up David, "No Andy, we're all cutting back here, so I think you can too."

Andy couldn't control himself and says, "What about Jane, what's she doing?" as he points his finger incessantly at her.

Jane remains calm and says, "You're right Andy, even though I pay for most of my own stuff, I should still contribute to the family bills. " She thinks for a moment and says, "... I'm willing to pay $200 a month."

"Actually Jane, I think you contribute by the work you've been doing around the house." says Elizabeth, "Andy, that reminds me, you really don't do much around here, do you?" She turns to David, "I think Andy could be responsible for the lawns and putting out the bins, what do you think?"

"That sounds good to me." says David, "Andy, do you have any other ideas on what you could do for your allowance?"

Andy's mind was a whirlwind, "What! I, I, I don't know what to say, I mean, you guys are really going to town on me, you're killing me here! From getting $80 a week, you're cutting it in half, I have to find a job and NOW, you want me to do work around the house as well! It's too much, I just can't take it." he says while crossing his arms and pouting.

"Andy, ANDY, listen to me." says David, "I know it's a big change and it may seem tough right now, but it's only because we haven't asked you to step up until now. Yes, it's going to take a bit of adjusting but chances are we probably would have cut your allowance soon anyway. I think we stopped with Jane when she turned 16 ..." He turns to Jane and she nods.

"Well, I don't like it. I feel like you're all ganging up on me, I thought you said we were a team and we'd all be better off, well I just don't see it." he says sulking.

"OK, I tell you what Andy, what if your mum and I give you a chance to come up with your own plan, you can present it to us and as long as it fits in with what we've been talking about today, we'll go with it. What do you say?"

Andy pauses for a while, "Well, I suppose that sounds OK." he says while wiping his eyes with his sleeves.

"Now Andy remember, the ball is with *you*, we'll wait for your plan and we'll hold off on your allowance until you come back to us with a plan, is that clear?"

"HUH! No allowance at all??"

"Yep, that's right. But just until you get back to us, so if you come back to us by say, tomorrow evening, it'll be resolved then. Do we have a deal?" David says while sticking his hand out.

Andy slowly reaches out and shakes David's hand, while nodding reluctantly.

"Great, it's a deal." says David, "OK, so what does the spreadsheet look like now, Jane?"

She turns her laptop around and shows everyone the screen:

Our Family Income
(Annual)

Description	Amount
Money In	
Wages – David – After tax	$67,600
Wages – Elizabeth – after tax	$18,000
Bank Interest	$0
Stock Dividends	$0
Rental Income	$0
Total	**$85,600**

Our Family Spending
(Annual)

Description	Amount
Money Out	
Electricity & Gas	$3,000
Gifts (birthdays, Xmas, etc.)	$1,500
Home & Contents insurance	$1,200
Home Phone, TV, Internet	$1,000
School Fees – Andy	$2,000
Club dues – D & E	$1,200
Home owners association dues/Body Corporate fees	$0
Health Insurance	$2,500
Medical, Dental	$1,500
Travel/holidays	$1,000
Mortgage/Rent	$31,200
Property rates, taxes & water	$2,800
Mobile phones – D, E & A	$720
ATM withdrawals/incidental spending	$1,800
Groceries	$14,000
Just in Case Funds	$0
Grooming & Clothing – David	$250
Grooming & Clothing – Elizabeth	$500
Grooming & Clothing – Andy	$500
Home accessories	$0
Car Fuel	$3,000
Car repairs	$1,000

Car insurance & Registration	$2,800
Donations	$0
Andy's Allowance	$2,080
Money saved for a goal – e.g. New Car	$0
New fun experiences	$0
Restaurants/dining out/movies/concerts	$1,200
Total	$76,750
Surplus	$8,850

"So we've saved around $9,000 over a year by making a few changes." David says, "That's good, but in order to pay off the mortgage in 5 years, the repayments need to be $5,600 a month. So with your mum getting a full-time job, that should net about $40,000 after tax, how does that work out Jane?"

She makes the adjustments:

Our Family Income

(Annual)

Description	Amount
Money In	
Wages – David – After tax	$67,600
Wages – Elizabeth – after tax	$40,000
Bank Interest	$0
Stock Dividends	$0
Rental Income	$0
Total	$107,600

Our Family Spending

(Annual)

Description	Amount
Money Out	
Electricity & Gas	$3,000
Gifts (birthdays, Xmas, etc.)	$1,500
Home & Contents insurance	$1,200
Home Phone, TV, Internet	$1,000
School Fees – Andy	$2,000
Club dues – D & E	$1,200
Home owners association dues/Body Corporate fees	$0
Health Insurance	$2,500
Medical, Dental	$1,500
Travel/holidays	$1,000
Mortgage/Rent	$67,200
Property rates, taxes & water	$2,800
Mobile phones – D, E & A	$720
ATM withdrawals/incidental spending	$1,800
Groceries	$14,000
Just in Case Funds	$0
Grooming & Clothing – David	$250
Grooming & Clothing – Elizabeth	$500
Grooming & Clothing – Andy	$500
Home accessories	$0
Car Fuel	$3,000
Car repairs	$1,000
Car insurance & Registration	$2,800
Donations	$0
Andy's Allowance	$2,080
Money saved for a goal – e.g. New Car	$0
New fun experiences	$0
Restaurants/dining out/movies/concerts	$1,200
Total	$112,750
Deficit	-$5,150

"Hmm, we're about $5,000 short of the target." David says with concern.

Jane looks at the spreadsheet for a moment and then says, "Dad, do you think you could ask your boss to give you a raise?"

He sits back and looks up, "Hmm, you know, it *has* been a while since I had a proper review at work, I think I can put together a case for why I deserve a raise. Good Idea Jane, thanks!"

"Yes, well done Jane." says Elizabeth, "There is however something that concerns me. While it's great that we'll be paying the mortgage off quicker, we're not going to have any extra for an unforeseen situation. I think we should find a way to at least accumulate a few thousand each year to cover potential situations cropping up.

In fact, what about Jane's 21st, that's coming up in a little over 6 months, where are we going to get the money for a party?"

Jane says quickly, "Mum, I don't really care about having a party. I can always just go out for a dinner with friends or something like that."

"Are you sure Jane? Twenty-One is a bit of a milestone, it's good to have a good celebration."

"No mum, I'm sure. I'm not interested in the big party thing, a small intimate thing with some close friends suits me fine."

Elizabeth thinks for a moment, "OK Jane, it's your choice but I still want to get you something in celebration of it, so we're still going to need to build that into the budget. In the meantime, just have a think about what you'd like."

David had been listening keenly and says, "I agree Liz, why don't you and I discuss it and work something out later. At this point let's focus on being in a position where the house can potentially be paid off in 5 years.

Up to this point, we've still had no real buffer anyway, so I think that if we stick with this plan for now and review it once you go full-time, then when everything else is implemented, we can see where we stand at that point. Is that OK?" he says empathically.

"I hear what you're saying, David, it's just that I'm a little uneasy now that I know the situation. OK, let's see how we go with our changes first." she finally agrees.

"OK, good. Now let's wrap this up ..." David says, while looking at the notes he's written, "So in summary, I'm going to ask for a raise, cut back on clothes and grooming, bring more lunches from home, cut back on entertainment and cut back on holiday costs. Liz, you're going to work full-time, cut back on coffees, entertainment and clothes and grooming also. Andy, we're going to wait for your proposal, and Jane, you'll continue to take care of yourself as well as some household chores. Are we all in agreement?"

Everyone agrees and he continues, "Good, then let's get together again in four weeks time and see where we're at, OK?"

They all agree and get on with the rest of their day.

Week Eleven – Gaining Clarity

"Hey Jane, come on in." Arturo says in his usual calm demeanour. After eleven weeks, he still spends a few moments looking into her eyes before they begin.

"So, anything you want to share, Jane?"

"Yeah, I had that conversation about debt with my dad and he realised that he felt really weighed down by the mortgage and that he'd like to find a way to pay it off within 5 years.

That led to him calling a family meeting, where we discussed where we were financially, as a family. The long and the short of it is that we cut some costs and my mum decided that she'd go back to full-time work to help pay the mortgage sooner."

"That sounds very productive, Jane. And has anything changed for you?"

"Uh, well, I don't think so. In fact I offered to pay $200 a month to contribute to the bills and they said that the work I was doing around the house was enough. They seem to have acknowledged that I'm being more responsible and they appreciate it.

My brother Andy, on the other hand, takes very little responsibility for himself and with the changes my parents are making, he's really finding it tough." She looks up and smiles as she remembers his little tantrum.

"Actually Arturo, there was something I wanted to ask you. My parents are aiming to pay off the mortgage within 5 years but by aiming for that, it'll leave them with no extra money for just in case something out of the blue comes along. Do you think it's wise to do that?"

"Well Jane, it's not so black and white. On the one hand, it's wise to pay off the mortgage as soon as possible, but on the other hand, it's not so wise to leave yourself without a buffer for some cushioning. I think that at this point it's probably a good idea to ask what the purpose of working is. So I ask you Jane, why work?"

Without hesitating, she says, "We work so we can live ... so we can survive and thrive."

"Yep, that's the generally accepted idea. But remember Jane, life is about joy, it's about appreciation for this moment and everything that it brings. I agree that sometimes a situation calls for something you initially have difficulty feeling joy about, but the key is non-resistance to what is.

Always remember, there's what is, and then there's *what you do* with what is. The situation only ever presents an opportunity for you to choose something that feels better to you.

Now, your parents want to pay off their debt within 5 years, is there joy in that? You and I aren't going to know the answer to this. I suspect the thought of being debt free feels good and that's good. The other side though, is that some sacrifices need to be made, which may not feel very good.

The key to it is this ... if life isn't joyful for 5 years, in the hope that it will be when the debt is paid off, then there's a major mismatch. Life is not about a better future moment, life is a continuum of now, and if you aren't joyful now, chances are you won't be joyful when the debt is paid off either.

Sure there'll be the temporary satisfaction of achieving the goal, but at what price? And I can tell you that the probabilities of something cropping up that wasn't planned for, and blows out the budget, are quite high.

So the bigger picture needs to be considered before committing to this sort of thing.

Here's what I'd ask your parents, and for them to write down their answers:

1. How exactly would life be better when they are debt free?
2. What would happen if something came along that stopped them from being able to pay off their debt within the 5 years?
3. How do they feel about the steps/sacrifices they need to take for the next 5 years?
4. Is that worth the pain now?

If yes, great, go for it. If no, look for alternatives, and find the path that is most joyful."

"Arturo, it sounds like you're leaning more on the side of not paying the debt as soon as possible, is that the case?"

"Not at all, what I advocate for is to live joyfully in this moment. Every situation involves positives and negatives. The positives to paying off the debt as soon as possible means that they'll be debt free sooner, the negatives are that they'll have to curtail their standard of living in the near term.

The positives to NOT paying off the debt as soon as possible means that they can maintain the lifestyle that they've become accustomed to, the negatives are that they're tied to the bank and have that weight around their neck for the longer term.

It really all comes down to which one feels better, in a given moment. But Jane, nothing is ever really black and white, there are always shades of grey and if we're willing to challenge our beliefs, other solutions are always available.

For example, have you ever wondered why some people are financially rich? Some might say these people have special talents or powers, and maybe some do, but for the most part, they're really no different than you and I. The only real difference is that they see life in a certain way and have a fundamental belief system that allows greater sums of money to flow to them. This belief system is generally either formed in childhood or developed through skills that are learned and honed through a diligent pursuit in the desire to want to do so.

The tricky part about developing these skills is that it can look like hard work, and this is where you need to be clear on what your true desire is. If you keep saying to yourself, 'Oh, when I have money, then it'll all be better.' Or, 'Oh, when I have X, Y or Z, I'll be better.' Then you're going to be working against yourself. The reason is because life is NOT about the future, life is all about right NOW!

Sure, you can say to yourself, 'hey, won't it be great when X, Y or Z show up', but if your dominant way of being is to struggle and resist against what is, you're not likely to go very far. You'll just hold your dream at arms length and focus on the struggle.

Jane, the future moment that is often craved for, comes out of who you are BEING right NOW. Your power lies in this moment, NOW. Things may not be as you want them to be right now but you can start to focus on feeling better and build up a belief that good things are possible for you.

Here's the sort of dialogue you can say to yourself, '*I'm alive now and I know that X, Y or Z are on their way to me. I feel excited by the steps I'm taking and I feel excited by how much opportunity is here for me. I'm amazed at how things have a way of working out for me, even when it looks like they don't!*'

Do you see where I'm going with this, Jane?"

"Yeah, I do, it's all about maintaining a good attitude, no matter what comes my way."

"It is, and, it's about noticing what's happening within you, otherwise you can do what I've said here and still be nowhere because you're using the positive as a veneer to cover up the negative. If you're not feeling good, chances are you want something to be different from how it is now.

It's one of the biggest issues in the Personal Development world. People say affirmations, aim to be positive whenever they can, but underneath they're really pissed off that life isn't how they think it should be. They do all this work in the hope that there'll be a pay off at some point.

That, is a big trap. There's never a pay off because there's ultimately no future moment that is better, it's all about this moment here, NOW!" he says as his right hand slaps firmly onto the desk.

"Be at ease and at peace now, and the 'stuff' takes care of itself. The paradox is that being at ease is the simplest thing we can do but most people are so caught up in striving for something that they can't allow themselves to be at ease.

When I said that stuff about being excited about the steps, the real key to it is the *feeling excited now* part, feeling good now is what it's all about.

When you think about the things you want, if you feel some negativity or angst that you don't have them, then it works against your desire. If you can think about them and feel good, then you've succeeded in this moment, the showing up of the stuff is a bonus, but the real gem is in feeling good now!

What this means is that life takes on a duality type of aspect. On the one hand, you know that all is well, through choosing to feel good now, and on the other hand, you also see that things may be contrary to that, i.e. that your circumstances still aren't great."

"Oh Arturo, you're doing my head in again ..." she says as she holds her head with both hands and shakes it from side to side, "OK, but how can you choose to feel good if plain and simple, you just don't feel good?"

"OK, good question. If you don't feel good, here are the steps:

1. Acknowledge what you're feeling by allowing yourself to cry, scream or whatever else needs to come out.
2. Sit with the feeling with the aim of seeing it be released from your body. Start at your feet and work upwards, releasing all the angst, frustration or sadness.
3. See it being blown away from you and falling to the ground, and then absorbed by the ground.

4. When you feel like an empty shell, take a deep breath in, seeing white light come into your body from the top and taking up every bit of space there is.

How does this feel to you?"

"Yeah, it feels good, I'll have to remember that one. OK, so back to my parents, are you saying that somehow they need to be at ease with their situation, enjoying life, while at the same time still working hard to pay off the debt, is that right?"

"Not quite. Yes, it's advisable to be at ease, but the *working hard* part is not at ease. Maybe another way of saying it is that you can have a plan that gives you a rough guide of the direction you're going in, but you're also at ease and accepting, that everything is being taken care of. And if it turns out that something hasn't been taken care of, you have what it takes to take care of it. Does that make it clearer?"

She looks up while nodding, "Yeah, it does ... it's not an easy thing to do, though. But I do feel that I get what you're saying. It's like you need to have one foot in the 'looking-forward' to things camp while the other foot stays in the camp where regardless of what tomorrow brings, I feel good now because somehow things work out for the best." She scratches her head, "But Arturo, what if there are some really shocking things that show up, how do you maintain the good feelings?"

"Jane, this is a process, and it takes a growing into, to truly trust that life really does support you. Yes, there are times when some wildly insane things happen but you'd use the technique I just shared with you and then you'd practice the, '*Hmm, isn't that interesting?*' technique. And of course, always aim to notice the breath as a way of putting a gap between you and the situation, so that you're not completely overtaken by the situation.

Now Jane, I want to be very clear about something, you can't change your parents, even if you can convey to them what I've talked about now, they probably won't change.

The best you can do is be an example for them, live as best you can, at ease and with awareness and trust that they will find their own way, that is best for them.

OK, we've covered a lot of deep stuff, the project for this week is to have that conversation with your parents and ask them to write down answers to the following questions:

1. How exactly would life be better when you are debt free?

2. What would happen if something came along that stopped you from being able to pay off your debt within the 5 years?
3. How do you feel about the steps/sacrifices you need to make for the next 5 years, assuming all goes well?
4. Is the potential future gain worth the pain now?

Then see how the conversation goes from there."

SHE ARRIVES HOME and says to her parents that she'd like to have a chat with them after dinner.

At dinner, not able to contain his curiosity, David says, "What did you want to talk to us about, honey?"

"Dad, I don't think we should do it over dinner, I think it'll be best if we do it later."

"Sounds serious, is it something I should be concerned about?"

"Dad! Relax, you're just going to have to wait."

"OK, OK, no need to get all huffy about it, I'm just curious."

Just then Andy pipes up, "I've thought about a plan for me and I want to discuss that with you guys too."

"Whoa, it's all happening." says David, "OK, Andy, tell you what, we'll have a chat with Jane first and then you, given that she asked first."

"Aw, why does she always go first?" Andy whines.

"Actually dad," says Jane, "that's fine, you can see Andy first while I tidy up after dinner."

After dinner, David and Elizabeth sit with Andy as he takes out a sheet of paper that he'd scribbled some numbers on. "OK guys, here's what I've come up with, l accept the half allowance but I want you to keep paying me this after my 16th as well. Jane got a full allowance up to her 16th, so I think it's fair for me to get the same amount as her."

"Just let me stop you there for a moment, Andy ..." Elizabeth interjects, "If you really want to keep comparing yourself to Jane, you're going to need to lift your game considerably. Have you noticed what Jane's been doing around here lately? ... And we didn't ask her to do this, she made a decision that she wants a clean room and that she wants to take responsibility for herself as much as possible. So are you sure you want to go down this path?"

He scratches his head, realising he might be digging a hole for himself. "Uh, OK, well, I'm just wanting things to be fair. You guys are coming down hard on me and I just want a fair deal, that's all."

"OK Andy, we'll hear what you have to say and chat when you've finished, please continue." says David.

He looks at his sheet and says, "OK, so I'll get a job and hopefully get at least $50 a week. As far as stuff around the house, I'll cut the grass and take the bins in and out every week. How's that?"

"Well, that sounds OK Andy ..." David remarks, "there's just a couple things that we need get clear though. First, this is a commitment you make, there'll be a timetable for cutting the grass, during winter it'll only be once every four weeks but during spring and early summer, it'll be weekly. With the bins, that happens weekly, and you'll need to go around the house and empty the bins into the outdoor bin also.

Second, when you get low on mower fuel, you need to tell me and we'll go together to get some. Keeping the mower clean and in tip-top condition is also part of the deal.

Third, you need to use the grass catcher and put the grass clippings on the compost heap.

If you don't meet this commitment, there'll be a consequence. The consequence will be no allowance for a week. Do you accept these terms?"

Andy scratches his head and mumbles, "Uh, I guess so."

"What was that Andy? Look, I'm serious about this. This is no different to a job that you get somewhere out there, if you don't do what you're hired to do, you're gonna get fired, it's as simple as that. So, do we have a deal?"

"Yeah OK, I hear you, sheesh."

He continues, "Now Andy, in relation to continuing your allowance after you've turned 16, your mum and I will need to have a chat about that and get back to you in the next few days, is that OK?"

"Yeah, OK dad."

"Good, tomorrow night we can draw up the schedule on the calendar, together." David says with a smile. Andy nods and goes off to watch TV.

David calls out to Jane, "Where would you like to do this honey, in the lounge or the dining table?"

She calls back, "Around the dining table is fine. Actually, if you could get a pen and paper for both you and mum, that would be good too ..."

The three of them sat around the dining table and Jane says, "OK, what I wanted to speak with you about was these changes that are being made to pay off the mortgage in 5 years. I was telling Arturo about it and he suggested that I ask you some questions."

"What sort of questions?" Elizabeth asks defensively.

"Well, OK, the first one is ... *How exactly would life be better when you are debt free?* But write down your answer before you share it with me."

"OK, but it feels like we're back at school." Elizabeth remarks

After a minute or so of writing David says, "I'm ready, how are you going Liz?"

"Almost done ... OK, done."

"Who wants to go first?" Jane asks.

"I will," David answers, "... Life would be better because I'd feel as free as a bird, I'd be able to work part-time if I wanted to, I'd have extra money to invest or spend on hobbies, I'd be relieved in not owing money anymore and I think I would just feel generally happier and at peace in not having this weight around my neck." He looks at Elizabeth with a smile and says, "Your turn."

"OK, well, I think life would be better because David and I would have extra money to do more things, we'd be able to pay for parties for Jane and Andy and give nice gifts. It'd also be good to have the choice to not work and spend more quality time with David and the kids."

"Great, thanks for that, the next question is ... *What would happen if something came along that stopped you from being able to pay off your debt within the 5 years?*"

"Hmm, tough question, Jane." David remarks.

After a few minutes, David sees that Elizabeth had finished and says, "OK, if something happens that stops me from paying the mortgage off in the 5 years, I think I'd be shattered, I've really got my heart set on paying this thing off in the 5 years and I don't really know what I'd do. I think I'd feel quite dejected, but I really don't want to think about that as being a possibility."

Elizabeth looks over at David with concern and says, "Well that really is my biggest fear, I think that we're putting all our eggs in the paying off the mortgage basket and if something happens, we're just so emotionally caught up in it, that I think we'd really struggle to deal with it. So to answer the question, I think that we would need to reassess the whole thing and deal with whatever it is that comes up."

"OK, and the next question is ..." but before Jane could finish, David interjects, "How many questions do we have to answer, Jane?"

"Not many, you're half way done. So the next question is: *How do you feel about the steps/sacrifices you need to make for the next 5 years, assuming all goes well?*"

David asks Elizabeth to go first this time.

"OK, I wrote, I can't say that I feel great about the steps or sacrifices that I need to make. I'm OK with going back to work full-time but if I'm honest, I wouldn't do it if I had the choice. I'm also not thrilled about the compromise for our summer holiday, I feel a lot of the prep work is going to fall on me and to drive for around 3 hours each day is not my idea of fun. So I don't feel so good about it. But I know it's important to David and I understand we all have to chip in and help out. I also hate the idea of not having some extra money to pay for things like nice gifts for the kids."

David looks at Elizabeth with surprise, "Wow Liz, um, I was hoping you would've felt better than that about it, I wrote ... I feel excited about the steps and understand that certain sacrifices need to be made in order to reach our goal. I feel excited about the fact that the family has come together and that we're united in a common goal. I know that it's not going to be easy but the thought of being free of debt feels really good!"

"OK, and the final question is ... *Is the potential future gain worth the pain now?*"

Without writing anything down, David says quickly, "Absolutely."

Elizabeth, with shock says, "What! How can you be so sure? There are so many variables, like, we need to be careful on how much we spend, you need to get a raise, I need a certain income, and if some unforeseen expense comes along, we have nothing to fall back on!"

He thinks for a moment, "You know, you're right, I've fallen in love with the idea of paying the place off so much that I guess, I'm looking at things through rose coloured glasses. The truth of the matter is that if we have a big expense come out of left field or if one of us is injured and couldn't work, then the whole plan falls apart." he says, looking down.

He continues, "... Maybe we do need to rethink this. I think that while I'd love to have the place paid off as soon as possible, it's more important that we all feel good about it, and from what I'm hearing Liz, you're not really doing this because you really want to. And the last thing I want is for you to feel resentment around this, like you have no choice or something. We're a family and I think we need to discuss this until we find a plan that we can all feel reasonably good about."

He turns to Jane and says, "Thanks sweetheart, interesting exercise. Once again you've given me something to think about."

"That's fine dad, but Arturo really should get the credit, he's the one that's helped me see things differently and I'm just passing that on."

"Well, you've still helped, and I'm thankful for that."

"Dad, there is one more thing that Arturo talked about today ..." she scratches her head, "I'll see if I can convey it well ... he said that it's important to feel good now even if things aren't the way you want them to be. He said that it's good to have the plans but it's more important that you feel good NOW and not be so attached to the outcomes.

I noticed that you said that you feel excited about paying off the debt but if something came along that stopped you from being able to pay it off, you'd be devastated ...

I don't know what the answer is for you, but what Arturo is saying is that somehow it's important to find a way to feel good regardless of what happens with the debt."

"Yeah, I get that Jane, I do understand that there's a balance required in finding a way to feel good even if things don't go the way I want. Thanks."

Later that evening, as David and Elizabeth get ready for bed, he says, "You know Liz, I know that you want to help alleviate the pressure I feel around this debt situation, but unless you can feel good about it as well, it's not going to work.

I think we need to revise the budget. I'm now thinking that if it takes 10 years to pay off the mortgage, then so be it."

She turns to him and says, "Have you looked at why you feel like this debt is a weight around your neck?"

"You know, I'm not really sure, it's like something awoke in me when Jane mentioned it and I suddenly became aware of this massive weight on me. If I ask myself why that is ... I'd have to say that it's the realisation that I haven't been very successful and I suppose ... that as a man, I think I should be a better provider for the family."

Incredulously, she says, "David! Are you kidding me? You're a great provider, and you're a great dad. You're here for the kids and you're here for me when I go through my difficult times. You've got a good job that pays a steady income and in my eyes, you *are* successful.

You don't need to compare yourself to the guys that run multi-million dollar businesses, that's not you, and to be honest, I wouldn't want you to be one those guys. I think those people sacrifice way too much family time in order to build their empires.

I love you as you are, you're a kind, caring, good man and you're all the man that I need, and want."

"Thanks Liz, I really appreciate hearing that. It's just that I do kick myself for not being a bit more financially savvy. I look at people that have invested in property and think that I could have done that if I'd been a bit more of a go-getter."

"Don't be so hard on yourself, no one knows what tomorrow brings. It turned out that investing in property when we bought this place would have been good, but we weren't to know that, and quite frankly, I'm not comfortable in taking that sort of risk either.

Look, we're OK, we may not be the richest people around but there's certainly a lot of people that are doing it tougher than we are ..."

"I hear what you're saying Liz, and maybe I need to find a way to forgive myself because I just feel all this pressure now. It's like I just realised that I haven't lived up to what my own desires were and now I feel stuck.

Maybe this is some sort of mid-life crisis, where I realise that I'm not as young as I used to be and that I'm not going to be able to live my dreams because I have to work for another 20 years to pay off the mortgage. It just feels suffocating."

"So what exactly *are* your dreams?" she says lovingly, "It's been quite a while since we talked about our dreams and desires ... I guess ever since the kids came along, our time has been focused on them, but now Andy is getting to an age where he doesn't need us as much and Jane is well and truly taking care of herself, so we can probably start to think about dreams again."

"Hmm, my dreams ..." he says as he stares at the ceiling, "I had always said that I wanted to spend time in tropical paradises, like Tahiti or the Bahamas. To have the freedom to get up and go visit different places, spend time with friends and learn to sail. What about you Liz, what would you say your dreams are?"

"Well, I think mine are quite simple, and maybe it's my maternal instincts, but I'd like to see the kids married and settled in their own homes. Maybe they'll have children and we can experience being grandparents also.

But apart from that, I'm not really fussed, I like working a few days a week and having the time to catch up with friends and maybe play some tennis with them. I like your idea of travelling but I can't say it's a dream of mine, but I'd certainly be there with you if you wanted to go."

He takes out a clean sheet of paper and a pen from his bedside table, "OK, so let's get clear about this, what's important to you is to have the freedom to catch up with friends and you like working two or three days a week. In terms of finances, you don't really need much more than what you have now, is that right?" She nods.

"OK, so if you found work for three days a week instead of going full-time, would that be something you could feel good about?"

She thinks for a moment, "Well, yeah, that'd be really good because I'm really not enjoying the thought of working full-time and to do an extra day would still be a step in helping out our debt situation, while not feeling demoralised in working lots of hours."

"Right," says David, "let's work with that then. I'm also thinking that instead of doing the daily trip to the beach that I came up with for our holidays, let's just go for a full week and cook ourselves, I think we can do that for about $2,000 in total, instead of going for the usual two weeks and eating out regularly. How does that sound?"

"That sounds great to me!"

"The other thing I can do is shop around for a better deal on our mortgage, I saw an ad the other day that was offering a fixed loan period for a lower rate than we pay now, so that should help quite a bit also."

"David, there is one more thing I'd like addressed though, I'd like to have some money set aside for things like major birthdays and possibly paying for Jane and Andy's weddings. It's important to me that we have some type of savings account in place, I think that if we set aside $250 per week for this, that should do it."

He scratches his chin and says, "Ooh, that may be tough to do, that's 13k per year of after tax dollars! But look, you're right, we do need some sort of savings account. Why don't we come up with some actual goals, and see how it pans out."

"OK, what did you have in mind?" she says.

"Well, let's see, we've got Jane's 21st in around 6 months, Andy's 18th in a little more than 2 years, then his 21st, 3 years after that, that brings us to around the 5 year mark and who knows, maybe Jane may get hitched some time after that also!

If we allowed 5k for the birthdays and 25k for a wedding, then we'd need a total of 40k over the next five years."

"And David, you're not allowing for our major birthdays! You'll be turning 50 in just over a year and then I'll be turning 50 in around 3 years! Ugh, that's not a pleasant thought!"

He laughs, "OK, OK, yes, we're both getting older. Look, for my 50th, I really don't want to make a big deal out of it, I had a good party for my 40th. I'm thinking it'd be nice for the two of us to go away somewhere."

"We could get a taste of that tropical paradise living you're dreaming of by going to Tahiti or maybe Bali, I think that would be a great thing for you to look forward to."

"That's a great idea Liz, but it won't be cheap, we'd probably still need to allocate close to 10k towards it."

"All I'm saying, my love, is that you're worth it. Have a think about it, look at the numbers, see how the spreadsheet looks and we can go from there. Oh, and while you're at it, allocate a reasonable amount for my 50th!" she says with a cheeky smile, "I'd like to have a nice shindig with friends, and maybe a small piece of jewellery from you would be nice too!"

Smiling, he says, "Okay Liz, I'll do that. I suspect that the figure you came up with of $250 a week is what it's probably going to take. But seriously Liz, I do feel really good about this.

I feel like the joy is coming back. I think I've been just going along with things without really questioning anything. But what we're doing now is planning for our next phase in life, and while I may not be living my dreams, working in partnership with you feels fantastic. I love you my darling."

She moves closer and says, "… And I love you, my wonderful man." as she kisses him gently on the lips.

The next morning David wakes up, turns to Elizabeth and says, "Oh, oops, we forgot to speak about Andy's allowance last night … OK, so what I was thinking to say to him is that after he turns 16, we'll put his weekly $40 allowance into a separate bank account until he's 18. He can then put that money towards a car, and he'd still need to do the lawns and take the garbage out."

"OK, I think that should be fine." says Elizabeth, "Maybe we can encourage him to save some money when he gets a part-time job also … Actually, why don't we do this, if he gets a job before his 16th, we stop the allowance altogether at that point and start the bank account for his car then. What do you think of that?".

"Hmm, it's a good idea, it's just that he'll most likely resist. The only way he's likely to go for it is if he's earning more than $80 a week!"

"OK David, I've got another idea, his bus fare is around $20 a week, we'll make his allowance that, and put the other $20 into the new bank account. That'll hopefully be an added incentive for him to find a job quickly. Also, we can all make our lunches together the night before, so that way there's no excuse that we run out of time in the morning."

"I like it Liz. let's tell him tonight ..."

At dinner, David says, "Andy, you know, your mum and I had that chat about your allowance and what we came up with is that we'll continue to pay an allowance to you after you turn 16 ..." Andy's face lights up, "but instead of you getting it directly, it'll go into a new bank account that you can put your savings into so that you can have some money to buy a car when you turn 18.

Now, between right now and the time you turn 16, we're going to make your allowance $20 a week for your bus fare and put the other $20 into this new account. When you get a job, you can add to this account with any extra money you get. So what do you think of that?"

He scratches his head, "Um, did you say you're going to cut my allowance in half, again?? You don't want to give me any money to live on at all!!"

"Just hang on a moment ... " says Elizabeth, "you don't need *money to live on*. The $80 we were giving you was used for your bus fare, buying your lunch everyday and for your general entertainment. And it hasn't been a bad deal for you, I might say. It's way more generous than what I grew up with, I can tell you that!

Anyway, we've now said that we'd give you $40, and the way I see it is that you have a choice, you can make your lunch with the rest of us each night, and then save $20 a week towards your car, or you can blow it. We're not going to force you to do this but I'm guessing you want as much money as possible in that account so that you can get a nice car. Am I right?"

Andy looks at both of them, with puppy dog eyes and replies, "But what if I can't get a job? How will I have fun with my friends? They all have money and I'd feel embarrassed if I didn't have any money."

Not knowing exactly what to say to him, Elizabeth says gently, "Andy, you're a smart boy, you always have been, I'm sure you can find a job. Employers are always looking for bright kids with a great attitude. If you can show them that you're a keen worker, I'm sure someone will give you a job. Also, if the only way to have fun with your friends is to have money, then something is missing."

Sensing Elizabeth's discomfort, David says, "Andy, look, we totally get that this is a big adjustment for you, but just know that it's temporary. You've got what it takes to find a job and you never know, you might really enjoy earning your own money."

Still looking forlorn, Andy turns to Jane and says, "So do you think I could get a job at your work?"

Jane had thought about this from the last time he'd asked and said, "Andy, I'm really not comfortable with both of us working at the same place. But I tell you what, get a job somewhere else and if you can be responsible in turning up on time and maintain a good attitude, then after 6 months I'll put in a good word for you, how's that?"

Andy was about to sulk when Jane reinforced, "Remember Andy, A GOOD ATTITUDE."

Andy blurts out, "OK, OK, I get it, it's time to grow up and all that stuff." He takes a deep breath, "... OK, I'll start to ask around tomorrow after school. And mum, dad, I accept the new bank account idea and that my allowance will just go towards my bus fare."

"Great, let's look at opening an account online in the next few days." says David.

The following evening David says excitedly, "I made that presentation for a raise today, the bosses are going consider it and will let me know next week."

"Good on you David ..." says Elizabeth, "I too have news, I spoke to my manager today and said that if it was easier for her, I'd actually prefer three days a week instead of going full-time, and she said there would definitely be a better chance for that than full-time at this point. She's also going to let me know next week."

Andy then says in a sombre mood, "Well, I went and asked for a job at a few places after school today but no one was interested."

"OK, well, good on you for trying Andy ..." says David, "it takes guts to do what you're doing. Stick with it champ, something will come up."

Jane then says, "So Andy, I couldn't help noticing that your shirt is hanging out of pants and your jumper looks messy ... is this how you went to ask for a job?"

"Jane! This is my school uniform, what do you want me to do, come home, get all dressed up and then go??" he says sarcastically.

"Andy, I'm not saying this to have a go at you. You know how I mentioned last night that A GOOD ATTITUDE is what's important ... well that applies in every moment." She gets up and says, "Watch me ..." she moves to other side of the room, pulls out one side of her shirt from her skirt and with hunched shoulders, moves towards the table, and in a goofy voice says, "Um, I was wondering whether you have some after school work for me ..." everyone laughs.

Then she walks back, tucks her shirt back in, stands tall and walks across to the table, confidently saying, "Excuse me, are you the manager here? ... I'll be turning 16 soon and am looking for some work experience after school. I learn quickly and have a positive attitude. Do you have anything available for me?"

"Do you see the difference here, Andy?" she says as she sits back at the table.

"Um, yeah, I get it. But that's not really me, I'm an easy going sort of guy, I don't want to act all fake just to get a job."

"Just hang on for a moment Andy..." Elizabeth interjects, "I understand what you're saying, you have a different style than what Jane has, and that's OK. But what Jane is showing you though, is two different ways of approaching the same thing. You can still find your own way of asking for a job but I think the point Jane's making is that if you stand tall with a neat appearance, it gives a better first impression. And as they say, you only get one chance at a first impression!"

"OK mum, I'll see what I can come up with, I get what you're saying, be more confident. But I tell you what, it's nerve wracking, my heart beats really fast and I feel a bit scared."

"Well ..." says David, "that makes you perfectly normal. That's why I said it takes guts to do what you're doing. Whenever we do something new and put ourselves out there for someone to potentially say *no* to us, it tends to bring out the nerves!

I'll let you in on a little secret ..." he says in a low voice, "I felt nervous and a bit scared myself, when I gave the presentation to my bosses earlier today. But the thing is, just because you're feeling a bit scared, you shouldn't let it stop you. If you really want something, then as they say, 'feel the fear and do it anyway'."

Andy was listening intently to David and was surprised to hear his dad say that he felt scared also, "Thanks dad, that really helps, I would've never thought you still feel that way at *your* age, I thought that when you're old, nothing scares you and you can do anything!"

"Steady on champ, I'm not that old ... OK, maybe compared to you, but anyway, the truth of the matter is that you *can* do anything, but that doesn't mean that you don't feel fear or nervousness."

"OK, OK. I'm getting it, I'll work on my delivery and try some other places tomorrow."

Later that evening as David and Elizabeth prepare for bed, David says, "You know Liz, I have some more good news, I've found a deal where we can lock in our home loan for 10 years at a rate of 5.5%. That means we won't be crushed if interest rates go up at any point.

Of course, we won't get the benefit of lower interest rates either, but it feels important to lock this in, so we at least won't get any nasty surprises if interest rates go up."

"That's great news honey ..." she says, "hopefully by next week we'll know about your raise and my extra day of work, then we can look at the budget again."

The following evening Andy comes home and says, "I didn't get a job today, but people seemed friendlier, one even told me to come back next month as something might open up soon!"

"Well done champ! So what are you going to do now?" David says.

"Well, I was thinking of waiting and taking it from there."

"OK, think about this for a moment, Andy ..." David says with serious note in his voice, "you're going to wait for a month, in the meantime no money is coming in and what are you going to do next month if they say that there's still no openings? You'll be in the same position you're in now. Are you willing to take that risk?"

"Um, now that you put it that way, it doesn't really sound so good. I guess, I was just hoping it would be easier than this ..." he scratches his head and says, "But, you're right dad!" as the realisation hits him, "I'll go out again tomorrow and keep looking and I'll look everyday until I find something." he says enthusiastically.

"Good on you Andy, I'm so proud of you, my darling boy." Elizabeth says with a big smile.

The following evening Andy arrives home and says excitedly, "Hey, guess what, I got a job and I start on Monday!"

"Way to go Andy, what a way to finish the week!" says David, "So what are the details? Where is it? What are you going to be doing? How much are they paying you? Etc."

"Uh, well, it's at the local green grocer, *Johnny's*, I'll be sweeping floors and doing general clean up stuff to start with, they're going to pay me $10 an hour and they said to come for one hour everyday after school and a couple of hours on Saturday mornings. I'm really excited, I should get $70 for the week! And get this, they liked my attitude!" he says with a smile from ear to ear.

"Andy, that's fantastic. You're on your way now, things are really looking up." says Elizabeth, "Jane will be thrilled for you also, when she gets back from work."

Week Twelve – Compounding

"Hi Jane, come on in." says Arturo. "I'd like to go through a model today that may help you get clearer on how to manage money. In fact, I use this model myself for budgeting!" He moves over to the white board a writes:

My Allocation Model:

Me	30%
Fun	5%
Goal	5%
Give	10%
Live	30%
Tax	20%

"What this means is that each month, I split my income into these allocations. I created separate online bank accounts for each group to keep track of the allocations.

The 'Me' is money I pay myself first, it's how I take care of myself and show myself that I'm the most important aspect. I put this money towards my 'Money Tree'. I'll explain the money tree concept in a moment.

The next 5% goes to 'Fun', I spend this every month even if it's on something frivolous. The point, is to send myself a message to look for new ways to have fun or experience something new every month.

Then, 5% goes to saving for some 'Goal', it could be for a car, a nice watch, or whatever takes my fancy. It could even be for an overseas holiday, it's really for anything I want that's a bit bigger and I need to save towards.

The next 10% goes to 'Giving', some call this tithing but I just call it giving, because you can give this amount to any person or organisation that you want to support financially. Like, a family member, a religion, a political party or anything else you want to support.

Personally, I like to support organisations that focus on providing people with a hand UP, rather than a hand OUT. But the important part is that whatever you give, you give freely, with no expectation for anything in return.

The message I send myself in Giving, is that I'm abundant, that there's always plenty of everything and that I'm happy to share the abundance that I AM.

Note also, you don't have to give 10% or anything at all if it doesn't feel right, you might want to give your time to a community organisation if you prefer, it's the same thing. It's really all about sending a message to yourself that you really *are* an abundant Being.

I then allocate 30% to living costs. For someone starting out, I'd recommend spending no more than 50%, if you go over 50%, it's important to find a way of either lowering your living costs or increasing your income. Ideally, it's a good idea to monitor this so you can put less into your 'Living' and more into your 'Me' account.

The way I did it was that I started with 50% for 'Living', 10% for 'Me' and 0% for 'Goal'. Then when I had the lifestyle I desired and my income kept increasing, I made it 40%, 15% & 5%, then 35%, 18% & 7% until it got to where I am now.

Note, this didn't happen overnight, it was a gradual growing and I continue to monitor it because from here, I plan to get it to 10% for 'Living', 30% for 'Me' and 20% to 'Giving'."

"Whoa, wait a sec, I'm getting confused with all these numbers, can you give me an example of this?" she says.

"Sure, let's say you make $2,400 a month, 50% goes to living, i.e. $1,200. For the sake of the exercise, let's say you don't need any more than $1,200 to live. Then 10%, $240 goes into your 'Me' account.

Then, let's say that in the following year, your income rises to $2,600 per month and your living costs are still around $1,200, this now represents 46% of your income. You can then increase your 'Me' account to 14%, or $364.

In this way, you get to build your 'Money Tree' at a faster rate. As long as your income rises more than your cost of living, you'll be able to get your percentage for 'Living' down. Does that make sense now?"

"Yes, OK got it, thanks."

"Good. Now, the final amount is for tax. Tax is one of those things that a lot of people don't like paying and without going into a philosophical argument, I tend to focus on the fact that I'm generating income and am a productive member of the community.

What the government does with what they collect from me, is none of my business because I'm not interested in trying to control them. They're elected officials and there's no point in resisting what is. Having said that, I don't pay any more tax than I absolutely have to, I'm always going to use the laws to legally minimise the amount I have to pay.

So is that all making sense so far?"

"Yep, sounds very calculated, I like knowing that all the money has a certain purpose. But what about the 'Money Tree' you mentioned? I'm really curious about that one."

"OK, good, the *Money Tree* is a term I use to describe something that pays me over and over again without having to do much work to support it. People often say that money doesn't grow on trees, well, I say it does! It just depends on whether you've planted a money tree SEED or not." he says with a cheeky grin.

"It's really no different than when you plant a fruit tree, let's say peach, it's going to take a few elements. You need, a peach seed, some fertile soil, a sunny spot and water. Once you have these things, you dig a hole, plant the seed and then water it regularly. Over time the seed germinates and a seedling is formed, but it can take a while before the seedling breaks through the soil, so a bit of patience is required at the start.

After much care and attention and after a few years, the seedling becomes a young tree that begins to give a small amount of fruit. With continued care, the tree grows bigger and stronger and provides even more fruit year after year. You eventually have so much fruit that you're able to preserve it, so you benefit from the fruit in the winter months also!

Now the really cool thing is that if you treat money like a fruit tree, you'll eventually get lots of fruit in the form of money! Are you still following this?"

"Yep, I understand the analogy, I just don't see how exactly I can grow my own *Money Tree* though!"

"OK, so to understand that, we need to discuss compounding and leverage. Have you heard these terms before?"

"Uh, I've heard of leverage, like a jack lifts a car, and I've heard of problems compounding, but no, I don't really know what you mean with money."

"That's fine, the concept is very similar. I'll talk about compounding first, I think it'll really blow you away.

I heard a story one time about a couple that had 9 children and these 9 children became adults and went on to have 52 children, then from those 52 children, 201 more children were born!

I don't know how many children those 201 children will go on to have but it's reasonable to think that it's going to be in the high hundreds. So at this point, the original 2 people compounded humans at a rate of 100:1 within roughly a 100-year period.

In other words, compounding is just a fancy way of saying multiplying, but you multiply a bigger number each time ... you know the saying, 'multiplying like rabbits'? Well there are a lot of things in nature that multiply or grow at what's called an *exponential* rate.

There's a number sequence known as the Fibonacci sequence, which explains this rate. It's quite easy and it goes like this ..." He moves over to the whiteboard and writes the following:

1, 1+1=2, 1+2=3, 2+3=5, 3+5=8, 5+8=13, 8+13=21, 13+21=34, 21+34=55, 34+55=89 and so on ...

"So the sequence goes, 1, 2, 3, 5, 8, 13, 21, 34, 55, 89, etc. Now it's said that in Fibonacci's book from the 13th century, he did a thought experiment with rabbits. He said that if you start with a pair of rabbits, male and female, and they mate and have a pair of rabbits, and if this continues, you end up with a rabbit population that matches the sequence I've shown you on the whiteboard. So the *multiplying like rabbits*, is really the compounding of rabbits!

With this in mind, when it comes to money, compounding works in exactly the same way as the rabbit experiment.

Imagine $100 as the first pair of rabbits and the interest that it earns are a baby pair of rabbits. This is how it would look if you had $100 generating 10% every year in interest:

After year 1, you have $110 (your initial $100 + interest of $10);
After year 2, you receive interest on the higher amount of $110 and so now you have $121 ($110 + interest of 10% = $11);
After year 3, you receive interest on $121 and you now have $133.10 ($121+ interest, 10% = $12.10)

It doesn't look like much, but when this is allowed to continue, the results are significant. In this example, after 20 years you'd have a figure of around $670, that's almost 7 times your original amount. And to make it even more impressive, you haven't had to do anything for it, it happened naturally by just letting it grow on its own!"

Impressed, she says, "That sounds pretty good Arturo, but 20 years seems like a long time to wait for the harvest!"

"Yep, and that's exactly why most people don't stick with this. As humans, we like instant gratification, we want everything now …" he says as he clicks his fingers for emphasis, "and yes, 20 years is a long time to wait to reap the rewards.

But as you know, I'm a now kinda person also and I think we can have our rabbit and eat it too!" he says chuckling. "The allocation model I've outlined on the whiteboard takes care of things because you'll be living and enjoying life NOW, while also putting a little away for this growth element.

That small 10% you pay yourself is money you'd probably blow if you weren't allocating it this way, so this *Money Tree* becomes a very nice bonus, years down the track."

"OK, I think I'm getting it. By splitting my money into the various allocations, I can plant the seed now for my *Money Tree*, and still have fun now. I'm not having to waiting for the fruit from the tree to give me pleasure, I'm enjoying the journey. And maybe I won't need to go through what my parents are going through because I'll have the money set aside!"

"Jane, once you know about compounding, and you have a system to enable that compounding to happen, you'll be in a position to make wiser decisions. Every dollar that flows to you will now have a purpose, so yes, you will have money set aside.

OK." he says with excitement, "It's time for a wild example. If I offered you $1,000,000 now or 1 cent today that doubled every day for the next 30 days, which would you take?"

She thinks for a moment and says, "Well the obvious thing seems to be to accept the million bucks now, but I get a feeling that this is some sort of trick question, so I'll say the 1 cent that doubles."

"That, would be the correct answer." he says smiling, as he opens a computer file and shows her the following:

"At the end of each day, you have the following:"

Day 1: $0.02	Day 2: $0.04	Day 3: $0.08
Day 4: $0.16	Day 5: $0.32	Day 6: $0.64
Day 7: $1.28	Day 8: $2.56	Day 9: $5.12
Day 10: $0.24	Day 11: $20.48	Day 12: $40.96
Day 13: $81.92	Day 14: $163.84	Day 15: $327.68
Day 16: $655.36	Day 17: $1,310.72	Day 18: $2,621.44
Day 19: $5,242.88	Day 20: $10,485.76	Day 21: $20,971.52
Day 22: $41,943.04	Day 23: $83,886.08	Day 24: $167,772.16
Day 25: $335,544.32	Day 26: $670,088.64	Day 27: $1,342,177.28
Day 28: $2,684,354.56	Day 29: $5,368,709.12	**Day 30: $10,737,498.24**

"So after 30 days, that little one cent, compounding at a rate of 100% turns into a golden goose of over 10 million dollars!!"

"Wow Arturo, that's incredible, it's like a super magic trick. I can see the numbers are right but I just can't believe that it really works out like that."

"Well, it sure does. But look at how it took 10 days to get to just $10. The next 10 gets you to over $10,000 and if you took this option, you'd be kicking yourself at this stage for not taking the $1M, but then look in the last 10 days, that's where the magic really happens.

The first 10 days of not much happening is why most people get bored and give up with it. In reality, this sort of thing happens in years, so if you can stick to the plan, even after 10 years of nothing much happening, you'll be truly amazed at how your *Money Tree* grows. This is a very long term plan with major benefits."

"Hmm, it reminds me of the tortoise and the hare story, slow and steady, wins the race." she says.

"Yep, that's a great example, Jane."

Just then, he takes out some sheets from the top drawer of his desk and hands them to her:

Live Example							
	Date	**Dividend**	**Shares**	**Total**	**Price**	**Value**	
Initial Investment	Jun-2000		1,000	1,000	$9.93	$9,930	
	Dec-00	0.35c per Share	24 shares	1,024			Dividend Reinvested
	Jun-01	0.33	21	1,045			Dividend Reinvested
	Dec-01	0.40	26	1,071			Dividend Reinvested
	Jun-02	0.39	22	1,093			Dividend Reinvested
	Dec-02	0.46	28	1,121			Dividend Reinvested
	Jun-03	0.44	28	1,149			Dividend Reinvested
	Dec-03	0.51	34	1,183			Dividend Reinvested
	Jun-04	0.47	31	1,214			Dividend Reinvested
	Dec-04	0.54	33	1,247			Dividend Reinvested
	Jun-05	0.51	29	1,276			Dividend Reinvested
	Dec-05	0.59	32	1,308			Dividend Reinvested
	Jun-06	0.56	28	1,336			Dividend Reinvested
	Dec-06	0.69	33	1,369			Dividend Reinvested
	Jun-07	0.62	30	1,399			Dividend Reinvested
	Dec-07	0.74	37	1,436			Dividend Reinvested
	Jun-08	0.62	45	1,481			Dividend Reinvested
	Dec-08	0.74	78	1,559			Dividend Reinvested
	Jun-09	0.46	42	1,601			Dividend Reinvested
	Dec-09	0.56	41	1,642			Dividend Reinvested

	Jun-10	0.52	39	1,681			Dividend Reinvested
	Dec-10	0.74	54	1,735			Dividend Reinvested
	Jun-11	0.64	52	1,787			Dividend Reinvested
	Dec-11	0.76	64	1,851			Dividend Reinvested
	Jun-12	0.66	58	1,909			Dividend Reinvested
	Dec-12	0.79	61	1,970			Dividend Reinvested
	Jun-13	0.73	50	2,020			Dividend Reinvested
	Dec-13	0.91	58	2,078			Dividend Reinvested
	Jun-14	0.83	51	2,129			Dividend Reinvested
	Dec-14	0.95	63	2,192			Dividend Reinvested
	Jun-15	0.86	59	2,251			Dividend Reinvested
	Dec-15	0.95	77	2,328			Dividend Reinvested
	Jun-16	0.80	75	2,403			Dividend Reinvested
	Dec-16	0.80	68	2,471			Dividend Reinvested
	Jun-17	0.80	68	2,539	$28.42	$72,158	Dividend Reinvested

"OK, so what you're seeing here Jane, is an investment of $10,000 in the stock of a real life Australian public company and all the figures are real. This company is considered a 'Blue Chip' company, which just means that it's a well-established, big company.

Notice how it starts with 1,000 shares and after 17 years, the number of shares grows to 2,539. The ownership in the company has more than doubled by allowing the profits that the company pays out to be put back into the company, in the form of reinvestment.

And also Note, $10,000 in the year 2000, has grown to $72,000! That's over 7 times your money in 17 years, and this includes the turmoil of the Global Financial Crisis in 2008!

It's also important to note that if those profits hadn't been reinvested, and therefore not been allowed to compound, the investor would've received around $22,000 in profits over the 17 years, and their investment would be worth $28,420. They still would be doing well but nowhere near as well as allowing the compounding to happen.

Now the super amazing thing is that if this company continues to grow at this rate for another 23 years, then after 40 years, that $10,000 investment will be worth around $1,000,000 or 100 times your money!"

"Wow, I like the sound of that, Arturo."

"Yep, and get this, it compounds out at a growth rate of 12.3% per annum without you having to lift a finger! The company simply accepts your instructions to reinvest your profits and then uses this money to make more money.

The key take away from all this, is that when a company pays you a dividend, it's important to reinvest it. If you don't, it's like chopping branches off the tree while it's just starting out, it stunts the growth and therefore limits the fruit that it'll produce each year."

"I'm really liking the sound of all this but can you please explain what a dividend is? I've heard the word but I'm not sure what it means."

"Sure, a dividend is simply a fancy word for the part of profit a company makes that's paid to the people that own the company, the shareholders.

When you buy a share in a company, you become a 'share-holder' and that means that you own a small piece of that company. You become a business owner, a silent one that relies on the managers of the company to look after your interest in the business.

Effectively what happens is that you've bought into a business that already has managers looking after the business and they're being paid to grow your money. A good company will do that well, year after year. These are the sorts of businesses you want to find and invest in.

Shall I go back to the key point on reinvesting the dividend again?"

"No, I'm with you now, it's like when you see those tree rings, after a big tree is cut down, it shows a bigger and bigger circle as it grows. So each year that goes by, the tree is getting a bigger girth by expanding at a consistent rate. I think I remember that from something in high school."

"Great! You got it, Jane, well done.

Now, I'd like to give you one final real life example to show you what's possible. You now know the results of what it looks like to grow your money at a rate of 12.3% every year ... Well there's a man called Warren Buffett, who became one of the very top richest people in the world by growing his money at a rate of around 20% per year over 50 odd years and created a fortune of over 75 Billion US dollars!

Interestingly, anyone could have bought a share in his company, Berkshire Hathaway, in 1987 for $2,900, and in 2017 that one share is worth around $250,000. This company pays no dividends, it just automatically reinvests profits in itself because they believe they are the best managers for that money.

This growth works out to about 86 times your money over 30 years or, 8,600%! Sounds pretty good, huh? You might think that to get that sort of return he was producing annual profits of 100% plus, right? But no, in actual fact, it works out at a compounded annual rate of only around 16%!

Well, I say *only* because compared to 8,600%, 16% seems like peanuts, but of course to make an average 16% after tax year after year, is nothing short of excellent. The point is, that by reinvesting that 16% each year, after 30 years, the money grew unbelievably. Most people find this hard to believe, but you can do the sums quite easily with a computer.

The important thing to note, is that if you can sit and allow your money to multiply, generating a return of 8—10% on all your money is excellent. Don't beat yourself up if you can't do what Warren Buffett can do, you can be extraordinary by generating half the returns he does, by following the basic compounding principles.

Now, if you're feeling excited about compounding, there is a way to guarantee, and yes, I say GUARANTEE, being a millionaire within 45 years by not having to learn anything about investing or the stock market. Here's what it takes:

1. Find a bank account that pays you 5% per year (this is the average rate of interest paid historically on deposits);
2. Deposit $500 every month without fail;
3. After 45 years you'll have contributed $270,000 of your own money, but it will have grown to $1,013,238 through the power of compounding!"

"I have a question Arturo, my bank account pays me essentially nothing at the moment, so how would this compounding work right now?"

"Good question, at the moment we have incredibly low interest rates, so yes, to compound through a bank account is very tough. There are other options though, that are much better than a bank account right now.

I'm going to share a special formula with you that a lot of people don't know about, it's also why I gave you those sheets on the real life example of compounding, I call it *The Easy Way to Invest*.

But before I go into that, I'll give you a summary of what we've covered so far:

1. Open up fee free online bank accounts for, ME (you), FUN, GOAL, GIVE and LIVE (TAX isn't needed if you get money in after tax dollars only);
2. Work out how much you're going to allocate to each;
3. Put in the relevant percentage of your income in to each of them.
4. Create your *Money Tree* with the money you allocate in the ME account

Actually Jane, our hour is almost up, so let's leave this until next week. The project for the week ahead is to work out your allocation percentages, I'll email a template that you can follow as a guide.

Next week I'll go through the formula for investing and if there's time, I'll go through leverage as well."

SHE ARRIVES HOME and David greets her at the door, "Hey Jane, how's it going? How was your session with Arturo?" he says enthusiastically.

"Yeah, all good dad. He spoke about creating a budget based on set percentages, like, a percentage for yourself and a percentage for living costs. You know, that sort of thing. He also talked about compounding and how money can grow incredibly when you let it."

"OK, I'd like to hear more about that. Do you think we can get together after dinner and chat about it?"

"Actually dad, I need some time to digest it all, myself. It was a big session and he said he's going to send me a template that I can work through. What if we get together after dinner tomorrow night?"

"OK, it's a date, honey." he says as he moves over and gives her a big hug.

At dinner David asks Andy, "So, how was your first day at the grocers, champ?"

"Yeah, it was pretty good, nothing too hard. I just had to sweep the floors and then do a spot mop on areas that were sticky from where fruit had fallen. The owners seem nice, they're a husband and wife team, they said if all goes well I'll be able to serve customers at the cashier's desk in the next few weeks."

"Good stuff Andy, I knew you could do it." says Elizabeth.

"Good on you squirt," says Jane as she lightly punches him on the arm, "... I'm impressed." Andy blushes while smiling from ear to ear as he ate his meal.

Later that evening, Jane saw Arturo's email and downloaded the template:

My Income Plan

(Annual Estimate)

Description	Amount
Active Income	
Wages	$0
Business/Other Income	$0
Passive Income	
Bank Interest	$0
Stock Dividends	$0
Rental Income	$0
Total Income	$0

My Spending Plan
(Annual Estimate)

Description	Amount
My Money Tree (At least 10% of income)	
High Yield Account	$0
Living Costs (No more than 70% of income)	
Electricity & Gas	$0
Gifts (birthdays, Xmas, etc.)	$0
Home & Contents insurance	$0
Home Phone, TV, Internet	$0
School Fees	$0
Club dues	$0
Life insurance	$0
Home owners association dues/Body Corporate fees	$0
Health Insurance	$0
Medical, Dental	$0
Travel	$0
Mortgage/Rent	$0
Property rates, taxes & water	$0
Subscriptions	$0
Mobile phone	$0
ATM withdrawals/incidental spending	$0
Groceries	$0
Storage unit costs	$0
Just-in-Case Funds	$0
Grooming	$0
Clothes	$0
Home accessories	$0
Car Fuel	$0
Car repairs	$0
Car insurance & Registration	$0
Giving (10% of income or what feels right to you)	
XYZ worthy cause	$0
Savings for Set Goal (No more than 10% of income)	
XYZ Goal	$0

Fun (No more than 5% of income)	
New experiences	$0
Restaurants/dining out/movies	$0
Total Expenses	$0

She reviewed the template and adjusted it with her figures:

Jane's Income Plan
(Annual Estimate)

Description	Amount
Active Income	
Wages	$14,700
Passive Income	
Bank Interest	$0
Total Income	$14,700

Jane's Spending Plan
(Annual Estimate)

Description	Amount
My Money Tree (At least 10% of income)	
High Yield Account	$1,470
Living Costs (No more than 70% of income)	
Gifts (birthdays, Xmas, etc.)	$300
Medical, Dental	$300
Mobile phone	$500
ATM withdrawals/incidental spending	$2,600
Grooming	$1,200
Clothes	$1,200
Car Fuel	$1,200
Car repairs	$600
Car insurance & Registration	$1,800
Giving (10% of income or what feels right to you)	
XYZ worthy cause	$600
Savings for Set Goal (No more than 10% of income)	
XYZ Goal	$1,930
Fun (No more than 5% of income)	

New experiences	$400
Restaurants/dining out/movies	$600
Total Expenses	**$14,700**

The following evening, David announces to the family that he got a raise and that after tax, it adds around $4,500 a year to his income. "That's great news David!" says Elizabeth, "… I'm hoping to find out tomorrow whether I've got the extra day's work too. Hopefully we can have a double celebration!"

After dinner Jane gets together with David and shows him the spreadsheet that Arturo had sent her. "… You see dad, what Arturo said was that you pay yourself at least the first 10%, as a way of rewarding yourself, and showing yourself that you're important.

Then he said you allocate 5% for fun because it's important to enjoy yourself along the way. He strongly said that it's all about this moment right now, if you're not enjoying now, you're probably never going to enjoy.

Then he allocates 10% for giving, like to charities, but he said you could give in non-financial ways too, like in doing community work. I've decided to give 5%.

Then there's allocating 10% towards a goal, like travel, a new car or something else that's bigger but isn't going to pay you anything to have it.

Then he allocates around 50% for living but this really depends on your income level. On the spreadsheet, he shows that the figure shouldn't exceed 70% if you're on a low income. And that's about it, so what do you think?"

"Well, it's interesting, there's a simplicity to it that feels really good. I'll need to review the family budget to see how it fits, but I think I'll stick with the existing one for now and adjust later. I do like the idea of paying yourself first though, I wish I'd have done that when I was your age!"

"Yep, that's something I'll definitely start doing straight away. Arturo said he's going to show me some special formula for investing, next week, so that should be interesting too.

The other thing Arturo went through was compounding, do you know about compounding, dad?"

"Yes, but I never really felt that I had enough money to do that sort of thing properly."

"Well, from what Arturo showed me, it doesn't look like it takes a lot of money to start. He said it's all about finding an investment that makes good profits and then you need to reinvest those profits that are paid to you, and then forget about it. Oh, and it needs to be in well-managed companies.

He told me about a man that's one of the top richest people in the world because he was able to invest and let his money grow.

I can't remember the details but he said that if you bought one share in this man's company ... Oh, Warren Buffett, that was his name. If you bought one of his shares in 1987, in 30 years it'd now be worth around 86 times more and it compounded at something like 16% per year!"

"Wow Jane, that's quite a stat, I *have* heard of Warren Buffett, I think he's even been called the greatest investor of all time."

"Well, Arturo showed me that it's possible for the average person to invest and get around 12% per year. The key, he said, was to always reinvest your profits so that it builds on your original money.

He told me about some 13th century man that did a thought experiment with rabbits, and how they could multiply, which is exactly the same as how money can multiply in a good investment."

"I'm impressed, Jane. I'll just have to hope that my Superannuation plan works like that. Actually, that reminds me, maybe I should review my Super to see how it's performing, and whether I can do anything better with it.

Let me know what Arturo says about this formula for investing and I'll see if I can do that with my Super Fund money also."

The following evening, Elizabeth announces that her work will be able to give her another day of work. "Woo Hoo Liz!" David screams out, "... that's fantastic, I'll have to update the budget and see where we're at."

The following evening, David shows the family the adjusted figures:

Our Family Income
(Annual)

Description	Amount
Money In	
Wages – David – After tax (Full-Time)	$72,000
Wages – Elizabeth – After tax (3 days per week)	$25,000
Bank Interest	$0
Total	$97,000

Our Family Spending
(Annual)

Description	Amount
Money Out	
Electricity & Gas	$3,000
Gifts (birthdays, Xmas, etc.)	$1,200
Home & Contents insurance	$1.200
Home Phone, TV, Internet	$1,000
School Fees – Andy	$2,000
Club dues – D & E	$1,200
Health Insurance	$2,500
Medical, Dental	$1,500
Travel/holidays	$2,000
Mortgage/Rent	$37,000
Property rates, taxes & water	$2,800
Mobile phones – D, E & A	$720
ATM withdrawals/incidental spending	$1,800
Groceries	$14,000
Just-in-Case Funds	$13,000
Grooming & Clothing – David	$250
Grooming & Clothing – Elizabeth	$500
Grooming & Clothing – Andy	$500
Home accessories	$0
Car Fuel	$3,000
Car repairs	$600
Car insurance & Registration	$2,800
Donations	$0
Andy's Allowance	$2,080

Money saved for a goal	$0
New fun experiences	$0
Restaurants/dining out/movies/concerts	$1,200
Total	$93,820
Surplus	$3,180

"OK, the adjustments I've made are the increases in income that your mum and I have, the mortgage repayments based on paying the loan off in 10 years and money for Just-in-Case, that will be used for special occasions.

Taking all that into consideration, we have around a $3,000 buffer as a further just-in-case. I love it, we've done some great work guys, we should all be proud of ourselves."

"I think we should celebrate, any ideas on how you'd like to do that?" says Elizabeth.

"let's go bowling ... " says Andy quickly.

"That's fine with me, maybe we can get some take away food afterward as well. Any objections or other ideas?" David asks.

Everyone agrees and David picks up his glass and gestures for everyone to clink the glasses together in celebration, "Cheers ..."

Week Thirteen – The Money Tree

After the usual pause of looking into Jane's eyes, Arturo says, "OK, let's get into it. This formula I'm going to be sharing with you will allow you to multiply your money like a professional, if you choose to. You may not generate Warren's 20% odd, but even at 10% per annum, your money will grow very nicely indeed.

And remember, unlike the example of the one cent that doubled everyday, the reality is that it takes many years to multiply money to the larger amounts. The difference in how much money your *Money Tree* produces from year 20 to year 30 is huge, and if you can go to year 40, it'll blow your mind."

Jane was becoming impatient, "C'mon Arturo, spit it out already, don't leave me hanging here." she says with frustration.

He smiles, "OK, I know I'm labouring the point a little, but if you want to build wealth, understanding this concept of compounding is absolutely critical.

Now, most people aren't all that interested in learning about how to invest, if you are, that's great, go for it. But if you're not, this little plan is the easiest way I know to have your *Money Tree* grow.

The formula goes like this:

1. Pick thirteen large, well established, strong companies that you like, and list them 1-13;
2. Put the money that you've allocated for investing, the *ME* account, into a stock brokerage account;
3. When you have $1,000 in that account, buy $1,000 worth of stock in the first company on your list;
4. When you accumulate the next $1.000, buy $1,000 worth of the next company on your list, and so on:
5. When you have $1,000 in all thirteen companies, you go back to the first company and do it all again for the next 30 years, at least."

"That does sound very basic Arturo, but I wouldn't have a clue where to start. Like, where would I find these companies or how do I even buy them?"

"No problem Jane, take out your journal and write down the following:

1. Do an Internet search for *Barron's Best Online Broker*—You're looking for an ONLINE Stock Broker that charges no more than $10 to buy stocks (and no other fees);

2. Open an account with them and if you have any difficulties, call their help desk;

3. When you've accumulated $1,000 in your *ME* account, transfer it into your new brokerage account;

4. Look at the list of companies, which I'll be giving you, and pick THIRTEEN that you like. You can also do a little research to make sure you're comfortable with what the company does. Yahoo Finance is a reasonable resource to use;

5. Write down the list of Thirteen companies on an Excel spreadsheet;

6. Buy $1,000 worth of stock in the first company on your list and keep a record of it, i.e. the date you bought it, the cost per share, number of shares and total cost;

7. When you save another $1,000, put it into the second company on your list, and so on;

8. Repeat this year over year;

9. When dividends are paid, let them sit in your brokerage account to form part of your next $1,000 purchase;

10. ALLOW THIS MONEY TO SIT THERE, do NOT touch it for at least 30 years;

11. After 30 years, you're likely to harvest substantial fruit from your *Money Tree* and if you leave it for 40 years, you'll likely have more fruit than you know what to do with!

Now you need to know, there'll be times when you'll be tempted to sell these stocks because there's either been a boom or a bust, DON'T DO IT. In fact you may even be tempted to sell and use this money for another asset, I strongly suggest you leave it alone. Just stick with the plan and let the probabilities take care of your wealth."

He takes out a file from his desk drawer, that contains a long list of companies and hands it to her ... "Please look at the lists Jane, the thing to note is that these are all U.S. companies, they're not better or worse than stocks in other countries. It's Just that the U.S. is such a big market in comparison with Australia that it provides much more choice ... So does this feel like something you can do?"

"Uh, I think so. I mean it does feel a bit overwhelming, there's actually quite a few steps involved here."

"That's OK," he says, "just do one step at a time. With selecting the thirteen companies, you can literally put the sheets on a wall and throw darts at them if you want and see how you feel about that selection. All these companies have proven track records and it's really just a matter of choosing the ones you like the sound of.

Another good way of picking your companies is to make a list of all the products and services you use everyday, then look at which companies provide those products and services, and invest in those companies. You already contribute to the profits of those companies, so why not let some of that profit find its way back to you?

The way to make a list is to look at the food you eat, the drinks you drink, the toiletries you use, where you do your shopping, the telecommunication services you use, the bank you use, etc. and then choose those companies to buy shares in. Chances are, these companies have dominant brands, that produce consistent profits, and that people use and enjoy everyday. Does that make sense?"

"It sure does, Arturo, and I really like it. I can see how it makes making a decision on which companies to choose much easier, thanks."

"Yep, and I also want you to know that lots of people would say you should study in detail everything you can before putting your money into any stock, and in principle, I agree. However, if you have no real desire for it, going with large, well established companies that have a long track record of success, is a reasonable bet..."

"But what if I stuff it up in some way and I end up not compounding my money?" she says with concern.

"Firstly, the companies on the list I gave you have a history of managing their businesses well, and they grow their businesses consistently, over time. Secondly, most of the products and services we use everyday are run by successful companies. Your aim here is to create a plan that conservatively allows you to grow your money at a rate of around 10% per year, over the long term.

I can tell you now, you're not going to be the next Warren Buffett by following this plan. But you're most likely going to vastly outperform the average investor because the average investor doesn't have the mental fortitude to sit and allow the magic of compounding to happen.

Speaking of Warren Buffett, he told a story once about the Coke company. He said that if you'd have invested in one share at $40 in 1919, when Coke first listed on the stock exchange, by 2011, that $40 investment, assuming you reinvested the dividends, would have been worth $5,000,000!

It's staggering, and I know it's 92 years, not 40, but it really highlights how a strong business can grow over time. That is one monster tree producing a lot of fruit, and in fact, it's continued to grow since.

The thing is, there are lots of examples like this. There's Disney, buying $1,000 of stock in 1957 and letting it ride for 60 years, would be worth around $2.5 million! Or then there's McDonald's, $1,000 in 1970 would be worth around $500,000 after 47 years.

The really amazing thing is that this growth happened without any extra money being added, it was just $1,000 that compounded by reinvesting the dividends that were paid by the company.

If you follow the strategy I've outlined for you Jane, you'll likely do even better because you're adding to your account along the way.

Let me show you this ..." He opens a file on his computer and says, "I've created a very conservative spreadsheet to show you what would happen if you put aside $500 a month i.e. $6,000 per year, and put it into the strategy that I've outlined.

I've used a compounding rate of 8%, which is considered to be the average return on the stock market going back over the long term..."

Year	Balance	Return	Deposit	Balance
1	0	0	6,000	6,000
2	6,000	480	6,000	12,480
3	12,480	998	6,000	19,478
4	19,478	1,558	6,000	27,037
5	27,037	2,163	6,000	35,200
6	35,200	2,816	6,000	44,016
7	44,016	3,521	6,000	53,537
8	53,537	4,283	6,000	63,820
9	63,820	5,106	6,000	74,925
10	74,925	5,994	6,000	86,919
11	86,919	6,954	6,000	99,873
12	99,873	7,990	6,000	113,863
13	113,863	9,109	6,000	128,972
14	128,972	10,318	6,000	145,290
15	145,290	11,623	6,000	162,913
16	162,913	13,033	6,000	181,946
17	181,946	14,556	6,000	202,501
18	202,501	16,200	6,000	224,701
19	224,701	17,976	6,000	248,678
20	248,678	19,894	6,000	274,572
21	274,572	21,966	6,000	302,538
22	302,538	24,203	6,000	332,741
23	332,741	26,619	6,000	365,360
24	365,360	29,229	6,000	400,589
25	400,589	32,047	6,000	438,636
26	438,636	35,091	6,000	479,726
27	479,726	38,378	6,000	524,105
28	524,105	41,928	6,000	572,033
29	572,033	45,763	6,000	623,796
30	623,796	49,904	6,000	679,699
31	679,699	54,376	6,000	740,075

32	740,075	59,206	6,000	805,281
33	805,281	64,422	6,000	875,704
34	875,704	70,056	6,000	951,760
35	951,760	76,141	6,000	1,033,901
36	1,033,901	82,712	6,000	1,122,613
37	1,122,613	89,809	6,000	1,218,422
38	1,218,422	97,474	6,000	1,321,896
39	1,321,896	105,752	6,000	1,433,647
40	1,433,647	114,692	6,000	1,554,339
41	1,554,339	124,347	6,000	1,684,686
42	1,684,686	134,775	6,000	1,825,461
43	1,825,461	146,037	6,000	1,977,498
44	1,977,498	158,200	6,000	2,141,698
45	2,141,698	171,336	6,000	2,319,034

"Jane, what you're seeing here is that by following this strategy and saving $6,000 each year to add to your investment, you could have over $2.3 million by the time you're 65!

Remember, this is nothing special, this is simply saving $500 a month, buying $1,000 of stock every 2 months and earning an average of 8% on your investment for 45 years.

Now, does this seem like something you can do?"

"Wow, that looks amazing, I'd struggle to put $500 a month right now, but I can see there will be a time when I'll be earning more and so can save more. So yeah, I think I can do this." she says excitedly.

"OK, good, that's the good news. The challenge to keep in mind though, is that the stock market is a highly irrational place. The price of something doesn't really mean anything in particular, it's just what the underlying flavour happens to be at that particular point in time.

By buying slowly over time, the irrational behaviour of the stock market has less significance and you'll smooth out your results by doing this. Ultimately though, your commitment to the plan and the strength of the underlying business is what will grow your *Money Tree*.

There's going to be times where you over pay for a company and then there'll be times that you under pay. The market goes through cycles just like everything else in nature. So by sticking with the plan, you'll be able to average out all the ups and downs and do well overall.

In the Coke example I just mentioned, you need to know that the company went down to $19 in 1920, it lost over half it's price, but it survived and went through both world wars and continued to make a profit!

So what I want you to take to heart is that prices of stocks go all over the place, for any number of reasons. But over time, a good business has VALUE, and that value is eventually recognised and that's what ultimately has stocks appreciate in the long run."

"OK, got it. You know Arturo, just changing the subject, I've been thinking that maybe the time has come for me to leave Uni and find full-time work. I was looking through the allocation that I came up with and I'm really not earning enough to live the way I'd like to live."

"OK, I hear your concern, Jane. But before we talk about that, it's important to understand that what you earn doesn't have to determine whether you stay or leave Uni. Be clear that if you choose to leave Uni, you do it because it's no longer serving you in what your current desires are. Not because you can earn more by leaving. Do you get that?" he says with emphasis.

She thinks for a moment, "... OK, yeah, you're right. I can see that in the way I'm saying it, I make Uni an excuse for not being able to earn more. You got me, I realise now that I *am* looking for a way to leave without having to be fully responsible for my decision!"

"Good, I'm glad you realise that. You're looking for a back door so you can blame not earning enough as a reason for dropping out. OK, so now the question is: What feels like the right step to take and why?"

"Well, I feel a bit scared on how my parents are going to react to me dropping out, but my heart just isn't in it anymore, so I feel that I'm better off just working full-time at my current job, instead of continuing to live the lie of going to Uni without attending classes.

To answer your question, dropping out is *definitely* the right step to take, the why ... I'm not so clear about, but I just know that it is."

"Ultimately Jane, it takes courage to stand in the face of your fears and to follow your heart. You can't control the way your parents will react, but what you *can* do is be as clear as possible that this is the right step for you and then have a clear plan of how you'd like things to go when you drop out.

Now I sense you *are* clear on dropping out as being the right step but because you're unsure of what happens next, there's apprehension there.

Here's what I recommend, go back to the spreadsheet you did for survival and do a new one using the new spreadsheet that I gave you so that you can allocate more appropriately.

Once you've done this, think about where you'd like to be heading and what you'd like to bring to the world that fills you with joy.

OK, let's leave it there and talk about leverage next week. There's quite a bit for you to look at this week, did you want to repeat it back to me, just so we're clear?"

"Um, OK, the first thing I think I should do is revisit the spreadsheet for survival, putting in my allocations, then pick the companies to invest in and finally, think about what I could do, that's joyous in the world."

"Actually Jane, do it in this order, you can write this down:

1. The survival spreadsheet;
2. Prepare a plan on what feels like the right next step in relation to dropping out, do not tell your parents until you're clear;
3. Think about what you'd like to bring to the world.

If you have time, you can pick the companies you want to invest in also, but leave it if it gets too much. This isn't necessary at this point but just a 'nice to have'. Is that clear?"

"Yep, got it Arturo, see you next week."

On the way home, her mind was in a spin, she loved the *Money Tree* idea and that there might be an easy way to invest. But first, she had to address the whole dropping out thing.

She felt super clear that Graphic Design was no longer her path, it somehow felt hollow now but she knew that her parents wouldn't just accept that, she needed a plan of action. She decided to review the survival spreadsheet after dinner and go from there.

At dinner David asked her about the session with Arturo. "Oh, it was amazing, he told me about creating my own *Money Tree* and how you put the 10% that you allocate for yourself, into investing in stocks, through his easy-way style." she says with excitement and continues, "Basically, he gave me a list of some well-known U.S. company names and the idea is to select thirteen of these companies and then slowly build the *Money Tree* by putting $1,000 a time into each company."

With concern, David says, "I don't know about this honey, how can you invest in a company that you know nothing about? It sounds very risky to me."

"Well, he did say that all the companies on the list were good, let me think of the exact words he used ... he said they all have a history of managing their businesses well, so it was just a matter of picking the ones I liked. I'll show you the list, they're all companies like Disney, Apple, etc."

"You know Jane, maybe I'm just a little ignorant of these things and that's why I feel uneasy about it, but I think it might be wise to not put all your eggs in the stock market and you may want to consider other types of investment. Not that I know a great deal about it, but have a chat with Arturo about it and see what he says."

"OK, I'll do that, dad."

After dinner she got started on the spreadsheet and after modifying her survival spreadsheet ...

Jane's Income Plan
(Annual Estimate)

Description	Amount
Active Income	
Wages (after tax)	$30,000
Business/Other Income	$0
Passive Income	
Bank Interest	$0
Stock Dividends	$0
Rental Income	$0
Total Income	$30,000

Jane's Spending Plan

(Annual Estimate)

Description	Amount
My Money Tree (At least 10% of income)	
High Yield Account	$3,000
Living Costs (No more than 70% of income)	
Electricity & Gas	$900
Gifts (birthdays, Xmas, etc.)	$300
Home Phone, TV, Internet	$600
Mortgage/Rent	$10,000
Debt Repayment	$3,000
Mobile phone	$900
ATM withdrawals/incidental spending	$2,400
Groceries	$4,000
Just in Case Funds	$1,200
Grooming	$600
Clothes	$300
Public Transport Costs	$1,500
Car Fuel	$0
Car repairs	$0
Car insurance & Registration	$0
Giving (5% of income or what feels right to you)	
XYZ worthy cause	$1,000
Savings for Set Goal (No more than 10% of income)	
XYZ Goal	$0
Fun (No more than 5% of income)	
New experiences	$0
Restaurants/dining out/movies	$300
Total Expenses	$30,000

She came to the conclusion that if she continued living with her parents, after 5 years she could save a decent amount towards buying a home. She made further modifications and came up with the following ...

Jane's Income Plan
(Annual Estimate)

Description	Amount
Active Income	
Wages (after tax)	$30,000
Business/Other Income	$0
Passive Income	
Bank Interest	$0
Stock Dividends	$0
Rental Income	$0
Total Income	$30,000

Jane's Spending Plan
(Annual Estimate)

Description	Amount
My Money Tree (At least 10% of income)	
High Yield Account	$6,000
Living Costs (No more than 70% of income)	
Electricity & Gas	$0
Gifts (birthdays, Xmas, etc.)	$300
Home Phone, TV, Internet	$0
Mortgage/Rent	$0
Property rates, taxes & water	$0
Debt Repayment	$3,000
Mobile phone	$900
ATM withdrawals/incidental spending	$2,400
Groceries	$0
Just in Case Funds	$1,200
Grooming	$600
Clothes	$300

Public Transport Costs	$0
Car Fuel	$1,200
Car repairs	$600
Car insurance & Registration	$1,500
Giving (5% of income or what feels right to you)	
XYZ worthy cause	$1,000
Savings for Set Goal (Aim for No more than 10% of income)	
Saving for Deposit on a house	$10,000
Fun (No more than 5% of income)	
New experiences	$300
Restaurants/dining out/movies	$300
Total Expenses	**$29,600**

She decided to have any an early night and look at creating a plan in the morning.

The following day she went to the library and got to work on planning for the drop out. She realised that her primary focus was that she wanted to be fully independent. She liked the idea of being able to save by living with her parents but that couldn't be forever, she really needed to find a way to stand on her own two feet.

Just then, Mandy walked in and saw Jane sitting at a desk. "Hey Janey, how's it going?" she says quietly, "... I haven't seen you in class lately, what's going on?" she says with a cheeky grin.

Jane had kept the dropping out idea a secret but decided that it might be good to share it with Mandy, "Well, have you got a moment now?"

"Sure, I've got about 30 minutes before my next class starts."

"OK, well you know how Arturo's been helping me? ... Well, out of that, I've realised that I really don't want to be a Graphic Designer anymore, and I actually just want to drop out altogether. I feel like I'm wasting my time here, now."

"You know Janey girl, I had a feeling things would be changing for you when you told me that Arturo gave you his card, he does seem to have a certain affect on people he comes into contact with." Mandy says with a wry smile.

Chuckling, Jane says, "Well he's certainly had an affect on me, that's for sure. Look, I guess the thing is, I don't really know what I want to do, I just know that somehow my time can be better spent on something else.

Arturo is helping me be more independent and I feel good about standing on my own, somehow it feels as though I need to be helping other people stand on their own also. It's like I've been going through life half asleep and now he's helping me to wake up and live more fully, somehow!"

"Wow Jane, I haven't seen you talk with such conviction, like, ever! I don't know what he's been saying to you, but I like the new you!"

"Thanks. but I'm still shitting myself about telling my folks about dropping out. I just know they're going to crack-it with me for not finishing my studies."

"Is there anything I can do to help?" Mandy replies cheerfully.

"Thanks, I really appreciate it, but no, I don't think there is. I need to come up with a plan for what I'm going to do when I drop out. My folks aren't going to accept me dropping out if it sounds like I'm doing it on a whim."

"You know Jane, I don't know why, but I'm getting the feeling that I should tell my dad about your situation and see what he says. Arturo helped my dad a while back and I think he might have some insights into what you're going through."

"Uh, OK, I suppose that should be fine."

"Hang on, I'll go outside and call him now ..." A few minutes later she returns and says, "Yep, my dad laughed and said he understands exactly what you're going through, he said you should come around and have dinner with us tonight, if you can. He said 6.30pm would be good ..."

MANDY ANSWERED THE door upon Jane's arrival, "Come on in Janey ..." Mandy's two older brothers no longer lived at home and her mother died when Mandy was ten. Now she lives with her dad, Martin and step mum, Susan.

"Hello Jane, good to see you again." Martin says. Martin was a fit looking, mid 50's man, with bright eyes.

"Hello Mr Bosely, thanks for inviting me over." Jane says politely.

"A pleasure, but please, call me Martin, and this is my wife, Susan ... Take a seat, Mandy tells me you're getting some of Arturo's unique help!"

"Uh, yeah, he's helping me see things in ways I could never have imagined, that's for sure ... Um, I was wondering, Mandy tells me he's also helped you in the past, do you mind saying how?"

"Sure Jane, I met Arturo at a business function about eight years ago. I was working for a large bank at the time and he'd been hired to do some business consulting for the bank.

Anyway, to cut a long story short, we struck up a conversation and as it turned out he'd been asked by the bank to recommend a list of candidates to be made redundant.

On hearing this I suddenly felt that my job was under threat and that he'd be adding my name to his list. He noticed my anxiety and said to me, whether he adds my name to the list or not, I always have a choice, that it's up to me on whether I see myself as a victim or to stand in a place of responsibility ... "

She chuckles, "This is starting to sound very familiar, sorry, please go on ..."

"No problem. Anyway, it turned out that he did add my name to his list and it turned out to be one of the best things that could have ever happened. Up to that point I'd been quite complacent, I had a job that paid well but I was really just plodding along.

My wife had died a few years earlier and I was really feeling quite flat. It was as though I had given up in a way and was just going through the motions because I had to look after the kids.

What I realised later is that Arturo was helping me every step of the way, I don't know how he does it but somehow he knew what I needed and simply allowed me to find my way with it.

It turned out that I got a nice payout from my redundancy package, which allowed me to stay home and take a year off work to decide what I wanted to do. Arturo and I struck up a friendship and he helped me be more open, which allowed me to connect with my kids in a way I'd never done before.

When Mandy's mum was alive, I left it all up to her to take care of the kids and when she died, I was lost. I loved my kids but I still wasn't there for them. It was during that year off that I met Susan and I began my part-time business ..."

"Actually, Mr ... I mean Martin, what *is* your business? I don't think I really know. Mandy has mentioned that you work from home and you love what you do, but I don't really know what that is."

"It's true, I do love what I do and it feels magical at times. I work as a Toastmasters Agent. What that means is that when people or organisations are looking for a particular speaker for their function, they contact me and

I arrange the right person for the job. It's extremely satisfying and gives me lots of flexibility in the hours I work."

"Wow, I've never heard of that role before. How did you realise that that was what you wanted to do?"

"Well, I sort of stumbled onto it by accident, although as Arturo would say, 'there are no accidents!' Anyway, a friend of mine was organising his wedding with his wife-to-be and they mentioned that the Master of Ceremonies they'd hired had to pull out at the last minute.

I'd been involved with the local Toastmasters group for a number of years and would have been able to do the job myself but I also knew a number of people that would enjoy the experience also, so I made a few phone calls and organised the right person for the job.

Long story short, word got out that I had a knack for arranging good speakers at reasonable prices and the business was born.

You see the thing is Jane, sometimes you don't know what value you can bring until you open yourself up to an opportunity, by saying YES. I don't know what your path is but if you can give yourself the space for an opening, you might be pleasantly surprised."

"So let me ask you this, what would you say if Mandy wanted to drop out of Uni?" Jane says with a cheeky grin.

"Jane, Mandy told me you're not looking forward to telling your parents, but if you're wanting to use my answer as a gauge for what your parents will say, you're going to be disappointed. My desire for Mandy is for her to follow her heart, if she wants to change course, it wouldn't change a thing for me.

There would however be a reason for the change, no one changes their mind for no reason and I'd expect her to be open in sharing that reason with me."

"Hmm, that's a good point, I haven't really thought about my reason, I just know that I need to change course now and that's about it."

"OK, so spending some time on that might be a good step to take. Your reason will most likely help soften whatever reaction your parents may have with your decision to change path now." says Martin.

On the drive home Jane started thinking about why she felt this way, why the idea of dropping out was so compelling now. That's when it hit her. "Shit!! I've forgotten what I've seen with Arturo, that I'd be helping kids be responsible, independent and healthy adults. How could I forget that?? The question now is: how am I going to tell mum and dad that I've had a vision of helping kids?"

In the morning she remembered a dream where she was in a room full of desks and computers with kids sitting at the desks typing away. She was walking around the room and noticed one of the screens had a spreadsheet on it. Then a child called out to her and said, "Excuse me miss, how much does it costs to live?" To which she replied, "Not as much as you might think ... "

As she jumped in the shower she said to herself, 'What a weird dream, I wonder what it means?'

Later that morning she saw Mandy in the library again, "Hey Mandy, how's it going?"

"Yeah, good Jane. Oh, my dad said he really enjoyed that chat with you last night."

"Yeah, me too, it was good to hear how he's faced some tough situations and grew from it."

"Also, he wanted me to let you know that if you ever want to chat, you're welcome to call him."

"Thanks Mandy, that's great. By the way, I had a weird dream last night, do you have time now?"

"Sure, for a few minutes."

"... I was walking through a roomful of kids that were sitting at their desk typing away on computers. They seemed to be working on a spreadsheet of some sort and one kid called out to me and asked how much it costs to live, to which I said, "Not as much as you might think". Any idea on what it might mean?"

Mandy thought for a moment, "It seems symbolic in some way, I'm trying to think how your conversation with my dad last night might be related ... maybe it's some sort of clue into what you're supposed to be doing, you know, helping kids, that sort of thing. Anyway, I better go to class now, I'll catch you later Jane, sorry I couldn't help more ..."

Jane sat with the thought for a moment, 'Helping kids, how can I really help kids??' She sat back for a moment and thought about what she saw her future self say, 'helping kids be responsible, independent and healthy adults.'

'And how can I do that with a computer??' she said to herself over and over again. She then remembered that the kids were working on some sort of spreadsheet and that one kid wanted to know what it costs to live.

'What if I could create a spreadsheet that helped kids understand what it costs to live? And maybe with some planning they could create what they wanted rather just go along life hoping that things just turn out? Maybe I could call the program, *You, Creator.* Now, where would I start?'

Over the course of the afternoon she came up with a plan and decided that tonight was the night to tell her parents she was dropping out.

After dinner she said, "mum, dad, do you guys have some time now? I'd like to share something with you."

"Oh, can we make it in about half an hour Jane? There's a TV show I'd like to see." says Elizabeth.

"Actually mum, this is quite important, I think this should take priority."

She saw the look on Jane's face and said, "OK, that's fine, let's do it now."

They sat at the dining table and Jane could feel her heart pounding, "… Guys, you know how things have been changing for me, how I'm accepting more responsibility, how I'm stepping up more and more … Well, I've been thinking about my future and how my studies fit in with what I see for myself now, and the thing is, I don't see Graphic Design as something I want to do anymore …"

Elizabeth had just taken a sip of tea and spits out, "PHWHAT!! What are you saying? You don't have that long to go before you graduate. What's brought this on??" she says with an elevated voice.

Jane takes a deep breath and closes her eyes for a moment, "Look, I know this isn't easy for you to accept but I feel really clear about it. I've had a sense lately that I need to be helping children and so I want to explore that."

"Jane …" says David as he takes a deep breath himself, "this isn't something you should do on a whim. If you drop out, you'll be seriously damaging your employment options. Are you able to explore the helping children thing while completing your studies as well?"

"No, I can't. It's like Graphic Design was me in another time. Right now, I'm seeing the world in a different light and I need to follow what my heart is telling me. If you guys could support my decision, that'd be great, but if you don't, I'm sorry, I'm clear about it and I need to do what's right for me."

Tears start to stream down Elizabeth's face and she says, "Oh Jane …

you're making a huge mistake. There are people that would kill to be in your position and you're throwing it all away, on some, I don't know what exactly ... You'll just be known as the drop out ..." She drops her head into her hands as David puts his arm around her.

Jane could feel herself become calm now, "Wow, that's quite a reaction, why do you think this is affecting you so much, mum?"

Elizabeth screams out, "WHAT!! Don't you give me that psychobabble crap, young lady. I'm really angry and I think it's just best that you leave us right now." Jane gets up and calmly walks off.

David, consoling her, says "Liz, hey, it's OK, it'll be OK ..."

"What the hell are you saying, David! She's stuffing her life up, and you know it. I just can't believe she's going to throw it all away, just like that, it makes no sense ..."

"Well, maybe it does make sense, Liz. She's undergone quite a change over the last few months. She's stepping up around the house, she's helped us in dealing with our finances and she just seems to have a much more mature attitude to life these days. I really can't say that I'm entirely surprised by this. I'm disappointed, sure, but not surprised."

"Well, I *am* surprised and I *am* disappointed, she doesn't know how good she's got it. She's got an opportunity to get a good, respectable job, with the world at her feet, but no, she wants to throw it all away, on some ... some damn pie in the sky idea. She's just making a huge mistake, that's all." she says shaking her head.

"Liz, I know that you would have liked to have gone to Uni, do you think that by Jane dropping out, it may have put you in touch with the hurt you felt in not having had that opportunity?"

Elizabeth takes a deep breath, "Oh God, probably ..." she says angrily, "but I think that I'm like any other parent that wants the best for their children. She's a talented and smart girl and I just think she's throwing away a great opportunity, that's all."

"Maybe you're right Liz, the thing is that Jane's not a kid anymore. We always knew the day would come where she'd make decisions that we might not agree with. I'm at least super thankful that she's had the sense to not mix with the wrong crowd and take drugs or get pregnant!

I know this is still a challenge though, and I think that we need to trust that we've done enough to instil in her a good compass, that can help guide her, even if we can't see that right now."

"OK, OK, I hear you David, it's just tough, that's all. I guess I had all these plans for her. But you're right, she's an intelligent young woman and it's about trusting that she'll be OK, no matter what she chooses ..." Blowing her nose she says, "OK, let's go and speak with her and find out what she plans to do now."

David knocks on her door and calls out, "Jane, can we come in?"

"Sure, come in guys ..."

"Look Jane, I'm sorry for that reaction, it was a big shock and something I really never expected. But look, you seem to have made up your mind now, so what are your plans from here?" says Elizabeth calmly while wiping her nose with a tissue.

"Well firstly, I plan to see if I can work full-time at my current job, they've been giving me more responsibility and I think there's an opening to share the store manager role soon.

Also, I plan to create an online program that helps kids to get clear about what they want and how that translates in the real world. I'll need to do a lot of work on this but I plan to offer this as an online program that will hopefully grow into a good business."

"Right, wow, and when do you plan to put this all into action?"

"I'm planning on talking to Jamie, the store manager, in the morning and I'm going to start the online program straight away."

"My goodness Jane, and you're sure about this? Like, have you thought about what happens if things don't go as planned?"

"Well mum, as a first step, I'm hoping you guys don't kick me out of the house, that I can still live here ..."

"What!! Of course we wouldn't kick you out of the house ..."

"Well, this is your place and possibly because I'm not living by your rules, you might want me out of here. It was just a thought, I didn't think you would but I had to prepare myself to stand on my own if you did."

"Oh my God! No, put that out of your mind because you can stay here as long as you like, Jane."

"Thanks, that's a big help. Now if I'm not able to work full-time where I'm at, I'm going to look for other work, wherever I can. I aim to earn enough so that I can start to save and get to the point where I'm financially independent. So that's the basic plan.

"And what about Uni, when will you stop that?"

"Uh, well, I haven't been attending classes lately so I'm not going to go at all now. To be honest with you, I've been feeling for a while that I needed to drop out but I was scared about what your reaction was going to be and so I just went to the library until I just knew I couldn't lie to you this way anymore."

"Right. Well Jane, all I can say is that I hope you've thought this through, this could be a very tough path you've chosen."

"Mum, all I know is that I can't stay at Uni any longer, I need to change direction and trust my heart."

David had been quiet the whole time and now says, "Jane, I want you to know that your mum and I love you, no matter what. We would have preferred that you finish Uni but if this is what's in your heart, we'll support your decision.

We've both noticed how you've grown and matured in the last few months and we trust that if you feel this is the right path for you, that it *will* lead to something good."

Jane gets off her bed and rushes to give them both a big hug, "Thanks guys, I love you both so much." she says with tears streaming down her face.

The following morning she goes in to see Jamie. Jamie's in his late 20's and has been the store manager for a couple years. "Hi Jamie, how's it going?"

"Yeah good thanks Jane, what brings you in at this time of the morning?" he says with surprise.

"Well, I wanted to have a chat with you, is now OK?" He nods, "OK, well, I've made a decision to leave Uni, so I'm available to do more hours, if you have them. I can even work full-time if that works."

"Oh, right, that's a big decision Jane, has something happened to make you leave?" he says with concern.

"No, nothing has really happened, it was more a realisation that it wasn't for me anymore. I got a strong feeling that my path lies somewhere else now."

Jamie takes out his roster, "OK ... well, I can't give you full-time hours at this point but I can put you down for a few more shifts. I can probably put you down for full 10 hour days on Friday through Sunday, if you want ..."

"Yep, I'll take it, that's great, thanks Jamie."

"OK, it's Thursday today and this weekend is taken care of but are you OK to start this as of next week?

"Sure, put me down. I really appreciate that."

"No problem Jane, done."

Week Fourteen – Leverage

"Hey Jane, come on in ... How was your week?"

"Well, quite interesting really, I had dinner with Martin, and after that I felt strong enough to tell my folks that I was dropping out. Then, I got some extra hours at work. Oh, and I've also come up with an idea for creating an online program to help kids!"

"Wow, that is one eventful week!" he says excitedly. "And how did your parents react to your decision? Were your worst fears realised?"

Chuckling, she says, "Actually, it wasn't as bad as I thought it'd be, they weren't happy about it and my mum cried and carried on a little, but then they came around and said they would support me in whatever I felt was right for me!"

"That's great Jane, parents do have a way of surprising us when we're clear within ourselves.

OK then, let's get into this week's discussion. I've spoken about allocating your money in a certain way, I've explained the *Money Tree* and the formula for compounding, now the final piece of the puzzle to understand, is leverage.

You understand how a car jack allows you to exert a relatively small amount of force or energy on one side, which then creates a magnified force on the other side, and this gives you the power to lift the car ... OK.

Well, with money it's very similar, using debt, you can commit a relatively small amount of money and be able to buy something that has a lot more value. This is what happens when you borrow money to buy something like a house, your savings plus the banks money gives you the power to buy a house, something you wouldn't be able to do without the leverage you get from borrowing the banks' money.

I'll show you on the whiteboard. Lets say you buy a house for $400,000:

House cost . . . . $ 400,000
Your money (savings/deposit) . . . $ 40,000   (10%)
Bank money (borrowings) . . . . . $ 360,000   (90%)

The amount you borrow from the bank is considered to be your leverage, i.e. with your 10% deposit, each $1 of your own money, gives you the buying power of $10. That's leverage of 1 to 10.

In other words, $40,000 of your own money, gives you the power to buy something that's 10 times more valuable, i.e. a $400,000 house! This is a phenomenal deal and gives you the illusion that you have more money than you actually do.

While you can in fact make a lot of money this way, leverage is a double-edged sword, and has a potential down side also!

Leverage is fantastic when the thing you buy goes up in price, but if instead of going up, it goes down, then beware, that's where the pain begins.

Let me show you an example, let's say you buy the house for $400,000 and a year later you decide to sell the house and the price is now $440,000, it's increased by 10%:

```
House sale . . . . . . . . . . . . . . . . . $ 440,000
Bank loan repaid . . . . . . . . . . . . $ 360,000
Your money . . . . . . . . . . . . . . . . $  80,000
```

You sell the property and pay off the $360,000 loan and you're left with $80,000 in your pocket. That means you just made a $40,000 profit in one year! Or you could say that you've made a 100% profit on your original $40,000, which is called a 100% cash on cash return.

In other words, you've doubled your own money in one year, while the house only went up by a relatively small 10% in price. Great, right? ... Well now let me show you what would happen if instead of the house going up by 10% to $440,000, it actually went DOWN by 10% to $360,000:

```
House sale . . . . . . . . . . . . . . . . . $ 360,000
Bank loan repaid . . . . . . . . . . . . $ 360,000
Your money . . . . . . . . . . . . . . . . $        0
```

Selling at $360,000 means that you walk away with ZERO, after you repay the loan. You've now lost ALL your money, a 100% loss on your cash when the value of the house only went down by 10%!

Is this scaring you yet?"

"It sure is, I wouldn't want to take that risk at all."

"Sure, but it's not my intention to paralyse you from taking this type of risk, there are times when it makes a lot of sense to do this, it's just that you need to understand and be OK with the downside before entering a deal like this.

There are people that believe you can never lose with 'bricks and mortar', meaning that houses are extremely safe investments, and generally speaking, that's true. The problem happens though, when people get into something thinking they can make a quick buck and they borrow more on the basis that they can't lose. That's when they start to play Russian roulette!

Yes, there are people that have been successful with buying and selling homes quickly, but it requires studying and learning about property so that you go into it with a full understanding of what you'll do if things don't go as planned.

The key to leverage is always to look at the downside potential of what you get in to. If you can live with the consequences of things not going to plan, then that's a powerful place to stand. If you can't live with the consequences, then don't use the leverage, or at least don't put all your eggs in that basket.

Now, the real purpose of wanting to talk to you about leverage is for you to realise that you can leverage yourself also. i.e. you as a person have many talents, even if you don't know all of them yet, and you can leverage yourself to have money flow in.

I'm not talking about what happens when you get a job, that's not leverage because you're being paid for your effort on a 1 to 1 basis, i.e. one hour worked equals one hour of pay, you're limited by the amount of hours you can do in a day or week.

The leverage I'm talking about is what elite sports people do, actors do, musicians do and all celebrities do. In fact, now with the Internet, there are people using YouTube and other social media sites to leverage themselves in all sorts of ways. It's the ability to receive way more money than the time that's put in to what they do.

What this means is that they still do the work but they're paid in a way that has nothing to do with their time. So for every hour of work they put in, they could be paid the equivalent of 1,000 hours or 1,000,000 hours of standard pay!

Their income is not a direct proportion of their time, it's a function of how many people they *serve*. More people served equals more income, it's really quite basic when it's broken down.

Then, a point may come where so many people have been served that the people serving get paid without having to lift a finger. Bands like *The Beatles* or *The Rolling Stones* are good examples of this. The momentum of this leverage is so great that when these icons die, money continues to flow in, as is the case for Elvis Presley and Michael Jackson.

I know it sounds amazing but it's happening all the time, and in some cases, these people bring in even more money dead, than when they were alive because the publicity reminds people of the previous connection!"

"Wow, I never really thought about that before, the fact that you can die and still be paid! I'm guessing this money goes to the families or heirs, is that right?"

"Yep, whoever or whatever is in the persons Last Will and Testament, gets the benefit from that leverage. Also have you ever wondered how or why it's even possible that one person can receive so much?"

"Uh, no, not really. I guess famous people just get to be so well known and their popularity makes them more marketable?"

"That's fairly close. People that are in the public eye can command more money because they have a following, sometimes called fans, and it's the following that has the value.

It has value because the fans are the ones that buy the music or pay to watch the movies and advertiser's know this. This is why a company like Nike will pay big bucks for top sports people to promote their name.

It's also why people want you to 'Like' them on Facebook, or watch their YouTube videos. The more people they get following them, the more influence they have on what those people see, and therefore, the more valuable they become to advertiser's. Just like the well-known sports players!

In other words, the more people that know about you and like what you're doing, the more that they're likely to listen to what you have to say because the familiarity helps them trust you. And this means that you have more potential to sell something on behalf of an advertiser.

I saw George Clooney advertising coffee on TV one time, people unconsciously think, '... Ooh, if he's drinking that, it must be good, I'll buy it', or something along those lines.

The bottom line is that the personality is well-known and gives off a certain image that people identify with, it captures their attention and they buy what the personality is promoting. And in most cases, this happens without you even realising that you're being influenced in this way.

I know it doesn't sound great, but in George's case, he originally provided something that's of value to people, through his movies, and out of that value, people 'feel' a level of trust in him, like they know him, and as a result he benefits financially from that."

"That really sounds quite manipulative, I don't like that." says Jane indignantly.

"Well, that's one perspective, and you could be right but remember that no one can manipulate you when you are *aware*.

The point I'd like you to focus on though, is that there's leverage in many different ways. Imagine this, you stand in front of ten people, sharing a message that's valuable to them, now imagine standing in front of a thousand people.

Are you doing any more work by standing in front of a larger audience? No, you're doing exactly the same thing except sharing your message with many more people. Your lever would now be 100 times bigger and would definitely have a bigger impact, for no extra work!

This is what marketing is all about, getting the message out to as many people as possible. It's why companies are willing to pay huge dollars to advertise during popular TV shows, TV is like one massive lever.

Look at Facebook, it has around two billion subscribers! That means there's two billion potential customers, and companies are willing to pay big bucks to get their message in front of those people.

Now to give you a contrast, I heard a story about Mozart. At the peak of his career, he was paid the equivalent in today's dollars of about $150,000 a year. It's a decent amount but it's pocket change compared to what top entertainers are paid these days.

The reason that he made such a relatively modest amount is because he could only *serve* a limited number of people, he didn't have much leverage!

There were no record deals back then, all the music was live, so his leverage was limited by the number of people that could fit into the concert hall he happened to be playing in. If he didn't perform, he didn't get paid!

Nowadays though, as an individual person, entertainment is where the major leverage happens. Have a look at this, Jane ... " He pulls up a file on his screen and shows the following table to her:

Passion	Who	Service Provided	Leverage	Income*
Tennis	Roger Federer	Sports Entertainment	Fans = Endorsements	$64 million p.a.
Racing— Formula 1	Lewis Hamilton	Sports Entertainment	Fans = Endorsements	$46 million p.a.
Golf	Rory McIlroy	Sports Entertainment	Fans = Endorsements	$50 million p.a.
Singing	Lady Gaga	Music Entertainment	CD's, Concerts & Endorsements	$90 million p.a.
Acting	Robert Downey Jnr	Movie Entertainment	Fans = Ticket sales	$65 million p.a.

* Incomes based on search estimates 2017 and are in USD

The bottom line is that when you have a passion for something and you follow through with dedication, you naturally become someone that is extraordinary, and this becomes an attractive quality that others enjoy seeing. As a result, money has a tendency to flow to you.

Check out these companies with major leverage ..."

Passion	Who	Service Provided	Leverage	Net Income*
Social Networking	Facebook	Connecting people	2 billion people	$10.2 billion p.a.
Fast Food	McDonald's	Cheap, consistent, fast food	Stores world wide	$4.7 billion p.a.
Beverages	Coca Cola	Fizzy Drinks	World brand	$6.5 billion p.a.
Internet	Alphabet (aka Google)	Easy Net searching	People clicking on Adverts	$19.5 billion p.a.
Computers	Apple	Stylish & Innovative products	Cult following	$45.7 billion p.a.

Source: Yahoo Finance 2017, amounts in USD

"These companies are known by virtually every person on the planet and they provide services that many millions of people either want or use everyday. As a result, they are worth many billions of dollars.

It's not easy to get your head around just how much money one billion dollars is, but looking at Facebook's $10.2 billion, it works out at roughly $28 million every single day 24/7 and Apple generates $125 million every single day! This is net profit, clear of all expenses, that's really mind blowing when you think about it."

"Wow! I can't imagine that much money coming in every single day, that would be amazing to have in a year, let alone a day!!"

"OK, so let's come back to where you are now ..." He takes out a sheet from a file in his drawer, "I'd like to show you the options you have available right now, because it's important to understand the ways money can flow into you and how much potential leverage you have.

You don't need to be the next Lady Gaga to have an abundance of money flow in, in fact there are wildly wealthy people, financially speaking, all over the place that you've never heard of.

So let's look at the avenues available..." He takes the following sheet out and places it in front of her:

Options	Service Provided	Leverage Potential
Employee	To Employer	Limited and most cases, nothing
Self-Employed	To many people usually	Limited to time usually, celebrities/ entertainers are the exception
Owner-Operator	To consumers & employees	Limited to the owners personal organisational skills
Business Owner	To consumers & employees	Unlimited in theory
Investor	Source of Money for businesses to use	Unlimited (although limited to how much money can be put to work)

Employee: *Someone with a job, physically doing the work for an employer*

Self-Employed: *Someone that relies on themselves to find work, do the work and run their business. Examples of these are contractors, doctors, lawyers and accountants. Self-employed people cannot stop working for long, otherwise their income generally stops.*

Owner-Operator: *Someone that transitions from being self-employed, by employing others or systems to deploy a greater level of leverage, but still have a hands-on role in the business. The owner-operator can look like a business owner because their business can operate without them for a short period of time, however it tends to not operate as smoothly when they're not there.*

Business Owner: *Unlike the owner-operator, a TRUE business owner can choose to be active, or passive in the business. It makes little or no difference whether they are there to operate it or not. An example could be someone that buys a McDonald's franchise, they can operate it actively, or choose to allow a store manager to run it. If the business owner takes the passive role, they take on more of an investor characteristic.*

Investor: *Someone that puts their money into businesses and passively allows that money to be managed by others.*

"Jane, the important thing to understand is that while the *business owner* and *investor* levels offer the best leverage potential, they're positions that you generally need to grow in to.

A good strategy is often to be the best employee you can be while still working on the job, and then working on how to find new ways to leverage yourself, when not on the job. I'm not saying this is what you *need* to do, that's up to you to decide. It's simply a model that has worked for a lot of people in the past.

As a side point, I'd also like to say that while it's great to have your *Money Tree* working for you, nothing grows you *Money Tree* like a business. As you've seen from the businesses we saw earlier like Facebook, etc, creating you own business allows for leverage on scale that goes way beyond stock investing.

OK, so time for a quick quiz, JK Rowling, the person that created the Harry Potter series, where do you think she fits in with the 4 options?"

"Uh, ooh ... she's an author that then had movies made from her books. From what I can see she's sort of self-employed, or maybe an owner-operator but she also gets paid now regardless of if she writes, so I guess she'd have to be a business owner?"

"Well done Jane, that's a tough one because while she isn't an entertainer personally, she *has* provided entertainment through her novels and the movies that have been created from her novels.

So yes, she probably started off being self-employed and then when sales of her books took off and the movie deals were done, she moved into the business owner level.

OK, let's move on. You mentioned you had an idea to create an online program for kids, that sounds good and I'd like to hear more about it next time.

Your project for the week ahead is to focus on your idea to help kids and notice how passionate you feel about it, then give it a rating from 1 to 10, if it's not a 10, what would get you there?

When you're able to find a 10, consider how you might transfer this passion to as many people as possible and go for it. Your aim is to have as much fun doing what you do, as possible.

So in summary:

1. Find your passion level;
2. If not a 10, find out what's holding you back and find a way to get to a 10;
3. Find a way to transfer or share this passion with as many people as possible, i.e. serve them so they benefit from your passion;
4. Take the step that feels right, even if it's uncomfortable, and go for it.

And by the way, I know it's not always easy to take a step, if you can check within, you'll know if it's right for you. You can think of it this way, let's say you feel the desire to go sky diving, you're in the plane with your parachute, flying at 2500 metres off the ground but taking that step out of the plane is terrifying ...

At this point, the thing that helps you take the step, despite the intense anxiety, is the desire to experience the freedom of free falling and a belief that it'll be amazing. Without the desire being bigger, the fear of the step can consume you, and this is anything but joyful living. So get in touch with and feel the desire, then take the step.

OK, on that note, see you next week, Jane."

"HEY JANE, HOW was it this week with Mr Arturo?" David says jovially.

"Yep, good dad, we discussed leverage, as in how you can be paid so that you don't have to necessarily be paid strictly on time. Like, you can put in an hour of work but be paid many times over, as in the case of entertainers."

"Yeah? And did you ask about the other types of investment, like we spoke about last week?"

"No, I didn't, the leverage topic was pretty big and I didn't get the chance to ask about that. I'll see if I can ask next week."

David nods and walks off, seemingly disappointed that she hadn't asked.

Later that evening she got to work on thinking about her passion level. She loved the idea of being able to help kids but then wondered if this program would really achieve the aim. As she felt the doubt, she closed her eyes to see how passionate she felt about the idea. Instantly she felt that it was still a 10, and yet the doubt was still there.

'What's going on? I love this idea but feel doubt still!' Then Arturo's words came back to her, '... feel the desire and take the step.'

'OK, I've just got to take a step. What's the step?' She realised that she didn't know what the next step was. Her mind had gone blank and she didn't have a clue of what to do next. 'Well, no point fighting it, I'll go to bed and see if any inspiration comes to tomorrow.'

The next morning she felt refreshed after a good night sleep. She ate breakfast and went off to the local library. She sat in one of the solitary cubicles, took out her note pad and pen and closed her eyes, while focusing on her breath.

As she sat there quietly, noticing the air come into her lungs and then out, she began to get in touch with the feeling of excitement in helping kids. After a few minutes, an idea popped into her head.

She said to herself, '... If I can help kids learn the about saving, like, it's OK to have fun, as long as you put some aside, then that might be a good start for them.'

She spent the rest of the morning making notes and formulating a program that might be attractive to kids.

Week Fifteen – Investing

"Hi Arturo, before we start I need to ask you something that my dad's been hassling me about. I was telling him about your method for easy investing and he said that there were many investments other than stocks, anyway he said to ask you if it's wise to be putting all my eggs in the stock market basket."

"OK, let's talk about that then. Yes, he's right, there *are* many different types of investments and generally speaking, it's a good idea to spread your money across many asset classes.

The thing is, you need to start somewhere and by focusing on one area first, you give yourself the opportunity to build a foundation to grow from. If you try to learn everything at the same time, chances are you'll overwhelm yourself and get stuck at the analysis stage for fear of making a mistake.

Having said that, there are some basics to know that'll help you assess investments without being overwhelmed, here it goes:

1. It should give you a return in the form of some sort of profit;
2. It should be able to do this consistently, and;
3. In order for it to do it consistently, it must have a sustainable and proven model for success.

Whatever it is, you need to determine whether it can do these things. If you can't, then you either need to educate yourself more or simply stay away. It's really as simple as that.

Now, the model I gave you is for stocks because stocks have a high degree of transparency, relatively speaking. You can easily find their track record and get a good picture of which companies perform consistently.

Of course, you can only do this if you educate yourself a little though. I know that not everyone is interested in this type of analysis, so that's why I came up with a list of solid businesses to make it a bit simpler.

It saves you some legwork and it's the closest thing to a 'one size fits all', that I can think of. But Jane, it's important to know there's no guarantee this model will make you hugely successful either. It's a simple model that, in the absence of anything else, is likely to be better than handing your money to a so-called, 'professional' money manager.

There's nothing really fancy about this model, it's just the simplest way I know for a novice investor to build a reasonable portfolio, without doing a heap of analysis. Yes, your eggs will be all in the stock market basket, and I agree with your dad, ideally you shouldn't do that, but when you're starting out, it's OK to do it this way.

If you feel the desire to diversify at some point, then I'd say wait until you have around $20,000 in each of your thirteen stocks. After that, you can start considering other forms of investment.

In fact, you might eventually find that your income has increased to a point where you can put over 50% of it towards your *Money Tree* account. And when that happens, you might decide to look at property or even equity in private businesses.

Just be aware though, in order to accept responsibility for getting into bigger deals, you will need to educate yourself. Each asset class has its merit and it's up to you to do the work to understand how the asset works and what the potential pitfalls are. And of course, remember the basics...

Now, back to stock investing, please write this down:
- STICK TO THE SYSTEM,
- LET IT BE BORING,
- Save a thousand bucks and buy the next stock on your list, THAT'S IT!"

"Right, OK. Um, do you mind giving me a recap of exactly how the stock market works?"

"Not at all, the Stock market is really like any other market, there are people that want to buy something and people that want to sell something. What they are buying and selling though, are small pieces of a business called a *share* or *stock*.

All markets follow similar principles, you'll generally pay more for a higher quality item than a lower quality one and sometimes things go on sale, maybe even a fire sale!

But like any market, all that glitters isn't gold, there'll be people around that will try to sell you things that are worthless, if you're not aware. This is why it's handy to do some homework before handing your cash over.

The key difference with the Stock market, as opposed to any other type of market however, is that when you buy a stock, you're becoming a part owner of that business. You're not simply buying some vegetables that you'll cook up, eat and be done with.

You're entering into a relationship, where you, as a *shareholder*, own a part of that business. You expect the management to have a high level of integrity so that the company is managed well and generates profit ..."

"OK Arturo, let me see if I get this, say I buy $1,000 worth of Apple shares, I become a part owner of the whole Apple business. Even though it's probably a tiny part, I still own a part of the whole business. Is that right?"

"Yep, absolutely. As soon as you own just 1 share in a company, no matter what the value is, you are a part owner of that company. You entrust your money to the managers of that company and you accept responsibility that your money is considered to be at risk."

"Ooh, that sounds a bit scary when you say it like that, *at risk*. I mean, what exactly is the risk of losing that money?"

"OK Jane, I want you to take a couple things to heart. One, you can't know what tomorrow will bring, and two, we live in a world of probabilities, not certainties. This is why there's never a guarantee for a particular outcome, the best it can ever be is a high probability for a particular outcome.

The world gives this illusion of stability and safety, for the most part, but we don't realise how unstable things are. For example, the Earth spins at over 1,000 miles an hour but we're oblivious to it, other than the illusion of the sun rising and setting.

Or what about walking in nature, everything looks tranquil enough but if you become still you might see birds eating bugs, new plants growing, old plants decaying and a constant flux of birth and death, everywhere!

The reality is that your next step in any moment is a probability based on what you've learned up to this point. So when you invest in something, it's based on the probability that it'll continue to do what it's done in the past.

There's nothing to say that just because all has been fine in the past, that it'll continue to be fine, life doesn't work that way. Having said that, it's OK to make a calculated guess, and that's really what risk is all about, a calculated guess!

The reality is that TRUE RISK, can't be measured. Yes, there are all sorts of formulas that economists and mathematicians use to calculate risk, but what they ultimately come up with is meaningless. It's meaningless because their calculations assume a 'normal' world, but the world experiences 'abnormal' things all the time, that can't be predicted.

So my suggestion is that you understand that for the most part, it's reasonable to expect that the world will continue as it has for millennia, but there's also a chance that something could happen that couldn't have been foreseen.

Using your Apple example, Apple is an absolutely massive company, over this past year it had average sales of around 600 million U.S. dollars each and every single day, that's six with eight zero's!

That's staggering when you think about it, but do you think that such a torrent of cash guarantees continued success? Nope, it just says that right now they're a massive business that consistently manages to generate a heap of cash, and based on their past, the probabilities say that they're likely to continue to generate this cash.

Knowing that they produce so much cash on a daily basis, and that they've been doing this consistently for many years, do you think there's a risk that Apple could go out of business?"

"Uh, well, it seems really unlikely that a company that size could ever go bust, but I guess I don't really know."

"Remember Jane, the future is not knowable, there are NEVER guarantees for what tomorrow brings, that's why some level of risk is always present. But, in terms of probabilities, it's highly unlikely that a company like Apple will ever disappear.

It's not because of their size, it's because of the momentum they've built up over time. Through clever design and aesthetics, they've successfully created an image that people both trust and find desirable. This trust and desire has people feel comfortable in paying a premium to buy their products and until that changes, they're likely to continue their dominance.

Now know this Jane, all things are possible but not all things are probable. Is it possible that a lightning bolt comes through the window right now and kills both of us? Yes it is, but it's not at all probable.

If you can accept that ultimately you don't know how things are going to turn out but that you can trust in the probabilities that support a good outcome, then you can invest in strong businesses knowing that the probabilities are on your side.

By the way, I'm not advocating blind faith here. I'm not saying that you should just trust what I'm saying. You can't truly accept responsibility for your actions when you do that. What I'm saying is that it's important for you to get to a point where you feel good about investing in the businesses that you choose so that you can leave the managers to do what they do best, without being concerned about the stock price."

"Hang on a minute Arturo, what if something major *does* happen, like say, a nuclear war where half the population of the world get wiped out, won't that wreck these businesses?"

"OK, firstly, I sense this is your fear talking because it's very extreme, but yes, your right, the probabilities *are* that all of the companies on the list would be seriously impacted and some would even go bust, that IS a possibility. Secondly, if you try to safe guard yourself from every possible threat, you'll be cutting yourself off from the abundance that this world has to offer.

There's a saying that goes, *The world has a habit of not ending.* So, if you put all your eggs into the 'world ending' plan, you're likely to miss out on some great opportunities.

If you're concerned about this, then it's a good idea to put some money into gold and silver bullion, say 10% of what you have invested in stocks. If an event like the one you describe was to happen, you have the value of the precious metals to live on until the world corrects itself.

I don't mean to be flippant about your comment Jane, there are indeed those that argue that the likelihood of a world war happening is increasing. But, time and time again, people that have planned for catastrophes happening have wasted a lot of time and money.

There was the peak oil argument in the 70's, there was the Y2K millennium bug in 2000, and there was the end of the Mayan calendar in 2012. People that put all their eggs into those worst-case scenarios paid a significant price, through lost opportunities.

Look, it's OK to think the good times won't last, and it's even healthy to be sceptical when everything seems to be going one way. But when you hang your hat on a certain outcome, that's when it can get dangerous.

Remember that you have within you the ability to rise above any situation and you ALWAYS have a choice on how you see things. So, even if the world goes to *hell in a hand basket*, as they say, it's still up to you on how you respond to that."

"OK, thanks Arturo, understood. There is one more thing I wanted to bring up, I noticed that the types of companies on your list include companies that sell cigarettes. Surely that can't be right, do you really want to support those sorts of businesses?"

"OK, good observation, and I'm glad you brought it up. This is probably one of the biggest conflicts that caring people feel when investing in stocks, that is, how can you, in good conscience, profit by investing in a business that deals in products that can harm people …

This is tricky and requires you to be clear on what it is that you're doing by investing in the first place. Let me ask you this Jane, let's go back to the Apple example, do you think that Apple meets the criteria of a socially moral business?"

"Um, I think so, people get value from the phones and computers, and it doesn't seem to be hurting anyone?"

"OK, what about the electromagnetic field that their products emit? Or what about the impact on the environment from the rare metals required in producing the products? Or what about the landfill from obsolete products that get thrown out due to planned obsolescence? Or then there's the fact that they set up operations in countries where wages are lower, which could be called exploitation.

I could keep going but I think you get the picture of how a business that produces something that people enjoy and get lots of use and value out of, can be turned so that it looks like it's not such a good thing …

The point is, it's not possible for you to know the impact that every business has in the wider scheme of things. Chances are that every single business will have an element that is both beneficial to some people and detrimental to other people."

"Hmm, OK, I get that. But come on, cigarettes?? It's pretty clear that they're harmful to people, surely you've got to draw a line somewhere!"

He leans back and looks up "… You want a line, do you? What if I told you there is no line, that it's all a matter of perspective? What if the tobacco company provided great health benefits for its employees and their families, investing in communities, doing all the right things except that they provide a product that may cause cancer in people, would that change your mind?"

"No! My grandfather died from lung cancer because of smoking, those products *do* cause cancer, people die because of these products, so I don't see any positive at all!" she says with agitation.

"Jane, Jane, look, I can see that this is a sensitive topic for you but respectfully, you're blinded by your emotions, you're not seeing that it was your grandfather's choice to smoke, whether he made the choice consciously or not, it was still a choice he made and no doubt he learned to enjoy smoking, as most people that get addicted do.

What I think you're saying is that if the tobacco company wasn't there providing the cigarettes, your grandfather may not have started smoking and therefore he may still be alive today, is that right?"

Her voice softened, "Well, I guess so, I do feel quite angry about the fact that my grandfather died as a result of something that could have been prevented if the product wasn't there. Those products are addictive and I just feel these companies operate without scruples, they're damn parasites on our society!" she says angrily.

"Let me take you back for a moment. Do you accept that as humans, we have the freedom to choose whatever we want?"

"Um, sure, we do but ..."

"No, wait, if you accept that we have the freedom to choose what we want, then how do we, as humans, respond when someone tells us we can't have something?"

"Well, we usually want it even more and find a way to get it anyway." she says with a smile.

"Precisely, the outlawing of something doesn't make people stop wanting it, in fact it's been shown that often the outlawing of something makes people want that thing even more and only helps the black market thrive!

As humans, we don't operate well when we're restricted or have things imposed on us. We tend to operate at our best when we allow ourselves to be free and explore what feels good to us. And by the way, I'm not condoning substance addiction here. What I'm saying is that getting to know what supports you and what doesn't, only really happens when you're free to explore life as it is.

If you die in the process, then that's where your exploration led you, I'm not saying it's right or wrong, it's simply a path that is chosen in that particular moment. There's no point in blaming anyone because that *was* the choice in the moment.

Jane, understand that you cannot control the choices that other people make, nor should you even try. You're in charge of your own choices, allow yourself to make the best choices you can with the greatest awareness you can bring to any situation. That's the best you can ever do."

"But Arturo, I just can't see myself investing in something like a cigarette company, it just doesn't feel right to me, I understand what you're saying but I wouldn't be able to live with the thought that I'm profiting from that type of business."

"Good, so you're clear that you won't pick that industry then. That's fine, I'm not saying you should or shouldn't, it's entirely up to you. Some people will feel like that in relation to companies that provide fast food or maybe credit cards or even fossil fuels for producing electricity.

That's all fine, ultimately it's a business that provides something that people are getting some sort of value out of, in whatever form that takes, and you're free to invest in whatever you like."

"OK, I get it, it does feel good to have the freedom to choose what feels good to me, I do like, for example, the way technology companies have helped make life easier."

"OK, but remember Jane, when you're choosing your thirteen companies, you want to get a cross section of many different industries to give you some level of diversification. In the tech area, I wouldn't choose more than three out of your thirteen companies. In fact, a good idea is to pick the basics of what people need, like food and shelter."

"OK, got it. Oh, there was one other thing I wanted to ask you quickly, my dad has some money in superannuation, how would he go about investing in the style you've been talking about?"

"Well, with people that have a lump sum to invest it's a little trickier, they can certainly pick their thirteen companies and start putting the $1,000 at a time but I'd probably do it this way: I'd divide the lump sum in half and put the half into all thirteen companies, then I'd systematically buy $1,000 at a time, say once a week, until all the money had been put to work.

Let me give you an example, let's say your dad has $130,000 in Super. He'd divide it in half, giving $65,000, and then he'd put $5,000 into each of the thirteen companies, leaving a balance in his account of $65,000. Then, he would start buying $1,000 a week, under the same system I told you about, until he has put all his money to work. It would take him 65 weeks to put this remaining $65,000 balance to work.

"Right, got it, thanks Arturo, I'll let him know."

"One other thing Jane, if your dad is getting close to retirement, then he may not want to have all his money in stocks because stocks are always going to have their wild rides. He may want to research other asset classes that possibly pay a smaller return but are more stable.

This particular *Money Tree* idea is mainly for younger people, say anyone under 40 with at least 25 years before they want to harvest the fruit from their *Money Tree*.

OK, lets leave it there for this week. Your project for this week is to:

1. Pick your thirteen stocks;
2. Find an online broker; and
3. Set up an account with them."

"HEY DAD, I spoke to Arturo about putting all my eggs in the stock market basket."

"Oh yeah? What did he say?" David says suspiciously.

"Well, he agreed with you mostly, although he said at the start it's a good way to begin investing. He said that when I get to a point where I have around $20,000 in each of the thirteen companies, then I could consider other investments.

Although, he said that whatever I do, I need to educate myself before investing, so I can accept full responsibility for it."

"So he's saying that you should effectively have a portfolio of $260,000 in the stock market before investing in anything else??"

"Hang on dad, Arturo was quite clear in that he said I can do whatever I want, as long as I educate myself first. He's given me this plan as a basic starting strategy. He said this was the simplest way he knew for someone to begin investing without having to learn all the ins and outs of investing. He's given me a list of proven companies that are likely to be around for many years to come, as a result, I can simply put a $1,000 a time into them and let the money grow slowly over time."

David sits back, looks up and says, "Hmm, fair enough, I'm still not overly comfortable with the idea but it makes sense. Was there anything else?"

"Yeah, I asked about your retirement money and whether this system would work for you too and he said it was a little trickier for people in your position. He said you can choose your thirteen companies, put half of your money into those companies and then start putting $1,000 a week until the remainder has been put in.

He gave an example of, let's say you have $130,000 in your account, you'd allocate $65,000 to put in straight away. Then, do the remaining amount at $1,000 per week for the next 65 weeks."

"Hmm, and what if there's a crash or something, what happens then?" he says sceptically.

"Well, I did actually question him about what would happen if there was something like a nuclear war ..."

"That's my girl."

Smiling, she continues, "He said that if I'm worried about it, then it's a good idea to put around 10% of my money into things like gold and silver bullion. He also said that it's best to focus on probabilities rather than possibilities, as in the probabilities are that things work out well even though the possibility for something bad happening also exists."

"Hmm, OK, that's easier said than done but it does makes sense. I'll certainly consider it for our superannuation."

"Oh, one more thing dad, he also said that if you're getting close to retirement, you might not want to have all your money in stocks. He said that this *Money Tree* idea was mainly designed for younger people that have at least 25 years to let the money grow."

"Right, OK. Well that makes me wish I could have started when I was your age! Not to worry, please thank him for me when you see him next ..."

Week Sixteen – Luck

"Hi Arturo, my dad asked me to thank you for sharing the idea on investing in the stock market."

"Sure, no problem, glad to be of service. OK, today I'd like to discuss *luck* with you. I remember I'd said I would talk about it and that you'd get a kick out of it ...

Now, everyone talks about luck, good luck, bad luck, dumb luck, etc. But what really is luck about? Have you ever thought about it, Jane?"

"Um, no, not really. I guess I figured that there's stuff that happens and you just say, '... oh that was lucky/unlucky', or something like that."

"Right, that's pretty much it. There are things that happen that are out of our control and so when something happens that we feel we had nothing to do with, we assign it to luck! It's a lot easier to do that than to stand as the creator of everything that happens to you, isn't it?" he says with a cheeky smile.

"But the truth of the matter is that we're all little entities stuck on this rock called Earth, that's floating in space. We live day-to-day with this illusion of permanence, certainty and security, when in fact at any moment, we could be wiped out!"

"Whoa Arturo, that's a bit dramatic isn't it? I mean, sure that's possible but we'd go crazy if we lived with that in the back of our heads all the time."

"You're spot on Jane. As humans, we do actually know that we're quite fragile, but we don't want to think about it or admit it. The thing is, we're masters at finding ways to survive and thrive, so the way we get around the psychological issue of dealing with this uncertain world is to create things like luck!

It's too scary to accept that *we're* creating all of it because that would mean accepting responsibility for everything that shows up, and most of can't handle that yet!

So, this concept called *luck* is used as a convenient way to say, 'well, it's got nothing to do with me, it was just luck!' If it's something negative, it helps us to not be responsible. If it's positive, it's a bonus, we might be thankful for a moment, thank God or something like that. Either way it was out of our hands and we remain as children! "

"Sheesh Arturo, you really know how to hit between the eyes, I mean, do you really have to analyse everything so much?"

"Hmm, OK," he says as he leans forward, "... so you think there's too much analysing, do you?" He stares intensely at her, "Tell me why you feel that way, Jane."

She suddenly starts to fidget with discomfort, "Uh, well, I was just saying. I mean, what ever happened to just accepting what is, going with the flow and all that sort of stuff?"

He remains quiet and maintains his gaze. She closes her eyes, realising that she needed to re-centre herself, after a few moments she says, "OK, I guess I'm feeling a bit overwhelmed again and it just feels like hard work to have to analyse everything like this. I'm sorry, OK?" she says with an edge of irritation.

He gently says, "Jane, there's no need to apologise, there's no problem here. I'm here to help you and at times, that may feel uncomfortable, but you never need to apologise to me.

If you remember back to our first meeting, I said that this wouldn't be easy. I said that it's simple, but it's not easy. Within each one of us there are patterns of thought that we've picked up from past experiences and when we try to change those, we can find ourselves becoming resistant to the change.

Sure, it takes energy to analyse and question things, it's easier to stay asleep and go with the crowd. But if you want to *be* the one you were born to be, then it's going to take a yearning from deeper within that says, 'YES, I'M HERE TO EXPERIENCE ALL THAT I AM', and then embrace it all.

Embracing it means that you accept the journey and become curious about how crazy situations are at times and then take steps that feel good to you.

So I guess the question is, does this path that you and I are on, still feel good to you?"

She closes her eyes again and takes some deep breaths. She feels her heart expand and then says quietly but firmly, "Yes, this does feel right ..." while opening her eyes at the same time.

"You're right, Arturo, there's a part of me that would love to go home and just sit in front of the TV and forget about everything, but I know deep down that that's not the answer. It'd just be a temporary escape from reality and I now feel that I have a deeper knowing, that I'm here to help people in some way."

"Good, that's very clear. OK, so back to luck. Do you understand how luck is used as a scapegoat now?"

"Scapegoat? Uh, OK, what I understand is that we use the idea of luck as a way to explain things that happen and seem to be out of our control. What I've heard you say is that everything is our creation, so whatever shows up is what we've created, somehow. I still don't really get how this happens, but in order to accept responsibility for my life, then it's about accepting that it's all my doing."

"Not bad, and one thing to be mindful of, is that you can fall into the trap of feeling guilty for creating all the crappy things that you or others may be experiencing.

If you stand as the creator, then you must be responsible for that too, right? But this is one of the paradoxes because each one of us is a creator and we all come together in a complex tapestry of interwoven creations."

"Whoa, wait a sec Arturo, my head is spinning again." she says while holding her head and thinks about what he'd just said. "... So you're saying that even though I create my world, and it means that I created you to be here right now also, you have created your world and you have created me to be here with you too!"

"That's it Jane, you got it."

"I did? Wait, what did I just say?"

He laughs, "You said it beautifully Jane, each of us creates our own world, I created you and you created me, and from a wider perspective, there isn't a separation, we actually are all creating together. It's all one big tapestry, interweaving different threads of life and yet all part of the same ONE. So, even though it seems like we are operating as separate little entities, from a deeper perspective, we are all one!"

"Hmm, that's tough to get my head around, but OK. So how is it that some people seem naturally *lucky*, while others *unlucky*? Why are they/we creating like this?"

"Well Jane, the thing to remember is that in most cases, the creating happens unconsciously, we can aim for something, have goals, put effort in, but ultimately, we don't know exactly how it's going to turn out, hence ... *luck*!"

"I don't get it, so now you're saying that luck *does* exist?"

He laughs again, "Luck is just something that's used to explain that which we have no real answer for. We *are* creators, whether we know it or not and so, if you can stand as the creator, the next time something happens, that you'd normally term as *luck*, you can simply say, 'hmm, isn't that interesting, there's something I didn't know I was creating!'

The idea is to not get too caught up in what shows up. Your aim is to notice your feelings, focus on your breath and take inspired action from there. If you feel like crying or letting out an emotion, that's fine, but noticing what gets triggered within you and letting it go is where the work is done."

"But what about kids? Like when a kid gets cancer or something, surely they haven't created that for themselves! Like, what's going on there? Or, what about when a baby dies in some sort of terrorist attack?" she says with agitation.

"OK Jane, maybe I haven't been clear enough yet. Being a child or an adult doesn't change things much. Sure, children generally don't carry the same burdens that adults do, but what I'm talking about happens at a level that's closer to thoughts and beliefs than a physical sort of thing.

Think of it this way, when we come into this world, we're born with a certain DNA imprint, that's a physical thing that can be scientifically proven. Now, many in the medical field believe that you can't alter your DNA, your genes are what they are. But, there have been tests done on cells that show genes turning on or off depending on what environment they find themselves in. They found things like healthy heart cells becoming unhealthy when mixed in a solution of unhealthy ones and even heart cells becoming liver cells when mixed with a majority of liver cells.

The bottom line is that our whole organism can change and adapt to the environment, it doesn't care about positive or negative, it's simply a response to the moment.

When a child develops cancer or a baby dies, they created unconsciously through their body's response to a given environment. It's something that we call genetics or bad luck or whatever, but the tapestry of life in that moment is causing the manifestation."

"Wow Arturo, you seem to have an answer for everything! How is it that you just seem to have this view of life that's so different to the way most people see life?"

"Well, it's not something I share often, but here it goes. I grew up in what would be considered a dysfunctional family, with a father that was physically violent, and a mother that was a drug addict. My mum began taking drugs as a way of escaping her reality but it soon became an addiction, which led to an overdose and she died when I was 9."

"Oh my God!! That's terrible!" she says with shock.

"Jane, I know it doesn't sound great but remember, we're all creating together in a this complex tapestry called Life. I'm not saying it was fun, I certainly copped some significant beatings from my father, but I learned to become extremely resourceful around him. I eventually learned what his trigger points were and how to run really fast the split-second one got triggered.

My mum, on the other hand, was a gentle woman and was often in a state of hallucination. She would say that 'Beings from another galaxy' wanted to pass information on to me, through her, and they asked her to put both her hands on my head, while she spoke what they said to her.

The consistent message that came out of her mouth during those times was that I was here for a specific purpose, that I had the ability to help others by seeing their brilliance, beyond their story, and that I would be able to see their calling in life, when I was ready.

I had no idea of what she was on about at the time but the upshot to all of it was that I became very sensitive and aware of what was happening around me and within me, and it not only helped me gain this ability, it also allowed me to find peace and ease in the moment."

"Wow, it sounds like you had a really tough childhood ... So this 'gift' you have, is really something you developed out of the hardship you went through as a kid, right?"

"Well, you could say that, but I really don't know what would have happened if my mum hadn't have been high so often. Whatever she experienced during her hallucinations, helped plant a seed in me that allowed a significant opening to happen. And, the by-products of all this are that I age at a slower rate than most people and that my immune system operates at a super efficient level. Oh, and I also realised that I'm not unique in this."

He now becomes serious and his gaze becomes intense, "Jane, from your perspective everything I've said could be just another one of my rants. The truth of the matter is that words don't teach, direct experience is what ultimately teaches. My aim here is to awaken something within you that allows you to experience the Truth for yourself."

"What? What are you saying, that I have some of those abilities too?" she says suspiciously.

"Jane, listen very closely, unless you are open to experiencing something for yourself, nothing I say will give you the reality of it. Being open to the idea that anything is possible is a great place to start. My aim is to simply help you be open to the possibilities.

OK, let's move on. I think we've covered enough for this week and your project is to come back to the breath every time you get lost in thinking about what we talked about today. See you next week, Jane." he says as he gets up to open the door for her.

On her way home, her mind starts to race. '... What was that all about? I've got abilities? Hmm!! OK, come back Jane.' she says to herself as she takes a big deep breath.

SHE ARRIVES HOME and David says cheerfully, "How did it go today, honey?"

Without stopping, she says hurriedly, "Uh, we'll talk later, dad ..."

He scratches his head as he watches her walk past, 'Hmm, that was weird.' he thinks.

Over dinner, he asks, "Jane, are you OK? You seem distant tonight."

"Um, I'm OK, it was just a bit of a weird session with Arturo, that's all."

"Do you want to talk about it?" Not wanting to bring up Arturo's abusive childhood, she says, "Uh, hmm, I suppose it's just that Arturo isn't your average person, in the way he sees life. He analyses every little thing and it seems a bit much at times, that's all."

"Well, I can't put my finger on it but you seem a little distressed or something, did anything specifically happen, Jane?"

"Well, we started speaking about luck, and most of us just accept that sometimes stuff happens and we call it bad luck, say. But not Arturo, he sees it that we're all creators and that whatever shows up is our creation." she says waving her hands in the air.

"Right, I see, that's a bit out there. It's not easy to accept we create everything." he says while thinking about what she'd said.

"Exactly, we don't mind the good stuff showing up and that maybe we created that, but the bad stuff is easier to just say it was this thing called luck! But ultimately, anything we don't have an explanation for, we call luck, and that keeps us as little children rather than responsible creators of our reality."

"Wow Jane, I see what you mean, he's certainly challenging. I don't know how I'd go if I was in your shoes. I mean there's just so much stuff going on day-to-day that it's tough to stand as the ultimate creator of it all. I guess all you can do is hear what he has to say but do your best to live in a way that feels good to you."

"Yeah, thanks dad. You're right." But as she agreed, in the back of her mind she kept wondering about what her own abilities might be.

Later that evening as she lay in bed, she thought about Arturo's experience with his mum and how messages were being passed on to him through his mum's hallucinations.

As she focused on this, she also became aware of her breath and she felt warm and relaxed. She then thought, 'What if Beings from other galaxies visit us all the time, but we just can't see them at this point??' It was crazy, she thought, and went to sleep.

The next day she awoke with a spring in her step, she'd had a dream of flying through space, visiting different stars and galaxies and it felt wonderful.

"Morning Jane, you seem cheery this morning, compared to last night, that is." says Elizabeth.

"Yeah, I feel good mum. I think I just needed a good night sleep, I'd had a big day yesterday. Anyway, I'm off to the library now, so I'll see you later ..."

Week Seventeen – Business

"Hi Jane, come on in." Arturo says chirpily. "How was your week?"

"Well, it was quite tough. I did get lost in the thoughts around what we spoke about last week and I often forgot to come back to the breath until I became quite anxious. I did have this dream though, where I was flying through space. I was visiting different stars and galaxies and it felt fantastic ..." she says excitedly.

He leans forward with curiosity, "Really? That sounds interesting, tell me about it."

"Um, I just remember having this thought before going to bed last Monday, something like, *what if Beings from other galaxies visit us all the time, but we just can't see them at this point.* Then I fell asleep and all I could remember was the joyful feeling of being weightless and flying really fast through space. There really wasn't anything else to it, it just felt really good and I woke up feeling quite refreshed the next day."

"And how does that thought sit with you, as in the thought that other things could be happening all around us that we have no idea about?"

"It feels crazy, it doesn't really make sense to me. Are you saying that that's true??"

"I'm not saying one thing or the other, all I'm looking to see is how open you are with it. The thing is, we live in a universe where all things are possible, so it really just depends on whether you can consider something as being possible for *you*."

"OK Arturo, I think I've heard you say a similar thing before. I guess it's just a bit too weird a thought for me at the moment, and to be honest, I'm still struggling with the idea that I might have some special abilities that I don't know about."

"Jane, it's more important that you check in with yourself to see what feels good to you. Always aim to focus on what's joyful for you and be open to possibilities. If something feels good, fine, if it doesn't, let it go and move on.

To do anything else with it is to create another story, another drama, and another bit of clutter in your head. It doesn't serve you, so come back to the breath, feel the joy and move on.

Always remember this Jane, words are just words. Yes, they can convey powerful messages and point to something real, but ultimately, unless you experience what those words are pointing to, they're not real for YOU."

"Right, OK, I think I'm getting that. It reminds me of politicians, they seem to say a lot words but most of it just seems to be hot air."

"Well, politicians really can't speak what's true for them anyway, they're part of a system that rewards them for maintaining an illusion, as in the illusion that government can take care of people.

Most people at this point, still like the idea of someone else taking care of them, they aren't prepared to do the work to be responsible for themselves, so government is necessary for them. Anyway, let's move on ... How's your program going? The one that involves helping kids."

"Um, yeah, I've been working on it. I've come up with the idea of introducing kids to the percentages that you've introduced to me, except even more simplified."

"OK, so what stage are you at with it? As in, do you have a plan for the product yet?"

"Well, I've been working on a number of variation packages, i.e. products that cater for different age kids, but that's about it. I still haven't developed a final product, if that's what you mean."

"OK, here's what I recommend you do, write this down:
1. Work out WHO you're going to sell these packages to;
2. Work out HOW you're going to sell these packages;
3. Find a successful online marketer to partner with and work out some type of profit sharing arrangement;
4. Develop the products, start with the simplest one first;
5. Test the product out to make sure your target market likes it and that the price is set at the right point;
6. Start selling as soon as possible."

"Right, that's going to be challenging ..." she says while feeling the overwhelm build up.

"Jane, please remember to keep coming back to what you felt when you got this idea, that's the light to help you get through the maze, we call business.

This isn't about forcing anything. Yes, it's challenging, but always break things down into smaller pieces and it'll come together.

Also, remember to ask for help if you get stuck, you have the option of sending me an email, if you want. And of course the Internet can be a great resource also."

"OK, thanks for that Arturo, it helps to hear that."

"Good, well let's leave it there for this week. For next week's meeting, I'd like you to do an updated financial statement, except just send me the actual position for the last month, not the annual. You know, the one where you put your current income and expenses. Also, please prepare your updated statement of Assets and Liabilities."

"Yep, can do." she says as she gets up to leave.

"Good. So we'll see how you're travelling right now, and please email it to me by Sunday evening."

"OK, got it Arturo, see you next week."

"HEY JANE ..." David screams out from the lounge as she walks through the door, "Come in here when you've put your things down."

"... Hi dad, what's happening?" she says as she walks into the lounge.

"Just wondering how your session with Arturo went this week, was there anymore stuff about *luck*?"

"No, we talked about business and the steps I need to take with the product I'm developing. I need to work out who and how I'm going to sell and then test the market, some how. I'm feeling a bit anxious about it at the moment, so I think I need to spend some time at breaking down the steps."

"Hmm, OK, good *luck* with that ..." They both laugh with David's play on words.

Week Eighteen – A Privileged life

CC Hi Jane, let's get straight into it ..." says Arturo as he takes out a folder and retrieves the print out from the email she'd sent him.

"Right, let's see what we have here ...

Jane's Income

(Actual monthly)

Description	Amount
Active Income	
Wages (after tax)	$2,210
Business/Other Income	$0
Passive Income	
Bank Interest	$0
Stock Dividends	$0
Rental Income	$0
Total Income	$2,210

Jane's Spending

(Actual monthly)

Description	Amount
My Money Tree (At least 10% of income)	
High Yield Account	$400
Living Costs (No more than 70% of income)	
Electricity & Gas	$0
Gifts (birthdays, Xmas, etc.)	$0
Property rates, taxes & water	$0
Debt Repayment—Credit Card	$550
Mobile phone	$75
ATM withdrawals/incidental spending	$260
Groceries	$0

Grooming	$60
Clothes	$120
Public Transport Costs	$0
Car Fuel	$113
Car repairs	$0
Car insurance & Registration	$120
Giving (5% of income or what feels right to you)	
XYZ worthy cause	$50
Savings for Set Goal (Aim for No more than 10% of income)	
Saving for Deposit on a house	$400
Fun (No more than 5% of income)	
New experiences	$0
Restaurants/dining out/movies	$60
Total Expenses	**$2,208**

... And the Statement of Assets and Liabilities:

Jane's Assets

(Things I Own)

Description	Amount
Things that don't pay me to own them	
Electronics—PC, Tablet, etc.	$1,000
Clothes, Shoes & Accessories	$700
Car	$5,000
Furniture & Fittings	$0
Things of value that don't pay me	
Cash at Bank at call	$357
Artwork & Collectibles	$0
Gold & Silver (Including jewellery melt value)	$300
Things that pay me to own them	
High Yield Bank Account—Money Tree	$400
High Yield Bank Account—House Goal	$400
Businesses	$0
Stocks/Shares	$0
Property	$0
Total Assets	**$8,157**

Jane's Liabilities

(Things I Owe)

Description	Amount
Things I might have to pay for in less than 12 months	
Credit Cards	$0
Short Term Loans	$0
Things I might have to pay for in greater than 12 months	
Credit Cards Long Term	$0
Long Term Loans	$0
School Loans	$25,000
Mortgage	$0
Car Loan	$0
Total Liabilities	$25,000
Net Assets	− $16,843

OK, looking good Jane, you've saved over 10% for your *Money Tree* and your *House* goal and you've cancelled your credit card debt! You're off to a great start. How do you feel about what you've created?"

"Um, yeah, pretty good. It's just that I know it's not really real. Like, I haven't paid for any groceries or rent or any of the other bills that normal independent people would pay for."

He stares at her intensely, in what feels like an age to her and then says, in a gentle voice, "Jane, you have the stars at your finger-tips and you focus on the dust at your shoes. Sure, your financial statement is different to that of another person, but don't think it's any less real.

The fact that you've prepared this financial statement and have become aware of how you're spending, and now allocating money towards your *Goals* and *Money Tree*, means you'll probably be able to stand as that independent woman sooner than you realise!

Look, there's no doubt that you're in a privileged position. There are lots of people your age that don't have the choice of living with their parents rent-free and they struggle week-to-week to get by. But never forget that life is a tapestry, we don't know why anyone else has to go through the circumstances they do.

All you can do is focus on being the best you can in the circumstances you find yourself in. From there, maintain a healthy attitude and look to add value wherever you can, and you'll serve yourself, and the whole, in ways you can't even imagine right now."

She looks down and says, "Hmm, you're right. I was putting myself down for being luck ... er, I mean, being in a position that's really quite fortunate compared to a lot of people.

You know, I guess there's a part of me that's really sad that other people have to do it so tough and I, I was calling my situation unreal as a way of somehow saying that I too was doing it tough."

"Well done Jane. You're getting to see how intricately the mind works. Now, let's go a bit deeper with it. At an unconscious level, you're uncomfortable with being in a privileged position, so you create a story that has that unconscious part feel in balance again.

Having this awareness now helps you to be clearer when you take the steps you take. So let me ask you, have you ever helped anyone, by being less than you are?"

"Well, I think the answer is obvious, of course not, but It's like when you see an ad on TV with a child in Africa starving, it feels terrible and you just want to find a way to help them."

"OK, so would it help them if you starved yourself?"

"Of course not." she says with agitation.

"So why put such an emotional strain on yourself? You can't help them by feeling bad for living in better circumstances, so why do that?"

"Well, I guess I feel guilty, like somehow because I'm in a better situation, I'm responsible for helping them in some way. I know it sounds weird, but that's how I feel."

"Jane, you're not alone in feeling this way. As humans, we don't enjoy seeing suffering, advertiser's know this and aim to hook us by pulling on those emotional strings. The thing is, without the awareness that it's an advertiser's tactic, it works it's way in so that you just get left with this feeling of guilt for being in a better circumstance.

It's a multifaceted thing that can look different to different people but essentially it's something that operates at a subtle level, and I'm not saying that we can't help these starving kids in Africa. What I *am* saying is that it doesn't help you or anyone else to be less than what you're capable of being.

Knowing this is just a doorway though, living so that you don't operate from a place of guilt requires awareness as well as a noticing of when you think or say things that don't feel particularly good to you.

Again, it's about being gentle with yourself and being curious about why you're feeling the way you feel."

"You know Arturo, it seems like there's all this stuff in me that I didn't know was there. Like, it feels as though every week you highlight something new for me. I mean, I knew I was complex but I didn't really know exactly, and now that I'm seeing it, it's a little scary and I can feel the anxiety wanting to kick in again."

"OK, think of it this way, as you go through life, it's like you're walking along a well worn, dimly lit path that you created in your early years. You bumped around a bit and worked out that this path was the safest you could find, even though you get tripped up on a few potholes now and then.

You then aim to patch up a few potholes and that seems to do the trick, only to find yourself stumbling on a never ending series of potholes as you continue down the path.

At some point you might think, 'I've had enough of this path, I've got to find another path', but you can't see clearly and even though you have your falls, it just feels easier to continue walking along the path you already know. It may not be great, but there's comfort in knowing it.

Then one day you fall hard and you say, 'Right, that's it, I've had it with this path, this time I'm really going to find another path.' That then has you try new things, but you realise that the new path has potholes too!

At some point you might realise that the path isn't the problem, how you see the path and your resistance to the path is the issue, and this becomes your work.

Right now Jane, you're starting to see that your path has more potholes than you'd realised. Your path is how you operate in the world and all I'm doing is helping to make your dimly lit lights a bit brighter, so you can choose what feels better to you. There's nothing to fix, as such, it's really all about seeing yourself as you are and not resisting what is.

OK, let's leave it at that for this week. For next week, I'd like you to prepare your financial statement on the basis that you're living the life of your dreams. In other words, show me what your dream life would look like, using the same spreadsheet you did your current position on. Will you do that?"

"Yep, that sounds like fun. OK, see you then ..."

Week Nineteen – Living the Dream

"Hey Jane, how's it going? How did it feel doing the dream financial statement?" says Arturo with a cheeky grin on his face.

"Um, yeah, it was interesting. I found that it wasn't as easy as I thought it'd be. Like, I know the sort of life I'd like to have but it wasn't easy working out where the money would come from to pay for it all.

I guess when I've thought about my dream life in the past, I'd always just thought there would be this big pot of money, like when you win the lottery or something, and then I'd just be able to buy a heap of stuff that way ...

But now that I have a bit more understanding of how money works, I realise that to live responsibly, I need to stand as the creator of my life. Out of that, I realised that relying on the lottery to take care of my dreams, felt like I was handing over my responsibility in some way.

So out of all that I started thinking, what *things that pay me,* do I need to own, so that I can be paid enough to then live the life of my dreams. And that was how I came up with the sheets I sent you last night."

"Wow Jane, that's beautiful, it brings a smile to my heart to hear you say that. You've really come a long way. OK, let's look at what you sent me ..."

Jane's Income
(Dream monthly)

Description	Amount
Active Income	
Wages (after tax)	$0
Business/Other Income (after tax)	$20,000
Passive Income	
Bank Interest	$200
Stock Dividends	$1,500
Rental Income (Net)	$2,000
Total Income	$23,700

Jane's Spending

(Dream monthly)

Description	Amount
My Money Tree (At least 10% of income)	
High Yield Account	$7,500
Living Costs (No more than 70% of income)	
Electricity & Gas	$200
Gifts (birthdays, Xmas, etc.)	$500
Property rates, taxes & water	$300
Mobile phone & Internet	$100
ATM withdrawals/incidental spending	$500
Groceries	$500
Just in Case Funds	$2,000
Grooming	$400
Clothes	$1,000
Travel/holidays	$2,000
Car Costs	$500
Rent/Mortgage	$3,500
Medical Insurance	$300
Other Insurances	$200
Giving (5% of income or what feels right to you)	
XYZ worthy causes	$2,000
Savings for Set Goal (Aim for No more than 10% of income)	
XYZ Saving Furniture, Art, etc.	$1,000
Fun (No more than 5% of income)	
New experiences	$600
Restaurants/dining out/movies	$600
Total Expenses	**$23,700**

"OK, so it seems that in your dream life you're not working in a formal job, you're getting most of your income from running businesses and you've got some passive income going, no doubt from your *Money Tree*.

On the expenses side, you're putting around 30% of your income into continuing to grow your *Money Tree*, good… and by the look of it, you're not living an overly extravagant lifestyle.

You're looking at generating an annual income of nearly $300,000 after tax, in order to live your dream life. OK, lets look at your statement of assets and liabilities …"

Jane's Assets

(Dream things I own)

Description	Amount
Things that don't pay me to own them	
Electronics—PC, Tablet, etc.	$10,000
Clothes, Shoes & Accessories	$20,000
Car	$50,000
Furniture & Fittings	$50,000
Things of value that don't pay me	
Cash at Bank at call	$10,000
Artwork & Collectibles	$100,000
Gold & Silver (Including jewellery melt value)	$100,000
Things that pay me to own them	
High Yield Bank Account Money Tree	$50,000
High Yield Bank Account Goal	$10,000
Businesses	$1,000,000
Stocks	$700,000
Property	$600,000
Total Assets	$2,700,000

Jane's Liabilities

(Dream things I owe)

Description	Amount
Things I might have to pay for in less than 12 months	
Credit Cards	$0
Short Term Loans	$0
Things I might have to pay for in greater than 12 months	
Credit Cards—Long Term	$0
Long Term Loans	$0
School Loans	$0
Mortgage	$200,000
Total Liabilities	$200,000
Net Assets	$2,500,000

With curiosity, Arturo looks up at her and says, "Hmm, so tell me Jane, why have you included a mortgage in your dream life?"

"Um, I think I just thought that everyone has a mortgage when they're buying a home. I wanted to make this realistic, I suppose. But now that you mention it, I can see it is a bit weird to include owing money in my 'dream life'." she says while looking down and feeling embarrassed.

"Jane, it's OK, this is just another one of those potholes in your mind. You have a belief that you need to go into debt to buy a home, that's very normal. By the look of it, you've made some assumptions that you'd be living this dream life at a certain point in your life, when you still had a mortgage, is that the case?"

"Uh, Well, yeah, I'm wanting to live this life as soon as possible so I'm thinking that this might be how my life is when I'm in my mid to late 20's."

"Right. So in around 5 to 8 years time, you think this could be the life you're living?"

"Actually, I'm not sure if I can make that much money in that time, I can't really imagine earning $300,000 a year!"

"Jane, I'm not questioning you to put a limit on your dreams, the truth is that it *is* possible for you to be living a lifestyle that's even more than this, in a very short period of time. But it really all depends on you. Remember, you're the creator ...

My questioning is to see if you can find a place within you that feels excited at the possibility of it, and that while you can't imagine it for yourself right now, maybe as you start to grow your business and your *Money Tree*, you'll start to see it as more of a reality."

"OK yeah, that feels good, I like the idea of growing my business in helping kids, all around the world. I suppose I really don't know how it'll go, I could be the next Mark Zuckerberg for a kids finance network or something!" she says as she bursts out laughing.

"Well Jane, that's not as incredulous as you might think. When you start to believe that you can be, do or have anything your heart desires, the world starts to become a magical place.

I have no doubt that those young Internet billionaires, would have all started with a belief in a dream. They probably didn't realise just how big their ideas were going to grow when they first thought about them, but it all starts with the seed of a dream. AND, a belief in yourself that you *can* actually create something significant that *serves* a lot of people.

Remember this Jane, we often *overestimate* what we can achieve in the short term and *underestimate* what we can achieve in the long term. This is because we're optimistic at the start but we often can't get out of our own way quickly enough to allow the abundance to flow in.

On the other hand, when we put some solid foundations in and allow that to grow, the momentum can have it grow much bigger than we'd first imagined. This is the reason why compounding is so amazing, it's growth upon growth upon growth. Before long you have a rabbit epidemic!" he says chuckling.

He now becomes silent and looks intensely into her eyes. After a few moments he says gently, "... Jane, this time that we're sharing is now coming to an end."

"Um, OK, is there a project you want me to do for next week?"

"No Jane, what I mean is that there won't be a meeting next week, or at all from now on."

"Huh? What? What do you mean? Why?" she says as the anxiety builds.

"Breathe Jane, remember, just be curious, there's nothing to fear."

"But I don't get it, why now? What's happened that makes you think that now is the time to end it?"

"It had to finish at some point, didn't it?"

"Um, sure. I just, I guess I thought, it would last for at least a little longer." she looks down, trying her best to focus on her breath.

"Jane, this relationship you and I have is tricky because my role is to help you get in touch with your essence, the one that's beyond your mind, so that you can experience more of who you truly are. As your mentor, I need to be very aware of when my 'help' starts to become a hindrance for you. You see, while it can look like help, and you're feeling good about me being here, if I don't let go, I become a crutch for you.

That situation doesn't help you or anyone else and can actually become quite harmful. The last thing I want to do is adversely affect you in your aim of being a healthy, independent and responsible woman.

I've mentioned before how this moment, NOW, is ALL we have, and right now, whether you realise it or not, you're ready to go forward without me!"

"Really? I don't feel ready. I feel like I'm just starting to get my head around all this. I mean, I haven't even finished the kids program yet, what if I stuff it up?"

"At the start of our session today, the way you explained your line of thinking in preparing your *dream financial statement,* told me that you're well on your way to standing as that independent woman you'd like to be.

At this point, YOU, as Jane, haven't caught up with YOU, as the one you truly are. That joyous, confident, powerful presence, that hides below the surface. I see the truth of you Jane, and you *are* ready."

"Well, those words are encouraging, but I guess it just all seems so abrupt, I mean, it seems to have just come out of nowhere!"

"As you sit more calmly now, can you get in touch with the one I described?"

She closes her eyes and focuses on her breath. She notices the air entering her nose gently and then leaving. After a little while she opens her eyes, looks at him and smiles, "... Yeah, I feel it, I *am* ready. I think what happened is that I got used to you being here and it feels like some sort of safety blanket, so in your words, the 'crutch' was definitely developing.

Thanks for what you've done for me, I'll never forget it. Is there some way I can repay you for what you've done for me?"

"Firstly Jane, it's been my pleasure, you may not know it yet, but you *are* a shining star. Secondly, I haven't 'done' anything in particular for you, you created the opening for me to be here. As the saying goes, *When the student is ready, the teacher appears.* And thirdly, you have no debt with me. By bringing more awareness to your daily life, you'll be choosing what feels more joyous to you, and you'll be standing as the creator you were born to be, and *that* is a great joy for *me*.

I do however want to make sure something is clear, do you recall why we've focused so much on the money side of life?"

"Um, I think it was because money is such a big part of daily living. Like, you can't do much without having money."

"It is and, you wanted to find a way for you to be more financially independent. It's important to remember, that money is a by-product, it's not something you go for, simply to have it.

If money for the sake of money becomes the be-all and end-all, then you become what I call a 'rich, poor person'. Where you have more than you know on the outside but have no foundation within. The result is that no matter what you accumulate in your life, you feel empty within.

By knowing that money is simply a by-product of living a joyful life, NOW, you give yourself the opportunity of being a 'rich, rich person'.

The foundation to living joyfully is in your awareness of the present moment, from there, it's in the noticing of what you do and whether it supports you or not.

Through this awareness, you can look at the pillars of maintaining a well functioning body, your vehicle. This includes the food you eat, the relationships you have, the sleep you get, the thoughts you think, the exercise you do and, the way you manage money.

It's all about being present and from there, establishing supportive practices that allow you the freedom to choose what you truly desire. The reality is that it's not easy to live joyfully if you don't have good health, loving relationships and money. It can be done, but most people get stuck in the lack of something when they don't have it.

So by focusing on money, the aim has been to help you establish one of the pillars, i.e. independence, so that you can use it to springboard yourself into living the life you were born to live. It's just one aspect and if you don't take care of your health and relationships at the same time, you'll get out of balance, and most likely, not live joyfully.

So remember Jane, bring your awareness to the present moment, notice your feelings and find the joy that you *are*. From there, practice living in a way that takes care of your body, your relationships and your money. Know that you are an abundant Being and that life supports you in ways you can't even imagine. I know I've ranted a little here, but is that clear?"

"Yeah, that's really good. I think it's easy to just get stuck in focusing on one thing, like the money, for example. So yeah, I'm glad you highlighted that. It's got me thinking that I do need to be more sociable. I've been so focused on these projects that I've hardly been going out."

"Good, it's important to remember that we're multifaceted beings, and we enjoy diversity. Now, before you leave, I'd like you to write down this summary:

1. Bring awareness in this present moment and have an excellent attitude in whatever you do;
2. Be at ease within yourself, if you notice that you're not, focus on the breath and consciously tell yourself to relax and that you're OK as you are;
3. Be curious about things with the aim of seeing them as neutral, resist no thing and in that, allow what is;
4. Be grateful as often as you can, the world can take on magical qualities when you open the doors of gratitude;
5. Everyday, aim to live in balance by eating well, exercising a little, surrounding yourself with people you like, and noticing how you feel about and treat money.
6. Allocate your money so that you save and invest in your *Money Tree*;
7. Let compounding do it's magic by following the *Money Tree formula*;
8. Don't borrow money for things that don't pay you to own them;
9. And most importantly, do what feels good to you, honour yourself and follow that which FEELS the best to you. From there, honour and respect others.

That's it Jane, go off and live and love life."

"Um, I'm just wondering, can I call you if I get really stuck on something?"

"Well, if you feel you're facing a situation where you don't know where to turn, then sure, call me."

"So I guess that leaves just one more question ... am I ever going to see you again?"

"I would say the probabilities are that we will see each other at some point, but as far as these types of meetings go, I don't know. I tell you what though, let's make a time for 5 years out and you can show me your financial statement at that point. How does that sound?"

"OK, It's a date, I'll put it on my phone, the first Monday of this month in 5 years ..."

They both get up and Jane quickly moves around the desk and gives him a big hug. "Thanks again, Arturo, I'll see you in 5 years!"

"Hi Jane, you're later than usual tonight, is everything OK?" David asks with concern.

"Uh, yeah, it's all fine. It went over time tonight because it turned out to be the last session I was having with Arturo."

"Huh? That sounds sudden, did something happen?"

"No, he just felt that I was now ready to stand on my own and so it was time to finish our time together."

"Hmm, are you OK about it, sweetheart? I know you were enjoying those sessions."

"Yeah, it was a bit of a surprise to start with but as he explained it, I actually felt he was right."

"OK, so where to from here?"

"Well, there's no change, I'm still going to be working on the same things as before, except now I won't be using Arturo as a 'crutch'."

"Is that what he said? That you were using him as a 'crutch'!" he says with disdain.

"No, relax dad ..." she says chuckling, "He said that that's what can happen if the break isn't made at the right time."

"Well, I still think it's a bit sudden and he could've done it over a couple of weeks or something like that to make the break a bit softer."

"Sheesh dad, if I didn't know better I'd say that *you* were the one that wasn't seeing him anymore instead of me!"

He turns his nose up and walks off indignantly.

Five Years Later

"Hey Jane, great to see you ..." Arturo says with a big smile.

She walks quickly towards him and gives him a big hug. "It's good to see you too." she says as she presses her cheek into his shoulder.

"Take a seat, you're looking great ..." he says as he stops and looks into her eyes. She remembers the long stares at the beginning of their sessions and she takes the time to enjoy his eyes also.

After about 30 seconds, she says, "... You know Arturo, you look exactly the same as when I saw you last. It's like you haven't aged at all! Actually, on that point, do you mind if I ask how old you are? I've been curious ever since you said that you age at a slower rate than most people."

"Well, you can probably add at least 10 years to whatever number you think I am."

She looks sideways at him, "Hmm, well I still think you look like you're in your mid thirties, so I'll add the 10 years and say, 45?"

"Close ... I'm 52.

"What? No way! You're almost my dad's age? ... That's incredible, I've seen 30 year olds that look older than you. How is that possible? I was saying 45, thinking that that was a real stretch!"

"It works like this, Jane, when you start to use your energy more efficiently, and I mean mental energy mainly, the cells of your body remain in balance and therefore don't age pre-maturely. Cells have a life-cycle just like everything else and when the cells of your body are in harmony, they simply live longer, the by-product is that the aging process slows down.

The truth of the matter is that I haven't done anything superhuman to look younger, it's just that most people look older because they place greater stresses on their cells through worry, blaming, complaining and general unease on a daily basis.

They resist what is, they judge things as wrong and they attach themselves to things in the hope that, *the thing* can give them some thing. On top of all that, everything they do is mostly an unconscious reaction to the environment they find themselves in. They often live in a state of fight or flight mode and experience very little peace.

I'm simply what a normal person could be if they learned to release the senseless chatter in their mind's and lived more in harmony with their own rhythm, rather than trying to bend themselves to fit into an insane world. And of course, that requires being more conscious in this NOW moment.

So anyway, enough of my rants, tell me about you, how's the last five years been for you?"

"OK. Wow, where do I start? ... It took me around a year to get the kids program finished and then about another 6 months before I found a way to sell it. Sales were very slow to start with but I was constantly looking for new ways to market it and I also created some add on products as well. So that's going well now.

I'm still working at the same fast food place and I plan to let that go as soon as I consistently make more from my business, on a monthly basis, than I do from the job.

I must say, I had thought five years ago that by now I wouldn't be working in a 'job' anymore, but the business has taken time to establish, and if I'm to be honest, It's really been a big learning curve for me.

I've had to learn about Copy-Writing, Internet Marketing, Affiliate Marketing, website set ups, payment systems, it was all a bit overwhelming at times but I would come back to how you helped me deal with the overwhelm and then take small steps.

As I look back now, it's been really exciting and I've had a heap of feedback that it's making a big difference for kids, which is so cool.

I really have to thank you again, Arturo, I couldn't have done any of this without you. I really hadn't seen this sort of life for myself, I thought I was going to be a Graphic Designer, get a job and that would be it."

"Well Jane, it was a privilege and a pleasure, as I said, you're a star!" he says with a cheeky smile. "... The reality is that not everyone is willing to let go of the illusion of security and embrace the uncertainty of what you've chosen. It takes a high level of trust in yourself to take that leap of faith and find out whether you've got what it takes to fly.

You might remember I said that this is all simple stuff in theory, but it's not easy to actually live it. In your heart, you're a limitless Being of light but until you're willing to trust your heart, your fear of loss or threat of survival will drive you and keep you in a loop of pain until you *do* choose to let it go.

Jane, always remember that you are the one that has created this for *you,* I was here the way you needed me to be, to help you on your journey, but it was all you. Ok, so let's see what your financial statements look like now ..."

She takes out her Income Statement and places it in front of him:

Jane's Income

(Actual monthly)

Description	Amount
Active Income	
Wages (after tax)	$3,550
Business/Other Income (after tax)	$2,100
Passive Income	
Bank Interest	$85
Stock Dividends	$185
Rental Income (Net)	$0
Total Income	$5,920

Jane's Spending

(Actual monthly)

Description	Amount
My Money Tree (At least 10% of income)	
High Yield Account	$2,000
Living Costs (No more than 70% of income)	
Electricity & Gas	$0
Gifts (birthdays, Xmas, etc.)	$100
Mobile phone & Internet	$60
ATM withdrawals/incidental spending	$600
Groceries	$0
Grooming	$140
Clothes	$200
Travel/holidays	$0
Car Costs	$900
Rent/Mortgage	$0
Medical Insurance	$220

Other Insurances	$0
Giving (5% of income or what feels right to you)	
XYZ worthy causes	$250
Savings for Set Goal (Aim for No more than 10% of income)	
Saving for Deposit on a house	$1,000
Fun (No more than 5% of income)	
New experiences	$150
Restaurants/dining out/movies	$300
Total Expenses	**$5,920**

"... This is looking really good, the thing I really like is that you're saving significant amounts of money. It looks like last month you put over 30% of your income into your *Money Tree* and almost 20% toward the deposit on a house! That's excellent. How do you feel about that?"

"Yeah, it feels great to be able to save so much, I'm really wanting to move out as soon as possible. I really appreciate being able to live rent-free but I know that I'm going to have to move out soon, because I'm still itching to experience being fully independent."

"Well, can I make a suggestion?"

"Sure."

"I recommend that you rent before you buy. Buying a house is often a larger expense than people realise and if you don't do your sums properly, you can end up pouring buckets of money down the drain.

In Australia, the main sum to do when buying a place is this, look at how much it'll cost you to rent an equivalent place and if the house/apartment/whatever, costs more than TWELVE times what you're paying in rent every year, then renting is most likely the better option.

For example, if you were looking at a place that would cost you $20,000 in rent per year, then the purchase price shouldn't be more than $240,000, in order to make buying, the better option. It's a simplistic calculation, but it means you won't overpay for a property."

"Oh-Kay, I'll keep that in mind, less than 12 times rent is the ideal buy point. Even though $240,000 for a property seems impossible right now!"

"Yep, I know it's not a reality right now but in order to have the figures work, that's what's needed. The other thing to remember is that when you rent, you need to put aside the money that you're saving by not owning a property, so that you don't become a victim of the property market.

For you, you need to be clear that if you decide to rent, you rent on your terms, you retain your power and continue with your plan on growing your *Money Tree*. Does that make sense?"

"Yep, what I hear you say is that just because it might cost less to pay rent, than to buy a place, I should still save that money so that if I decide to buy a place at some point, I have that extra amount available."

"Good, now let me show you what it looks like with some figures ..." He moves over to the whiteboard and says, "Let's say you've saved a 20% deposit for a house that costs $500,000, you have $100,000. Now let's say that to rent the same type of house, costs you $20,000 per annum. So the choice you have is:

1. Buy the house by borrowing $400,000 from the bank at say 5% and putting down your $100k deposit, or;
2. Invest your $100k in some relatively safe stocks that pay 5% in dividends, and then rent a place to live in.

This is what those choices look like on an annual basis…" He writes:

BUY		RENT	
Interest on loan	$20,000	Rent on House	$20,000
Maintenance Costs	$ 5,000	Dividend Income	$ (5,000)
Total Cost:	$25,000	Total Cost:	$15,000

"By buying the house, you pay $10,000 each year over what it would cost you to rent, and this is assuming no principle is paid off the loan!"

"Hmm, that looks interesting but isn't the house going to be rising in value each year as well?"

"Well Jane, that's an unknown. It might, but it could also stay flat or even go down a little. Just because property has risen strongly before, doesn't mean it'll continue."

"But owning a place means that no one can come along and kick you out, so there's a certain amount of security in that. It also feels good to know that a place would be mine."

"You're right, in our Western society, we like the idea of security, that we 'own' something solid. And if you need that security in the external circumstances, you get the privilege of paying $10,000 a year for that 'feeling'.

Remember Jane, I'm not saying that one is right or wrong, it really comes back to what's right for you. Does one thing support you more than the other, and can you be OK in trusting that you *are* secure within yourself?"

"OK, what I hear you say is that it's not necessarily in the house that I have my security, that it's in me. And if I buy a place, I'm paying a fairly big price for the idea of being secure. So the question to ask is, is it really helpful to me to buy a place when I could be saving that money and generating more income with it?"

"You got it Jane, if you reinvest that $10,000 saving each year, you'll have the compounding machine working for you also! And then if/when you *can* actually buy a home for less than 12 times rent, You'll have the money there to buy it without needing to borrow a large amount."

"Yeah, I like that. I'm really starting to get what you're talking about."

"Good. So when do you plan to move out?"

"Well, I actually haven't put an exact date onto it, I've just been focused on saving and getting my business income to match my job income. But now that you mention it, I realise that if I quit my job, then the business income will need to cover my new living costs as well. That's going to be quite a stretch."

"Absolutely. So what's the plan?"

She looks down for a moment and then says, "Well, I still want to quit my job when my business income matches my job income, so I'll stay at home a little longer and focus my efforts on building the business up and then move out when my income is $5,000 a month."

"That sounds much better. Okay, let's see the next statement ..."

She takes out her Statement of Assets and Liabilities and places it in front of him:

Jane's Assets

(Things I Own)

Description	Amount
Things that don't pay me to own them	
Electronics—PC, Tablet, etc.	$4,000
Clothes, Shoes & Accessories	$5,000
Car	$25,000
Furniture & Fittings	$0
Things of value that don't pay me	
Cash at Bank at call	$5,000
Artwork & Collectibles	$0
Gold & Silver (Including jewellery melt value)	$12,000
Things that pay me to own them	
High Yield Bank Account Money Tree	$2,000
High Yield Bank Account—House	$32,000
Businesses	$0
Stocks	$86,000
Property	$0
Total Assets	$171,000

Jane's Liabilities

(Things I Owe)

Description	Amount
Things I might have to pay for in less than 12 months	
Credit Cards	$0
Short Term Loans	$0
Things I might have to pay for in greater than 12 months	
Car Loans	$20,000
Mortgage	$0
Total Liabilities	$20,000
Net Assets	$151,000

"OK, that's looking good too, you're building the assets up nicely. I'm curious about one thing though, why have you got a loan on a car?"

"Well, I really wanted to upgrade my car and I was speaking with an accountant that said I could get a tax deduction on the borrowings if I used the car for business purposes, so I decided to do that."

He looks up, searching for the right words, "... Hmm, yes, I accept that you get a tax deduction, but how does the car put money in your pocket?"

"Well it doesn't really, but I need a car to get around in ..."

"Jane, do you recall that during one of our meetings I said not to borrow for things that don't put money in your pocket?"

"Yeah. But the accountant ..."

"Stop ..." He puts his hand out. "This is a good time to point out that 'experts' don't necessarily know what's best for you. A tax accountant will look for ways to minimise your taxable income, that's their role and most are good at that, but you need to assess whether it's still right for *you*.

It's nice to get a tax deduction but that should *always* be secondary to the reason for making a purchase. Think of it this way, if I said to you, give me a dollar and I'll give you fifty cents back, at the most, when you do your taxes, would you do it?"

"No, that makes no sense."

"Exactly, it makes no sense to spend a dollar only to get a smaller amount back and yet that's what many people do all the time. Coming back to you borrowing for the car, you're paying interest on a loan i.e. the dollar, and getting a tax deduction, say fifty cents back. Meanwhile, you've got a car that's losing value. It's a double whammy of loss!"

"I see what you're saying, but I still need a car, so how could I have upgraded my car at that time without borrowing?"

"Well, there are two ways. One, you wait and save for it as a goal, or two, if it's an emergency, you use your *Just-In-Case* money."

"Hmm, I think I need to get another account for *Just-In-Case* money. I've kinda just let that go!"

"OK Jane, and perhaps I could have picked that up earlier because I did notice that you deleted some rows from the template, I'm sorry about that. But yes, absolutely, revisit the template and set up the accounts that you need.

Ideally, the *Just-In-Case* money should build up to a point where you could live off it for at least 6 months if you had to. In your case, that means around $30,000."

"Actually Arturo, I have to accept responsibility for this, I did delete those rows because I wasn't using those at the start and I simply forgot about it. I'll take care of it tomorrow."

"OK. Well Jane, it looks like you're definitely on your way to being financially independent. And how are the other areas of your life going, as in health and relationships?"

"Well, I tend to not be as anxious these days, I focus on my breath and aim to not resist when things don't go the way I'd planned. Overall, I feel that I have a more positive outlook on life and I've maintained my health.

As far as a relationship goes, I'm still single, I find that most guys around my age, tend to not see things the way I see them. I think that ever since I met you, I find that I'm looking for deeper connections now, and most young guys seem to still just want to drink and party all the time."

"... Actually Jane, when I said relationships, I was referring to simply the relationships with the people around you, not necessarily a personal relationship. I'm getting the feeling that this is a concern for you though, is it a problem that you're 'still single'?"

"Hmm, you know, it's not really a 'problem' as such, but there's this thought in the back of my head every now and then that says, 'what if I'm too weird for most guys now?' But then I feel that I'm young and there's plenty of time."

"That thought in the back of your head needs to be addressed. From what you've just said, I think this is bigger than you want to admit. If you don't address this now, you might find that you'll get to an age where you'll feel that you're not so young anymore, and you're 'still single'! Then what?"

"You always have had this ability to see through me ..." she says while smiling. "You do have a point, I think I *am* justifying why it's OK that I'm 'still single'. It's not easy when I meet guys and they just don't seem to be on the same wave length."

"Jane, I'm not going to give you relationship advice, except that everything flows from YOU, as the creator. Whether it's money, relationships, health, it's all here for YOU when you find ease in this moment and allow the joy that you are to be here. Do you see that?"

"You make me laugh ... yeah I see that, it's all coming back to me now. I think what might be happening is that I've been focusing on standing as this independent woman for so long that I may have built up an image of what the perfect guy should be like!"

"Right, so when you meet a guy, your filters are limiting you from being there simply as the joy that you are. That's very normal, but it's important to remember that you *are* the joy, no guy, possessions or circumstances can make you better than you are in this moment.

The real journey is all about learning to be in a state of ease in this present moment. Whatever external situations you face don't matter all that much when you're grounded in the present moment. And, if this perfect guy is to show up, it'll have the best chance of happening when you're at ease within yourself, in appreciation and in love with this moment."

"Thanks Arturo, that's a great reminder. While I remember this from our talks all those years ago, I think a layer of it got buried. I felt my heart open as you said the words, and yes, being joyful now is what feels good."

"Great, was there anything else you wanted to share?"

"Nope, I think that covers it."

"Good. Well Jane, go off and rest in BEING."

She gets up and walks over to hug him, while saying, "You still speak like a weirdo, you amazing man ..." They embrace for a few moments and as she walks away she says, "I hope to see you again some day, old friend ..."

Glossary of Financial Terms

Borrower: Someone that borrows money from a lender.

Broker: A person or company that acts as a middleman between two parties, e.g. a Stockbroker acts as the middleman between a person looking to buy stock and a person looking to sell stock.

Business: This usually refers to an entity that operates to provide either a product or service for a fee, with the intention of producing a profit.

Business Owner: A person that owns a business but doesn't have to be there for the business to operate effectively. They are free to come and go as they please.

Company: A business structure that has a separate legal presence for the purposes of providing a product or service.

Compounding: The ability for something to multiply or grow, but where each level of growth adds to the previous number, e.g. 2x2 = 4, 4x2 = 8, 8x2 = 16, 16x2 = 32, etc. Each level is growing by a factor of 2 but it gets to 32 after only 5 levels of growth. Therefore, there has been growth on top of growth, just like the way rabbits multiply.

Debt: Money that is borrowed from a lender.
- **Helpful Debt:** Money borrowed that is used to generate a return for you;
- **Unhelpful Debt:** Money borrowed that does NOT generate a return for you.

Dividends: The amount of money that a company pays to Stockholders from its profits.

Employee: A person with a job, i.e. someone that is physically doing work for an employer.

Employer: A person/company that hires people to do a particular job.

Expenses: Money paid out by you, usually on a regular basis.

Income: Money received by you, usually on a regular basis.
- **Active Income:** Money you receive by actively doing something for it, by providing a product or service;
- **Passive Income:** Money you receive by not doing anything actively for it, usually through investment of some type.

Interest: The amount of money that is paid on a loan, either by you (if you are the borrower) or to you (if you are the lender).

Investment: Money put into something that will give the investor an income/return.

Investor: Someone that puts their money to work with the expectation of a return.

Lender: Someone that lends money to a borrower with the expectation of repayment.

Leverage: The situation where a relatively small effort on one side causes a larger effect at the other side. For example, in finance, a bank may lend you $4 for every $1 you own, when you buy property. In this case, if you have $40,000 you can borrow $160,000 to buy $200,000 worth of property. This effectively allows each dollar to buy something that is worth $5. Your leverage is 5 to 1

Money Tree: A concept that refers to the ability to put money into an investment where the return is reinvested back into the investment, to create a greater investment and therefore a greater return, over time. The idea is that just like a fruit tree gives you fruit, when the tree is mature, the money tree gives you money.

Mortgage: Essentially the same as debt except that it refers to the debt associated with property.

Owner-Operator: Someone that actively operates their business by employing others or systems to deploy a greater level of leverage. The owner-operator generally has to maintain an active role in the business, for the business to continue to do well.

Return: The amount paid on an investment, usually expressed as a percentage of the investment.

Self-Employed: Someone that relies on their own effort to find work, do the work and run their business day-to-day. Self-employed people cannot stop working for long, otherwise their income generally stops.

Shareholder: A person that owns stock in a company.

Stock/Shares: The entitlement to a piece of a company.

Arturo's Reminders to Jane

- You always choose what you choose because that's what you believe is the best path for you in that moment, whether that's a conscious choice or not.
- You're doing this because there is joy in your NOW moment and a clean environment is a natural extension of that joy, not because someone else has asked you do it.
- There's what happens and then there's what you do with what happens.
- I'm not forcing you to do anything here, you have a choice, what do you choose?
- True choice only comes when there's a gap between you, and what you perceive. If you can see yourself as whole and safe, beyond the physicality of things, then whatever is happening around you is just a play of forms and nothing can truly hurt you.
- This isn't about getting a right answer, simply be curious and notice what comes up.
- These relationships don't just happen automatically, they take work and a willingness to reflect on what the other has triggered for *you*.
- To truly grow up and be an adult means that you have all that it takes to take care of YOURSELF and that you're free of needing anyone to take care of you in any way.
- You never have to do anything that doesn't feel right for you. Right now, your old conditioning of what you consider as possible or not is causing you to feel anxious. But you *can* choose what feels good and go with that. Just focus on this moment, here and NOW.
- You don't have to do anything that doesn't feel right in this moment, and most importantly, YOU NEVER NEED TO RUSH. When the step feels right, you take it. If you're feeling overwhelmed just stop and regroup until you feel clear on the step to take.
- The mind needs things to match it's understanding, it doesn't like things not matching and will discount them, unless YOU CHOOSE something else.
- You have the power to choose, when you have the AWARENESS.
- We don't want to make the credit providers wrong, they're

providing a service and it's up to us to realise whether the temperature is being turned up!

- Nothing you buy is going to give you lasting happiness.
- Life is about joy.
- Unlike the example of the one cent that doubled every day, the reality is that it takes years to multiply the money to bigger sums. The difference in how much money your *Money Tree* produces from year 20 to year 30 is huge, and if you can go to year 40, it'll blow your mind.
- This is nothing special, this is simply saving $500 a month, buying $1,000 of stock when you have it and earning an average of 8% on your investment for 45 years.
- No one can manipulate you when you are *aware*.
- The future is unknowable, there are NEVER guarantees for what tomorrow brings, that's why some level of risk is always present.
- You have within you the ability to rise above any situation and you ALWAYS have a choice on how you see things.
- In most cases, we create unconsciously, we can aim for something, have goals, put effort in, but ultimately, we don't know exactly how it's going to turn out. Hence... *luck*!
- Words are just words. Yes, they can convey powerful messages and point to something real, but ultimately, unless you experience what those words are pointing to, they're not real for you.
- Keep coming back to what you felt when you got this idea, that's the light to help you get through the maze, we call business.
- You're the creator.
- We often *overestimate* what we can achieve in the short term and *underestimate* what we can achieve in the long term. This is because we're optimistic at the start but we often can't get out of our own way quickly enough to fully allow the abundance to flow in.
- Money is a by-product, it's not something you go for, simply to have it.

- Bring your awareness to the present moment, notice your feelings and find the joy that you *are*. From there, practice living in a way that takes care of your body, your relationships and your money. Know that you are an abundant being and that life supports you.
- We're multifaceted beings, and we enjoy diversity.

Resources

If you would like the templates that Jane used: Now spreadsheet, Survival spreadsheet and Money Tree spreadsheet.

Simply go to: **StudentIsReady.com/spreadsheets**, Put your primary email address in, and you'll automatically be sent the spreadsheets.

About The Author

Angelo Campione is a former CPA, and the sudden death of his brother-in-law in 1995 caused him to reassess life and to question what the purpose to life was. He pursued many different paths, which led to experiences in meditation, health and nutrition, Internet Marketing, financial markets trading and psychology.

Through a series of serendipitous events, he has since co-founded a Technology Investment group that supports new technology innovations, and now intends on making a significant contribution to the wider community through this association.

Website: StudentIsReady.com

www.ingramcontent.com/pod-product-compliance
Lightning Source LLC
Chambersburg PA
CBHW081808200326

41597CB00023B/4191